VISIONS
2 0 2 0

VISIONS
2 0 2 0

VISIONS
2 0 2 0

VISIONS
2 0 2 0

VISIONS
2 0 2 0

VISIONS
2 0 2 0

VISIONS
2 0 2 0

VISIONS
2 0 2 0

VISIONS
2 0 2 0

VISIONS
2 0 2 0

VISIONS
2 0 2 0

VISIONS
2 0 2 0

FIFTY CANADIANS IN SEARCH OF A FUTURE

M. G. HURTIG LTD. / PUBLISHERS / EDMONTON

VISIONS
2020

Edited for the CANADIAN FORUM *by*
STEPHEN CLARKSON

M. G. HURTIG LTD., PUBLISHERS

10411 Jasper Avenue

Edmonton, Alberta

Printed and bound in Canada

Acknowledgments

Camels are not the only offspring of committee creativity. This book is very much the product of the *Canadian Forum's* editorial board which together decided on the project, worked out its general thrust and cooperatively took responsibility for approaching potential authors for their response to our challenge. My thanks go first of all to Ian Burton, Michael de Pencier, Ian Drummond, Dennis Duffy, Edith Fowke, Jack Granatstein, William Kilbourn, Hilda Kirkwood, Thomas Martin, Kenneth McNaught, Kay Morris, Michael Sidnell, Peter Stevens, Melville Watkins and Milton Wilson for their help in personally approaching authors and in evaluating contributions. Particular thanks go to the managing editor, Abraham Rotstein, who, once having cajoled me into the editorship, supported the endeavour from inception to completion.

I am grateful to Christine Purden for her assistance in the preliminary editing of the text, and to the Canada Council for funding her collaboration.

To Harold Town, one of the many great Canadian artists to have contributed his black and white drawings to the *Forum* over the years — we are delighted to have his illustrations gracing each section of the book.

It is, of course, to the authors themselves that we owe our greatest thanks for taking up our challenge to foresee the unforeseeable.

There is a limit beyond which an editor cannot devolve duties or share responsibilities. For the selections and rejections, the arrangements and orderings, the editorial continuity and the tone of the volume the buck stops at the editor's desk. He may be but midwife to a collective labour, but he shares nevertheless the suffering and exaltation of the act of creation.

S. C.

Contents

letter to kyra on her first birthday

PART I   OBSESSIONS:

1   **the continental menace**

DENNIS LEE

5   **1838, 1970, 2020.**

MELVILLE H. WATKINS

6   **Multinationalization: Can We Stop the Process?**

JOSEPH R. STAROBIN

11   **Canada-America: Just One Guess**

STEPHEN GRANT

16   **Memory of a Canada-hunting Republican**

ANDREW WERNICK

21   **The Return of the Empire Loyalists**

JOHN ROBERT COLOMBO

26   **Robert Ripley Jr.'s "Believe It or Not!"**

DENNIS DUFFY

30   **Canadiana**

JEAN-PIERRE WALLOT

34   **A Visit to the Museum**

CONTENTS

PART II   OBSESSIONS:

39   the world scene

J. L. GRANATSTEIN

43   A World without War?

GEORGE WOODCOCK

46   Prophecies and Pontifications

IAN DRUMMOND

**53   The Great Gold Crisis of 2018:
          The Gold Goes Ouest**

DOROTHY FARMILOE

**58   Report of the Fact-finding
          Committee on Food**

JAMES REANEY

59   Supergenmot

ADRIENNE CLARKSON

**62   Fable Class at the Company:
          The History of the Red-toed,
          Hollow-chested Snackbuster**

A. P. THORNTON

**66   Your World, and Welcome to It
          (the 33rd Earl of Chesterfield writes
          to one of his sons)**

PART III   REALITIES:

73   the social fabric

CHRISTINA NEWMAN

**77   Some People, Places and Attitudes
           that Won't Appear in My Next
           Paradise**

CONTENTS

HARRY G. JOHNSON

81   The Economic Future of Sex

ROBERT FULFORD

85   The Future of Death

JOHN T. McLEOD

88   Looking Back on IIIth

EUGENE FORSEY

94   Trade Unions in 2020?

DONALD MacDONALD

94   The Future of Unionism

HUGH HOOD

103   Places I've Never Been

PART IV   REALITIES:

115   the political loom

ROBERT STANFIELD

119   Man and Government

MICHEL BRUNET

123   Quand un historien se mêle de lire dans la boule de cristal

RAMSAY COOK

128   No More Fun and Games

WALTER L. GORDON

132   The Future Politician

THOMAS A. HOCKIN

136   The Shape of Government and Politics in Canada in 2020: Some Speculations

ABRAHAM ROTSTEIN

141   **The Great Moral Addiction**

PART V   HOPES:

145   **canada, true north
and free**

WILLIAM THOMPSON

149   **2020 Hindsight**

WILLIAM NICHOLLS

158   **Canada — World Melting Pot**

GREGORY BAUM

161   **A New Renaissance?**

HERMANN REBEL

165   **2020 Visions of an Electric Mutant
German Historian Guitar Player
Berkeley Expatriate Prophet**

JOHN McCUAIG

170   **Software and the Imploding Spastic
Inevitable (home hints for 2020)**

PART VI   HOPES:

175   **man liberated**

LEONARD SHIFRIN

179   **The Withering Away of Welfare**

LLOYD DENNIS

183   **Learning in the Age of Wonder**

MAX CLARKSON

189   **The Victory of the NIMs over
the GEBs**

CLAUDE BISSELL
193   The Role of the University President

JOHN M. ROBSON
196   MIRV

JOHN O'NEILL
200   Sociology as a Skin Trade

PART VII   CONTEXTS:
207   the new technology

PHYLLIS GOTLIEB
211   SCORE / SCORE

MICHAEL IGNATIEFF
222   Symbiosis

ERIC KIERANS
227   Technology and the Polity

WILLIAM FRENCH
232   A Book Review Editor's Utopia

WILLIAM READY
**236   Publishing in Canada:
Its Death and Resurrection**

ROSS MENDES
240   Inside the Machine for Living

VINCENT TOVELL
244   From Tranquility, via Florence

PART VIII   CONTEXTS:
249   **our moving history**

KENNETH McNAUGHT
253   **The Future of the**
           Winnipeg General Strike

CARL BERGER
257   **A Canadian Utopia: The Cooperative**
           Commonwealth of Edward Partridge

MICHIEL HORN
263   **Visionaries of the 1930s:**
           The League for Social Reconstruction

DONALD EVANS
268   **One Step Enough**

271   **letter to kyra:**
           conclusion

275   **who are these guys?**

Illustrations

"Stop and Go"   2
brush, pen, ink and wash on paper
1963
8 3/4" x 5 3/4"
"Inscape Detail"   40
brush, pen and ink on paper
1961
8 3/4" x 5 3/4"
"Smoke — Flag Down"   74
brush, steel pen, ink concentrate, wax
and carbon smoke on illustration board
1966
40 1/16" x 30 1/16"
"Ego Screen"   116
brush, pen, ink and zinc print on paper
December 1963
8 3/4" x 5 3/4"
"Easter"   146
brush, ink, wash and knife on paper
1961
8 3/4" x 5 3/4"
"Fence Jump"   176
brush, bamboo pen and ink on paper
May 28, 1961
8 3/4" x 5 13/16"
"Water Furniture"   208
brush, pen, ink and knife on paper
May 26, 1961
8 3/4" x 5 13/16"
"Reflection for Kaz"   250
brush and ink on paper
1963
8 3/4" x 5 3/4"

(by permission of Mr. Town; courtesy the Mazelow Gallery, Toronto, and Herzig-Somerville Limited, Toronto)

letter to kyra on her first birthday

Toronto

March 18, 1970

Dear Kyra,

A year old today! As you were blissfully unimpressed by candle, presents, and everything else about your birthday party except the other kids and the icing on the cake, I'm going to celebrate your becoming a whole number by writing this letter for you to read much later – fifty happy returns later to be exact. In 2020, when the Canadian Forum celebrates its centenary and you are fifty-one, I hope you will pick up your copy of Visions 2020 (or order a print-out on your video console from the central microdata bank), take a serving of your favourite relax-and-perceive crystals and read through this kaleidoscript.

Leafing through the pieces myself, I am trying to imagine how they will strike you in the target year. There will certainly be enough to chuckle about, though what strikes me as hilarious in Jack Robson's MIRV or perceptive in Christina Newman's female utopia may appear as outdated to you as Emmeline Pankhurst's cause does to us. What I find a hopeful projection of educational revolution by Lloyd Dennis may well appear to your society as tragically naïve as the League of Nations' peace illusions do to us now. Let me explain the why and wherefore of Visions so you will at least be able to put yourself back in our mental shoes of 1970.

In wondering how to celebrate the Canadian Forum's fiftieth anniversary – a major literary event for us in Canada – the editorial board was reluctant to construct a self-congratulatory monument to its own historical ego. (We were in any case planning a large anniversary issue of the Forum for April 1970. An anthology of the best from the first five decades was also in the process of compilation.) So rather than reflect on the old days, good or bad, we thought it more consistent with the Forum's objective of probing latent issues to produce a special volume looking ahead to the future.

There was some risk in this venture. Canadian thinking has never been celebrated for its daring–theoretical or utopian. Survival having been our main preoccupation, we have had no real Canadian Dream, apart from the one fulfilled by the final silver spike of the Canadian Pacific Railway. Adopting the title Visions 2020, we invited contributors to react in a short article, story or poem to the question of what the next fifty years will bring. We didn't request an attempt at a literal 20/20 accuracy in the authors' visions of the future. We urged them "to take an imaginative leap, transcending the pedestrian by envisaging the future, the fantastic, the utopian." Depending on their mood and inclination, we wanted to ask some writers how, if they could, they would put the world, Canada or man together anew – a historian's world, a revolutionary's Canada, a social reformer's man. Others, we hoped, would attempt a forecast based on their particular expertise. A political scientist could predict whether our political structure would survive, an educator might venture a judgment on whether the education system would be transformed. What would happen to different professions – the book review editor, for instance, or the university president?

No, we were not pretending to assemble a scientific work. Herman Kahn, the American merchant of social science fiction who has published a celebrated book of predictions, The Year 2000, will be dead or deep frozen by the time you read this. When I think of the future myself, I find it – as did many of those we asked to write on 2020 – increasingly difficult to project a scenario of society fifteen years hence, let alone fifty. The future as a concrete target is losing its relevance to us. The increasing rate of social and technological change, the deepening sense of the fragility of our society, the uncertainty about our planetary survival all conspire to make the target of the next fifty years little more than an intellectual mirage unless we turn the future upside down, using it as a mind-expanding device to think about the present.

The study of the future may eventually become a high-ly refined science. You must understand that, as I write these words, futurology is still considered the rather wild hobby of some adventurous intellectuals. It is not a gener-ally accepted part of the social scientist's equipment. We still do not conceive the present as the process of be-coming the future. Even in our politics we react to prob-lems piecemeal by pragmatic adhocery, not planned programs. We haven't yet learned to make judgments about what to do now by choosing among the alterna-tive futures that are available. The future has been de-mystified but not harnessed. It holds no mysteries. We have manned the moon and mastered the molecule. The laser is being tamed. We have done most things imagined by poets and prophets – except to use the future in guid-ing our present. Visions' job is to start changing this blindness to the future by confronting Canadians with the alternatives they face.

But what is our uncertain future will, barring global holocaust, be your very observable past. As a period piece, Visions 2020 should be an intriguing document. These articles won't serve as much of a historical guide for the period 1970-2020, but they should give you a real insight into the state of mind, A.D. 1970, from which the intervening five decades developed. They will project a slide show of the world into which you were born. "If this was your contradictory conception of the future back then," you may well exclaim, "there is no difficulty explaining the problems of the 1970s!" In the final anal-ysis we are fifty authors answering a collective Rorschach test about the future as we search for our present.

We had no illusions that out of this approach would come a homogeneous book unified by style or content. Our aim was to produce a collection of perceptions that would provoke Canadians to contemplate what they are becoming with more than the perfunctory grunt of social conscience. We were not planning a collector's item whose table of contents would read like the social register of Canada's intellectual establishment, though we did invite many prominent figures to respond to our challenge. Many of these names that are household words in 1970 will probably mean very little to you in 2020. Eric Kierans and Robert Stanfield may be mere footnotes in your grandchildren's history text. On the other hand, student contributors like Michael Ignatieff or Hermann Rebel may have achieved by age seventy-two the stature of sages to the nation.

You won't be surprised to learn that with such a project there was many a slip between editorial intentions and publisher's product. Although we exploited all the personal contacts of every Forum editor, we had no idea what we would get. I hope your taste is eclectic enough to appreciate all the book's elements. Some pieces we have accepted were considered by different editorial readers as both "refreshing" and "paranoiac," "brilliant" and "drivel." What some consider without interest is for others an original perception from a different intellectual world.

Articles came written in the future tense and in the past, in the hortatory mood and the conditional. They were naïvely optimistic and gloomily despondent, sober and sardonic, prophetic and historical. There was no way they could have a common approach or a unifying trait. The apocalyptic did not all deal with the same problem, nor did the straightforward concentrate in one area. Many of these contributions defy simple categories. Yet out of them, four pairs of themes have emerged. There are two dominant obsessions and a concern for a number of realities; at the same time as the authors are inspired by definite hopes they see the future within two specific contexts.

Obsessions. Hovering over the idea of another fifty years you will find two recurring obsessions: that Canada will be dragged under by America's social disintegration and relentless expansion (part I: The Continental Menace) and, even if it resists, that world civilization will have difficulty withstanding obliteration, whether nuclear or political (part II: The World Scene).

Realities. *Apprehensions about our cosmic problems don't prevent thought about the more immediate realities of life. Many authors express a number of concerns about the institutions on which society will be based. Some have written on the social realities – the future of death, for example, trade unions and the role of women (part III: The Social Fabric), others on the specific problems facing our governmental structures (part IV: The Political Loom).*

Hopes. *In counterpoint to both obsessions and realities, there are recurring patterns of hopes focussing on two aspirations: that Canada will be a twenty-first century version of the true north, strong and free – free of civilization's discontent (part V: Canada, True North and Free) – and that specifically our social and educational values will change, allowing men to realize their creative potential (part VI: Man Liberated).*

Contexts. *Finally there is concern for the contexts in which we build the future. How will we use the new technology – or be used by it? (part VII: The New Technology). And how do we relate to our past while we envisage the future: will we move backwards into the twenty-first century or will our future be constructed as a conscious product of our developing history? (part VIII: Our Moving History).*

It is in these thematic sections that you will find our visions in varied styles, the fantastic, imaginative nightmare alongside the sober, analytical essay, followed in turn by the poetic and nonlinear. I'll continue my letter at the beginning of each section, explaining who the authors are and why their contributions were significant to us back in 1970. But there is only so much a kaleidoscope artist can do. He can assemble brilliant colours and match them in differing shapes. It must ultimately be the viewer who discovers his own vision from the cre-

ations of others. In 2020 as in 1970, what you, as reader, take from this volume will depend on what concerns you bring to it.

PART I. OBSESSIONS:

the continental menace

DENNIS LEE

5 **1838, 1970, 2020.**

MELVILLE H. WATKINS

6 **Multinationalization: Can We
Stop the Process?**

JOSEPH R. STAROBIN

11 **Canada-America: Just One Guess**

STEPHEN GRANT

16 **Memory of a Canada-hunting
Republican**

ANDREW WERNICK

21 **The Return of the Empire Loyalists**

JOHN ROBERT COLOMBO

26 **Robert Ripley Jr.'s "Believe It or Not!"**

DENNIS DUFFY

30 **Canadiana**

JEAN-PIERRE WALLOT

34 **A Visit to the Museum**

overleaf "Stop and Go" *by Harold Town*

Letter to Kyra (*cont'd.*)

This book is going to press when Pierre Trudeau's government is awakening to the realities of American control. If you are reading this section in 2020 as a Canadian, Kyra, then the warnings that are expressed by its authors will have been heeded in time. For the moment, it is hard to find much comfort to dispel the gloom inspired by the American menace, all the more fearsome as its own political structure shudders and begins to crumble.

Dennis Lee's poem on William Lyon Mackenzie makes the simple statement that we need radical and nationalist leadership. One conclusion from Melville Watkins' analysis of the long-run weakness of the international economy dominated by unviable multinational corporations is that the new Mackenzies must give this leadership in the struggle to retain some cohesion in the world. More gloomy views are presented by recent arrivals in Canada who have less equanimity about Canadian survival. Joseph Starobin, a spokesman for the old American Left, is the least pessimistic. There is still a chance for Canada to deal with the question of dependence as long as we pursue the target of reducing American control within the country. With this possibility in mind, the tactics of political alliance become of paramount importance: the Left must work with the middle class to gain this basic objective. In the opinion of the new American Left, the game is already lost. U.S. economic control is so great that Stephen Grant has no doubt about the final outcome. The process is beyond recall: friendly, efficient, good neighbourliness administered by his "Canada-hunting Republican" will simply grease the movement to continentalism. For Andrew Wernick as a neo-Maoist, no historical process is beyond reversal. In his Marxist acid trip, he sees the revolution breaking out in the United States while central Canada becomes the fortress of reaction.

You will see elements of the same obsession with U.S. power in poet Colombo's believe-it-or-nots. It may sound preposterous to talk of building a great Chinese wall along the Canadian-American frontier, but (believe it or not!) the Americans are already (1970) arming their border guards. After these hallucinations, Dennis Duffy's "Canadiana" nightmares of the marines taking over appear quite within the realm of the possible. They obviously are for one historian, Jean-Pierre Wallot, whose museum of the future has Canada as the northern fragment of an American imperial federation, with Montreal unilingualized, Quebeckers made "equal with North Americans" and Toronto having absorbed the rest of Ontario.

1838, 1970, 2020. DENNIS LEE

The Compact sat in Parliament
To legalize the fun.
And now they're hanging Sammy Lount
And Captain Anderson.
And if they catch Mackenzie
They will string him in the rain.
And England will erase us if
Mackenzie comes again.

The Bishop has a paper
That says he owns our land.
The Bishop has a Bible too
That says our souls are damned.
Mackenzie had a printing press.
It's soaking in the Bay.
And who will spike the Bishop till
Mackenzie comes again?

The British want the country
For the Empire and the view.
The Yankees want the country for
A yankee barbecue.
The Compact want the country
For their merrie green domain.
They'll all play finders-keepers till
Mackenzie comes again.

Mackenzie was a crazy man,
He wore his wig askew.
He donned three bulky overcoats
In case the bullets flew.
Mackenzie talked of fighting
While the fight went down the drain.
But who will speak for Canada?
Mackenzie, come again.

Multinationalization: Can We Stop the Process?

MELVILLE H. WATKINS

In 1926, foreigners controlled seventeen percent of the capital employed in manufacturing, petroleum and natural gas, mining and smelting, railways, utilities, merchandising and construction. Forty years later, in 1966, foreign control in these same sectors had risen to thirty-four percent. What will it be in 2020?

There are dangers in literal-mindedness, but let us begin that way. If the future is a continuation of the past, our fate is sealed, for the historical trend is clear. A 1965 Twentieth Century Fund study cites "the steady increase in non-resident, especially U.S., control which is seemingly unaffected by depression, boom, war or peace." Commentators in the past have often predicted that the end of the process was in sight; they have been consistently wrong. A steady upward drift in the extent of foreign control has presumably been built into the Canadian economy, given the existing extent of control by giant foreign-based firms over markets, capital, innovation, policies and politics. Reversal of the trend would appear to be ruled out in the absence of a really major change in Canadian policy or American expansionism or both.

If we broaden our perspective to consider the probable role of the multinational corporation globally, matters do not change at first glance. Consider the following predictions culled from a vast literature:

— Within fifteen years, the world's third industrial power will be not Europe but American industry in Europe.

— The coming decade will be one of intensified corporate multinationalization as both U.S. corporations and non-U.S. corporations try to establish worldwide markets and protect themselves from the challenge of others. (It might be presumed that Canada, with its open-door policy, would become increasingly a warring ground for foreign-based giants bidding to take over Canadian firms.) The world faces not *le défi américain* but *le défi international*.

— Within a generation, four hundred to five hundred multi-

national corporations will own about two-thirds of the
fixed assets of the world.
— By the year 2000 at the latest, U.S. corporations will
control seventy-five percent of the output of the non-
communist world.
While these predictions are not all consistent with each
other, they all point in the same upward direction. In the
midst of such a global thrust, there would seem to be little
hope for Canada.
Yet almost without exception, those who so predict hedge
their bets in ways that go beyond mere caution. There is a
sense of limitations to how far the process of corporate multinationalization, or of Americanization, can go without creating
tensions and conflicts that threaten to bring the process to a
halt, or even to bring the whole edifice down as if it were a
house of cards. Doubts abound:
— There was once before an international economy that
was the wonder of the world, but in this century it came
apart at the seams, first in war, then in depression,
then again in war.
— A multinational corporate economy not matched by an
equivalent development of a global polity is unlikely to
be stable in the long run, and "world government" does
not seem imminent.
— If the nation-state does wither away in the face of corporate multinationalization, serious contradictions will be
exposed: from where will the corporation as a crea-
ture of the state derive its legitimacy, and who will fill
those functions, like the maintenance of full employment and the operation of the welfare state, which the
state now fills and which go far beyond the limited com-
petence of the corporation?
— Unless and until the nation-state withers away, will there
not be a limit to how far the citizens of any nation-state
will permit corporate multinationalization to go, as they
watch national sovereignty being persistently violated and
national independence being steadily eroded?
— Corporate capitalism may prove to be dysfunctional
and nonviable — if it has not already done so. The
United States, the most advanced capitalist economy, is

even now characterized by a number of serious problems — its contribution to the balance of nuclear terror, poverty and black ghettoes at home, imperialism
and genocide abroad. Multinational corporations notwithstanding, most of the world lives in poverty; the gap
between rich countries and poor countries is widening
and few poor countries are demonstrating any real ca
pacity to develop economically.

But it is one thing to sense danger, another to imagine an
alternative path, other than chaos, to 2020. Consider the
possibilities:

— If the problem is multinationalization *per se*, then a possible alternative to multinational capitalism imposed
from without is national capitalism and, ideally, one's
own multinational corporations. This is what Japan already has and what Servan-Schreiber advocates for
Europe. But unless there is an indigenous bourgeoisie
with historic roots and a national commitment, the very
power of the multinational corporation would seem to
preclude its emerging in the future. As for Canada, its
business class, even at its peak prior to World War I, favoured home rule within the British Empire to real independence and relied throughout on American branch
plants to provide jobs and leadership for the new industrialism. Its national commitment has declined dramatically in this century, till it is now a thoroughly emas-
culated bourgeoisie.

— If the path of independent capitalism seems bleak for
individual countries, prospects may improve by building
capitalism in conjunction with the state and within regional blocs with larger markets rather than for single
countries. State capitalism in Canada would face ideological opposition from both the Right, which wants private
ownership, and the Left, which wants true socialism,
but its historic roots go back at least to the CPR and,
though now improbable, it cannot be ruled out. The
option of joining a regional bloc is greatly complicated
for Canada by the difficulty of finding one to join other
than North America — which is, of course, what posed
the problem in the first place.

— If the national bourgeoisie cannot be relied upon, a possible response to the multinationalization of capital is the multinationalization of labour. At the simplest level, this would mean multinational unions. Working against this option is not only the difficulty of its achievement — the business unionism of affluent countries has shown little interest in global solidarity — but the possibility that it wouldn't much matter since national unions have hardly impeded the evolution of corporate capitalism. In any event, Canada has already travelled this route, with North American unions to match North American capitalism, and the pressure within Canada is at present on the side of autonomy for Canadian unions. At its grandest level, the multinationalization of labour would mean the smashing of both the corporations and the nation-state to build international socialism. Whatever its appeal, it now seems no more than a distant hope.

— If the problem is corporate capitalism itself, a less distant hope is socialism within one country. The struggle for independent socialism can, in principle, mobilize both grassroots sentimental nationalism and the new radicalism evidencing itself in Western countries; it can appeal both to a national past and a noncapitalist future. As a strategy, it can gather back power from without the better to redistribute it within. It is probably the only serious alternative to the dominance of the multinational corporation, by promising integration and planning within one country as an alternative to integration within one industry across many countries, and by replacing the priorities of corporations as unilaterally determined by them, with communal priorities democratically established at every level.

There is no denying that a fine line exists between forecasting and fantasy, and I cannot deny my own preference. But one's hopes notwithstanding, an independent socialist Canada can hardly emerge without a long and difficult struggle of uncertain outcome. There is no reason to expect corporate capitalism to wither away with only a whimper. It has frequently demonstrated its viability historically through its capacity to co-opt and repress and, if it ends, it may be with the disastrous bang of a cold war gone hot or of a reassertion within capitalism of the national rivalries which twice this century have plunged us into world war.

So viewed, an independent socialist Canada should be preferred by default if nothing else. In fact, for myself, it is our last best hope.

Canada-America: Just One Guess

JOSEPH R. STAROBIN

If the projection of where Canada will be fifty years hence were simply a matter of extending its present historical parabola, one might make more than an educated guess. "If we but knew where we stand and whither we are tending," said Lincoln in his House Divided address, "we should then know what to do and how to do it." Yes, but even knowing where we stand today does not necessarily say much about "whither we are tending." Canada's future will be the resultant of the interaction of variables; her looming internal crisis with its imponderables must be charted in relation to the internal American crisis, whose outcome will be the function of even greater imponderables.

And what strikes a guest who is privileged to teach here is the vast double dialectic now at work: as the relations between Québecois and Anglo-Canadians press insistently for a redefinition, with all the signs pointing to a Quebec that will be "maître chez soi," the long, painful search for Anglo-Canada's self-identity must accelerate and the nationalist self-deinition of Canada will not be denied. Whatever the precise form that an autonomous Quebec works out with the rest of Canada — and even René Lévesque's party does not envisage isolation — Anglo-Canada will change the terms of its relation with the United States. Whether in anger with the Quebeckers, or in acquiescence or frustration, the Anglo-Canadian response is bound to be her own fuller emergence to nationhood and this spells conflict with the United States at a moment when it will be undergoing profound travail.

I take it for granted that the extraterritoriality of American corporations within Canada cannot long continue. New development will have to be on changed terms. The reconquest of decision making should be easier, since a new Europe will make its own weight felt; Latin America will be thrashing around with its developmental problems in the context of a century-long hostility to the United States, while great trans-Pacific changes loom as Japan becomes more dynamic and as

the unprecedented project of industrializing a proud and am-
bitious China, equipped with nuclear weapons, gets off the
ground. Thus, the crisis of Canada's sovereignty will be stimulated by her own constitutional crisis in the midst of profound
world changes. But Canada's bargaining position should improve.

If Canada's Left is to exert leadership in these matters (as
so many young people of diverse origins clamour that it must),
some weighty questions of strategy come forward. A country
so rich in development potential is bound to attract immigrants by the millions but these newcomers will represent increasingly an ethnic quality quite different from the past. The
Left in Anglo-Canada today still draws on the essentially British Fabian tradition commingled with the radicalism of those
earlier ethnic groups which came of age in the teeth of the
Great Depression and at a time of the highest prestige of
the Russian Revolution. What happens to this Left under the
impact of a socialist-corporatist tradition peculiar to Quebec?
What happens to it with the influx of a new kind of immigrant
not easily assimilated to the Scotch-Irish radicalism nor with
any radical experience in his homeland, coming here to participate in an anticipated boom of which continued American
economic and cultural influence seems a major ingredient?
The cultural pluralism which Professor Douglas Verney has
analyzed so well in several scholarly papers must give way to
a "melting-pot" process — or is this prospect easily dismissed as
another Americanism which is outmoded on its own soil and
which Canada can escape? The new migration is unlikely to
share the implicit anti-Americanism of either the traditional
Left or the tory-radical. The constituency of the movement
for Canada's self-assertion will be changing at the moment
when this self-assertion must accomplish great tasks.

Even today this makes itself felt in Canadian labour, which
is able to win higher living standards by direct action against
American-owned corporations, quite apart from the political
constellations which this labour movement supports. Trade union
leaders may take part in NDP conferences. Their locals may
finance NDP electoral campaigns on a nationalist program. But
Canada's best-organized workers, in getting what they want by
nonpolitical means, may not be enchanted with the problems

entailed in achieving independence. The project of a frontal
challenge to American hegemony which Melville Watkins has
projected with such magnetism thus faces immense inner difficulties. It cannot be achieved without a bitter battle with
Canada's managerial and owning class and yet it would need
the support of that conservative-nationalist tradition, the George
Grants who would cease to lament and come out to fight, with
whom the owning class is intertwined. And it would need, certainly, the backbone of a working-class/farmer alliance which
is now able to bargain directly, by extrapolitical action, with
the American-owned corporate structure as it stands. And this
would take place in the midst of a great wave of new migrants,
assimilating on new cultural terms — wanting to become Canadians all right but not wanting to contradict their chief
motive for migrating, which is to ripen the fruits of development
quickly and without the sacrifice that a nationalist-socialist
strategy must entail.

To stress the difficulties does not deny that the project is
worthwhile. It simply raises the problem of strategic postulates. At this point the American context with all its variables
needs some analysis. I hope I will not be accused of a perni-
cious continentalism (or worse) if I ask how an "independent
socialist Canada" falls into place with a variety of American
probabilities maturing at the same time. It is possible, of
course, to anticipate a socialist revolution within the United
States; in that case all the equations have to be run through a
different computer. Maybe my middle-aged eyesight, so strained by hallucinations of another age, does not see what seems
so evident to many young people. Let us not rule out anything
in the next fifty years. But such a revolution, dovetailing with
Canadian nationalism, seems most unlikely, assuming all the
time that American socialism would live easily with its Canadian counterpart. Or the United States can be viewed as a sort
of enraged bull who has seen "red" everywhere (Mr. Trudeau
projected the image in Washington of an elephant), a bull
whose blood is drawn in Vietnam, who staggers down the
corrida while Bolivian and Peruvian picadors do their job and
while Russia cancels out her nuclear threat and China comes up
like thunder across the Pacific; at the same time, the Black
Panthers devastate urban life and Canada's *coup de grâce*

is somehow delivered. In this scenario the moment of truth is a progressive outcome. Yet quite another outcome seems to me more probable. The American Samson, utterly shorn and blinded by impotent passions within a crumbling Fortress America, goes through a phase of fascism that would make the McCarthy era of the early fifties seem something like a pin dropping in an art museum. Such a prospect should bring no cheers anywhere.

The real issue within the United States is how to get it to accept the terms of a new relationship with a swiftly changing world short of internal socialization, for which the subjective factors are in nowise ripe, and yet avoid a seizure of power by the extreme Right. Nor is this an exclusively American problem. And it is not because of cowardice on the part of American progressives that the problem has to be posed in these terms. If Americans were able to resolve the problem alone, the problem would not exist at all. But they cannot resolve the problem. The net impact of their failure would affect everyone if there were not some broad, rough, historical concert of the *strategic* as distinct from the purely tactical moves of all the other "limited adversaries" that are involved in it. All adversaries are limited ones in our time. It is one thing for outraged Canadians to clear the airwaves of cultural pollution from across the border, to refuse the gamesmanship of the ABMs, to ease out American political science professors who put their shoes on the tables of their hosts . . . but it is quite another thing to project an evolution for Canada which assumes that its part in the next fifty years is something analogous to Vietnam, or Peru, or even Gaullist France.

The possibility of a unique piece of social and political engineering involving its distinctively Canadian elements and not derivative from the experience of other peoples is precisely the challenge. I am asking what the trajectory may be of an active, determined but also far-sighted and strategically responsible Canadian national movement on which no limits are placed except those which arise from a cool analysis of its own internal problems and which is obliged to take into account the real choices within American life itself at the same time.

To this question it is easy to oppose slogans. It is easy

to dismiss the question as irritating. But Canadian-American relations are bound to be a laboratory of something different than what we have seen until now; I have called it elsewhere a radical "postcontinentalism," with the "magnetic field" of Canada's competitive nationalist energy exerting an influence on the United States. Stormy or peaceful, the co-existence of Canada's growing nationalism with the realities of an America that must be brought safely out of its present dilemmas to a stage where its technology can serve and not dominate other peoples will require a strategy that is unique. If the older Left did not have it, a mindless New Left will not give the answers either, with all due respect to the steadfastness of the former and the exemplary courage of the latter. Nor will this be a process, this transformation of the American leviathan into something with which everyone can live, in which too many mistakes can be made. Those who realize the fragility of contemporary civilized life and who stand for a successful, living passage through the perils of the next fifty years must emphasize that nobody will be able to afford *postmortems*.

Memory of a Canada-hunting Republican

STEPHEN GRANT

It is 8:00 o'clock in the morning. An elderly man walks to a cabinet, takes two pills quickly. Bacon and eggs. He takes a cylinder from a pneumatic tube container, opens it and takes out a piece of microfilm. He places it carefully into a Projectoview, pops another pill which he will let melt in his mouth (coffee) and settles down to read the news. He has been going through this routine for some twenty years since his retirement from the Continental State Department. The date is July 1, 2017.

He quickly scans the news; the major item is a piece on the Medina Air-o-way dispute. Finally, he comes to his favourite column, innocuous in its fourth column status but, for him, remembrances of things past. It is called "You'd Better Believe It" and contains tidbits of unusual pieces of history, folklore and the like. Today's piece is particularly interesting.

"Our Northern Sector would be 150 years old today," the item reads. "Formerly known as 'Canada', it became a 'nation-state' in 1867 and part of our Glorious Union on this same day in 1990."

How clearly the old man remembers. As a key American figure in the developments leading to the Great Merger of 1990 . . .

How long ago it was. I remember them well. All the talk of good neighbourliness. We weren't exactly friends, but not enemies either. Continentalism was an inevitability, a good thing, too; I'll never understand why some of them fought it. Didn't they realize it was for their own benefit? They took pride in giving us their best brains in the fields of science and technology. Of course, we reciprocated by giving them our plant managers, and they didn't seem to mind that our dissidents and hippies went along.

In many ways, though, we were quite close. I remember the history books saying that we had the longest unprotected border in the world. We did, in fact, until we had to stop the

flow northward when the brain drain reversed and we started
losing *our* brightest minds and draft fodder. The border
made no difference though; an American businessman was the
same as a Canadian one, only more aggressive. Since the business of the continent was and still is Business, there was no
reason why we shouldn't have gotten along — at least superficially.

The old Merchant-Heeney approach made life so uncom-
plicated. We gave them protection in the form of NORAD; they
gave us their resources. It was a fair deal. And we helped staff
their university faculties in return for their providing solid research on CBW, among other services to our common cause of
freedom and democracy.

It makes me ill even now to think that for God-knows-what
reason they elected a socialist government in 1985. Fortunately, it didn't last long or else all our carefully laid groundwork would have been undone. Except for that and a brief
revolt in Windsor in 1995, everything went smoothly. In 1990
we legalized the *de facto* continental situation and now our
Glorious Continent numbers four sectors. Sixty states under the
old system. It is remarkable, though, that except for the Windsor Revolt, no marines were used. That was *after* Unionization!

The first important step for us was the Sharing-the-Wealth
pact of 1972, technically called the Canadian-American Resource Pact (CARP). We paid the price, but we wanted, needed
and by God (in Whom we trusted) we were going to keep the
use of those resources. The Columbia River Treaty started it
all, but there was no end. Their cynics cried that the country
was being sold out; Watkins and his socialists cried imperialism
and Walter Gordon whined about neocolonialism. I never liked
those words; the treaty meant exactly what we called it — sharing the wealth!

Two other issues were particularly important: Arctic sovereignty and pollution. The first was a flash-in-the-pan, the
second a ploy. We let the Canadians tough-talk us into allowing Canada to exercise authority in the Arctic, symbolic authority at any rate. Essentially, we had won as soon as they
thought they had. Our shipping in the Arctic was five times the
size of theirs. Besides, we had set up our submarine bases

there — on my instigation if I remember correctly. Finally, when we gained control of their shipping lines, the Arctic became ours legitimately.

Pollution was the real *coup*, though. It was a pressing issue at the time, or so it seemed. We let them put restrictions on our companies as they did with their own. Extraterritoriality was forsaken for this momentous event. We let them cut down automotive transport; we encouraged our oil companies to purify production while still maximizing profits. We might even have persuaded our people there to stop breathing if they had wanted an antibreathing campaign. What a joke! We did nothing about forest and river controls, however. They didn't either since the paper and water lobby was too important for them to ignore. We didn't mind as long as we got the profits.

As it turned out, when we made it clear that the resources were theirs to keep but ours to use, their controls saved us the time and trouble of purifying the stuff ourselves. And the best part of the whole bargain was that they thought they were the Boss, a phenomenon which made them more cooperative than before. That, too, didn't matter after 1990. The only problem is these damn gas masks. Still, we drive cars, don't we? That's the real mark of an advanced civilization. . .

The old man finishes the news. There is to be a testimonial dinner tonight commemorating the twenty-seventh anniversary of Unionization. He turns the machine off, puts the film back into the container and sends it into the tube where it will be destroyed. The Continental government discourages history these days. Still, he is possessed by memories of Canada . . .

I remember the dinner we had twenty-seven years ago. For my part in the affair I was invited to the head table. I declined; others had done much more than I. I remember, though, that in my day I offered some pretty sound advice to the department. On my advice we supported the Liberal party and kept it in power until Unification in 1990. That was designed to keep our economic base while establishing political control. The Liberals had no qualms about selling their country down the river quite literally. What was more, supporting the Liberals meant that labour and its affiliates were kept out of power, except for the slight aberration in 1985 when it was already too late. (Some said "almost" instead of "already."

How naïve!) The Liberal party took the guts out of labour and other "radical" nationalistic movements which appeared to threaten the continental system — a false alarm, really, since we had long ago ensured that the Canadian labour movement was an authoritarian extension of our own. That was why the 1985 election was sham, pathetic optimism, not victory for the Canadian nationalists.

We even supported Schreyer in Manitoba. Occasionally we had problems with Quebec, but after 1990 and the Great Cultural Assimilation we solved the Quebec question, ultimately less of a problem than the blacks turned out to be. We never had to use mace with the Quebeckers. The whole key, it seems in retrospect, was to give the Canadians the *impression* of independence; they didn't really want anything else.

In foreign affairs we allowed them to trade with the Chinese Commies. (Some now call them Eastasians!) Hell, we even gave them their own sphere of influence in Africa; they repaid us by Americanizing "their" countries for us. (Mitchell Sharp was quite a help!) They sent advisers in economics (our Rostowian economics), equipment (our advanced technology) and military strength (our new weaponry) to such potentially self-willed countries as Tanzania and Ivory Coast. Their antinationalistic bourgeoisie helped establish the technocratic Third World bourgeoisie in power, stifling the indigenous socialist movements and saving the day for Western freedom and democratic values. They deserve belated credit for that.

At home, we educated our continental managers in Canadian history so that the inevitable takeover would not spark any cultural resentment. For the rest of Americans, however, we didn't teach much about Canada; it didn't have much of a history anyway before Manifest Destiny caught up with it. Besides, we offered great opportunities for their young to study here and learn about democracy first hand.

The most striking thing in education, though, was the extent to which Canadian students knew so much about our heritage and so little of their own. No, on second thought, it isn't surprising, but it's all part of our collective heritage now.

From my heyday in the Continental State Department (formerly just State) until Union in 1990, I remember them

hurting us ౸ly once and that was more emotional than anything else. They left NATO in 1976, our two hundredth anniversary. They could have chosen the time better, that was all.
As for NORAD, however, there was no exit. Still, those really were
the days when Partnership meant Opportunity and what an
opportunity it was! We didn't miss it for the world . . .

The old man comes out of his reverie, smiling, content.

The Return of the Empire Loyalists

ANDREW WERNICK

Drop a cap of Marxism. The walls dissolve into windows and the chair is a time machine.

Turn on the sound:
"The *Canadian Forum* offers *you,* a bourgeois intellectual trying to make it back into the People you never came from, a chance to present Your Point of View (as a Student Radical) of What Canada Will Be Like in Fifty Years' Time."
The studio audience gorged on spectacles of plastic guns and cellophane domestic crises and battles of mice and teevee gladiators waits in narcotic silence for another bunch of petit-bourgeois illiterati to make semipublic fools of themselves.

Break for advertisement:
"From the Land of the Quiet Whisper, the Editorial Board — makers of Punch and Judy shows, deckchairs, polite conversation and deaf-mutes — editors of *Forum* magazine ('The magazine that's made with Mind in You'), present an off-peak-hour attempt to
Make You Guess
Make You Think
Record the snores of a colonial intelligentsia and deduce their dreams to test the pessimistic theory that the narcosis is complete, that visions are repressed, that blackboards are wiped clean, that ordinary people like you and me (middle-class kind of academics, junior faculty M.A., Ph.D. don't you know) have
Nothing To Say.
(We're hibernating. It's a nightmare where you are. DON'T WAKE UP.)
Will Technology Take Over?
Will we arrive at 1984? (When?)
Brave New World (Shakespeare isn't it? — Well it's not here. — Oh no, it's not here . . . it might be Over There, but it's not there. — Besides, we live in a class society . . .

bosses and workers: remember reading about it? — Oh yes,
that's right. Anti-imperialist struggle. People's War — *Wrong
Line*. Canada is not a colony. — I'd better read the *next*
one.)
Will We Go Like China? (Oh come on. Don't be ridiculous. China's further away than Quebec. Godard said so . . .
and he's a petit-bourgeois film-maker so he ought to know.
— Besides, China is only the arsenal of world revolution.
She does not export it. — Who are the Chinese people
anyway? They're on the other side of the page aren't they?
— World, man, world. They're on the other side of the
world.)"

Quote from the ultimate Marxist Text-book:
"Truly to reject relativism one would have to say that the
Chinese are the right side up and we are upside down. The
visual inversion of the social senses, evident for instance in the
widespread belief that the reason we have a society that pits
everyman against everyman against everywoman against everywoman against everyman is because of our fallen or evil or
competitive human natures, is a structural phenomenon. The
roots of this phenomenon lie in commodity fetishism which
is universalized in the domestic sector of imperialism developed to its highest stage."
Right On, Brother:
Hurtling through time, consumers and producers unite to
overcome their schizophrenia by becoming political actors taking seriously the proposition that they should take control of
the direction of their own lives.

The mediamen try to drive the telewedge between their split
selves and persuade them to consume themselves as a spectacle — the spectacle of themselves overcoming the split. A
strategic task: the successful treatment of revolutionary narcissism.
Besides, there is an impulse to act — unemployment rises,
taxes increase:
    Is it a recession?
    No. A government-induced cooling-off of an overheated
economy.

Why are they creating unemployment?
To fight inflation?
What's causing inflation?
Rising labour costs.
Do you mean rising wages?
It depends how you look at it. Actually real wages are falling.
Oh I see.
Anyway, the public suffers.
Who are "the public"?
The ruling class.
I see. But isn't the rate of inflation highest in the service sector?
Yes I suppose it is. There aren't any unions in the service sector to speak of and wages are disgustingly low. That's why we're having a prices and incomes policy.
To prevent prices from rising?
No, wages.
Why?
Profits aren't high enough.
What about the unions?
Oh, we need their help to discipline their own membership.
Very clever. Who thought of the whole idea?
University economists.
I thought that the real problem was that there's a war going on?

Switch to the Great Temple of Woodstock, where the Doors of Janus have been kept closed since 1941. There has not been one day of peace since the American Empire began to expand into the Pacific.
The state-financed peace religion has spread throughout the population after it had replaced the old Gods as the official state religion.
(How do you unite the people against the imperialist ruling class when the people are stoned? — Far out, man. I mean, far out.)

President Wallace addresses the psychedelic multitude:

"This society needs peace. I was a peace candidate and I intend to carry out my mandate." (Tumultuous applause. Scat-
tered cries of "Yeah. Yeah. Like, give peace a chance, man.")
"Unfortunately, there are many of our people who oppose
peace, who want to stir up the fires of racial strife, who want
to disturb the right of ordinary folks to Do Their Thing.
"Let those who have, do their thing. Let those who have not,
hustle themselves into freedom. We will not tolerate those who
oppose social peace, racial peace, economic peace, class peace,
peace on the campuses, peace in the factories, peace in the
offices, peace in the communities, peace in the streets. There
are people who are not peaceful. WE WILL EXTERMINATE THEM.
"We will crucify Barabbas in the name of Jesus Christ who
preached An Honourable Peace, Peace in Our Time, Peace
on Earth to All Men of *Good Will*. Shalom."

Shalom. Israel occupies Cyprus to preserve peace in the Eastern Mediterranean. Guerrilla warfare disturbs the peace in
Latin America, Southeast Asia, Africa. The legions are sent
out to impose peace.
(GIVE US BARABBAS!!)
Look! We've arrived. It's 2020 and the maple leaf flies from
every building. See, I told you the two-stage theory was correct. Canada finally had a bourgeois-national revolution.

Click on the radio:
"There were disturbances in many cities today as Canada
celebrated its tenth anniversary of independence. Rival groups
of students clashed in IBM University. They were dispersed by
military police, after arrests."
"What's going on, Mr. Jones?"
"It was all very predictable really. Canada legalized dope.
Toronto became the centre of the growing peace religion. Then
Quebec seceded under the PQ. The anti-imperialist forces —
workers and students — increasingly came into conflict with
the American-dominated new Quebec bourgeoisie.
"The Maritimes, geographically separated from Ontario, ac-
cepted the logic of the north-south economy by leaving the
Canadian federation and joining the U.S. in a customs union

which finally led to their becoming the fifty-first state. Likewise with B.C. and Alberta.
"Ontario absorbed a rising tide of immigrants, pro-British elements from B.C. and the Maritimes, fewer children from the States, political refugees from Italy after the revolution and an increasing number of older Americans who saw no future for their businesses in a country that was rapidly degenerating into civil war. As the revolution in the States spread, red bases were established on the eastern seaboard and consolidated as right-wing refugees left their homes and businesses for points north.
"A loose confederation of autonomous liberated areas was formed — which was joined by Quebec after a successful socialist revolution there. Major corporations moved their operations south to Georgia, Louisiana and Mississippi, and north to Ontario and Manitoba. The American capital was moved to New Orleans, but even it became ungovernable as urban guerrilla warfare spread through its streets.
"Mutinies in the American army gave opportunities for national liberation struggles to establish base areas in Latin America.
"Canada (Ontario and Manitoba) became the effective centre of monopoly capital in North America. The West and the Maritimes, which had become the fifty-first and fifty-second states of the Union, decided to amalgamate with Ontario and Manitoba and at a special constitutional conference, Canada declared its independence. What happened to Saskatchewan? — Nobody knows.
"The nationalist students, who had been celebrating Independence Day by a ceremonial burning of the American flag, were attacked by several hundred radicals who claimed to be in support of the provisional revolutionary government in Washington."

Robert Ripley Jr.'s "Believe It or Not!"

JOHN ROBERT COLOMBO

(from the *Canadian Forum*, January 1, 2020)

Quebec was once part of Canada!

*

The 49th parallel — which separates Canada from the United States — was once "the longest undefended border in the world"! The Berlin-like wall that now divides these two "friendly countries" was erected by the U.S. government to keep draft dodgers from seeking sanctuary in Canada. It runs from the Bay of Fundy to the Strait of Georgia. Over ten feet thick at its widest point, the wall has a sentry post for each of its 3,989 miles, and is longer than any man-made object on earth — with the possible exception of the Great Wall of China!

*

An earthquake will rock the West Coast late this year or early next, according to the stars. Some astrologers even predict the possibility that Vancouver Island will sink into the Pacific Ocean.

*

Next month the Royal Commission on Bilingualism and Biculturalism will table its final report. During the last sixty years, the commission has employed well over two thousand persons, some of whom are now second-generation commissioners.

*

It seems impossible now . . . but only 261 years ago Voltaire, the famous French author, dismissed mineral-rich Canada in a phrase as "a few hundred acres of snow."

*

At one time *American* ownership of *Canadian* companies was a contentious subject. How the tables have turned, with the present wholesale takeovers of large U.S. industrial firms by stockbrokers on Bay Street and St. James Street!

*

Rumours that the Toronto publishing firm of McClelland &
Stewart will go under have been circulating for half a century
now and have no basis in fact.

*

Yellowknife, N.W.T., was once Canada's most northern city!

*

Revered and loved by one-quarter of the world's population,
yet barely known in the country of his origin, Norman Bethune
is no longer "a prophet without honour in his own country."
Against much opposition, the National Historic Sites Commission has finally announced plans to erect a plaque in
Bethune's honour. The plaque will be unveiled in Graven-
hurst, Ont., where the famed surgeon of China was born in
1890.

*

Former Prime Minister of Canada, Pierre Elliott Trudeau, is
now running a successful leper colony in the Republic of Niger.

*

British pornographer, John Clelland, was actually granted a
pension by the British Parliament on the condition that he
not write a sequel to his erotic masterpiece, *Fanny Hill.*

*

St. Jude has been named the patron saint of the Progressive
Conservative Party of Canada.

*

Hugh MacLennan's novel, *The Return of the Sphinx,* was
roasted by the critics when it was first published in 1966!
Twice filmed, the Canadian classic has now gone into its
thirty-third edition.

*

Art Notes: Iain Baxter and Greg Curnoe are Canada's best-
known artists abroad, an international poll recently indicated.
In the same poll, painter Harold Town placed a poor tenth . . . .
Mario Amaya, the first U.S. citizen to be appointed director
of the National Gallery in Ottawa, may become the country's
first cultural ambassador to the U.K. . . . .

*

Expo Opens Again! Just as it rebuilt the Fortress of Louis-bourg on Cape Breton Island — at a cost of over $12,000,000 — the federal government plans the painstaking reconstruc-tion of Expo 67, the world-famous international exposition held half a century ago in Montreal. The new Expo will rise above the snows of Baffin Island, near Cape Dorset, as a tourist attraction and slum-clearance project. The cost of the new Expo is estimated at three times that of the original fair.

*

"For many years we had a country with little or no art. Now it seems we are to have an art without a country." These words were penned by A. Y. Jackson — Group of Seven artist — when the continued existence of Canada was still in doubt!

*

It has been reliably estimated that there are more draft dodgers and evaders and their descendants in the Dominion of Canada than there are draftees in the entire U.S. Army.

*

It's hard to believe that Canadians once regarded Mackenzie King as their dullest prime minister. With the forthcoming publication of King's private diary, recently unearthed among the C.D. Howe papers in the Bank of Montreal vaults, it will be shown that the "bachelor P.M." was, in fact, secretly married — and to his London spiritualist!

*

At one time there were more legitimate theatres in London, England, than in London, Ont.

*

Robin Mathews, president of the University of Toronto, which boasts some 2,500 professors, half of whom are U.S. or U.K. citizens, once headed a Canadian Sovereignty movement. The Mathews group sought to expose the "scandalous" condition whereby Canadian taxpayers supported American professors to teach the youth of Canada American subjects.

*

"Antiques & Junque" — sign in front of a second-hand store in Peterborough, Ont.
                                                    *

Nobel Prize-winning author, Anthony Burgess, now eligible
for the Governor General's Award, once wrote: "John Kenneth
Galbraith and Marshall McLuhan are the two greatest modern
Canadians that the U.S. has produced." Burgess himself has
taken out Canadian citizenship and taken up residence on St.
Pierre and Miquelon, a Canadian protectorate and tax haven
for successful artists.

*

Niagara Falls once flowed the year round!

*

Who even remembers that the Spadina Expressway was at
one time a controversial issue? Recently completed, this multi-
laned, limited-access expressway now runs all the way from
the southernmost tip of James Bay to Toronto Island Astro-
port. Part of the way it tunnels under highly urbanized
areas. The Spadina Expressway is the costliest in North American history, and is second in length only to the Trans-Canada
Highway.

*

"Canada is Scotland's revenge," according to aphorist Scott
Symons.

*

Mazo de la Roche, Robert Service, and Stephen Leacock
remain Canada's best-known authors abroad. They have held
their own in international esteem for the last three-quarters of
a century. Younger runners-up include: philosophers Marshall
McLuhan and George Grant, literary critic Northrop Frye,
novelist Graeme Gibson, and poets George Jonas, J. Michael
Yates, and John Robert Colombo.

*

"If I paint what I know I bore myself; if I paint what you
know I bore you," wrote artist Franz Kline, who continued:
"So I paint what we both don't know."

*

Believe It or Not! . . . for decades the *Canadian Forum* was
a marginal operation with only a few hundred readers! Ownership and title once exchanged hands for the princely sum of
one dollar. The *Forum* — North America's most influential
weekly — now has a readership exceeding those of the *Atlantic Monthly* and the *New Yorker* combined!

Canadiana DENNIS DUFFY

". . . I think I grasp what you're getting at, Pat, and surely we can both agree that the intervention was handled somewhat clumsily. Forty years have passed, however, sufficient time for the situation to clarify, and while some may argue that the threat of a Commie takeover was not perhaps as immediate as it appeared at the time. . ."

"But there was a threat, eh? You're saying there was a threat."

"No question about it! Forty-four Commie agents were in Ottawa at the time, plus unknown numbers of sympathetic Wafflers, and at least a dozen of them had infiltrated the RCMP, Defence, etc. Now you aren't going to tell me they were simply going to sit there sorting files during the crisis! In time, they would have assumed leadership of the various groups formed ostensibly to protest the Union; their expertise and backing would have enabled them to carry on a lengthy terrorist campaign, and the intervention — or as I like to call it, the rescue — would have come a little later and been a lot harder on all concerned. After all, every one of them had been given Chicom training, and at least three were involved in the formation of Canadian Separatist paramilitary organizations."

"At any rate, Senator, it's all past."

"My point exactly. And I think we have all gained a new and I would hope more cordial view of one another in the years following the Union. Certainly our Continental government can adopt a more flexible posture in fulfilling its strategic requirements, confident in the loyalty of the Northern Tier. Frankly, it always struck many of us as anomalous that, after the neighbourliness of the Hickel-Greene Energy Treaty, Canada would wish to remain outside our federal system. We've always thought that your tradition of federalism made you naturally inclined to consider getting closer to us at some time or another.

"Finally, your states are now able to concentrate their ener-

gies upon internal problems, confident that their natural products will find a ready market in an ever-expanding continental economy. And many soldier boys and their lovely brides
can testify as to the benefits gained through integration on
other levels, if I may speak facetiously."

"Thank you, Senator . . . and now for a message of interest
to every viewer."

Shanghai was no picnic, and the Northern Legion was right
where the action was. The deeds of the Canucks that day
will forever bring a surge of pride to every heart in the True
North.

"After that hairy first day, when the jolly green giants
were dropping like flies," recalls Medal of Honour winner
Sgt. Clifford A. Purdy, "it was a real pleasure to return to
base and turn on with a stick of HI."

Thousands of good heads agree. The carefully selected blend
of the smoothest Acapulco fibres with the sauciest of Ontario
hybrids produces a joint giving a High, High, HI.

Take a tip from the boys in Chinksville, and say Hello to
a HI during your next break or bust. Extra good vibrations.

The leader of the pioneer train expressed his satisfaction
with the facilities for constructing the new settlement at Cleav-
erville, and during the raising of the Leafs and Stars declared
that "our children's lifetime" will see a new centre of Black
Culture arise there, the greatest since Timbuctoo.

He brushed aside persistent rank-and-file complaints about
scanty rations and overcrowding in the transport planes during
the long flight. "We have a few malcontent Pantherites around
still, but we'll get their fat maws closed before we've been
here too long."

Gratification was expressed with the beauty of the rugged
scene, the grandeur of the task to be accomplished in the creation of a new settlement. "The Black Man will create here a
far more productive and tension-free environment in the
Northwest Territories than he ever could in the war-torn slums
of Detroit and Newark."

For the present, the so-called Indian regulations concerning
liquor and firearms remain in force, until statutes defining

the status of the new communities, especially as regards military service, have been drafted.

"Isn't it true that some members of the legislature are threatening to tie up the university budget if this move goes through?"

"Well, I ought to say that I think the vice-chancellor is at this very moment convincing them of the folly of such action. It makes no sense whatever to retain a top-rank graduate faculty in an out-of-the-way centre of higher learning. There just isn't enough to work on here. My colleagues and I feel our move to Milwaukee will upgrade our situation on both a personal and professional level, as well as encourage this university to concentrate upon those aspects of technical and practical education in which it has traditionally excelled. Furthermore, the problem of dissident students is significantly lessened in Milwaukee, as the firm handling of last year's library read-ins demonstrates. All in all, we look forward with confidence to the move. It marks a significant moment in the Union."

"Shit no, man, we don't want those freaky, ex-draft-dodger profs screwing up our northern campuses," declared the fiery coordinator of the Northern Students Federation. "Like when they skulked up here they copped out on the real scene, the curtain raiser. They're irrelevant now. This land has changed, we've changed, and they keep on rapping about the Good Old Canadian days, the Old New Leftie thing. We've got our files on those old farts, and we're turning them over to the University Surveillance Committee. Unless the committee acts immediately upon our non-negotiable demands, we plan direct action against these fossils."

He informed the 30,000 Minutemen that the city welcomed them and trusted that the hospitality extended would encourage them to meet here in future years. "The blending of the borders must involve the blending of the peoples," His Honour remarked to great applause.

"We are a great convention city," the mayor remarked, "and we cannot but recall how impossible all this would have been years ago. We can but hope that we will see you frequently in years to come, and that our own Canuck units will enable Minutemen International to smother subversion everywhere."

Today's special convention events include a parade up Yonge St., during which the latest Minutemen Patriotic Patrol vehicles will be displayed, followed by a riot-control demonstration for crippled children at Varsity Stadium.

In honour of the convention week, Toronto bars have been permitted to remain open until two a.m.

The suicide was attributed to disappointment over his failure to interest the Academic Publications Authority in his reportedly controversial manuscript on the origins of the Second Asian war.

The Vice-Chancellor of the Higher Learning regretted his inability to attend the funeral services and lamented the affair as "yet another instance of the tragedy that overtakes the eccentric scholar who deals himself out of the mainstream of political thought."

A Visit to the Museum   JEAN-PIERRE WALLOT

> time: provincial day, July 1st, 2020
>
> place: Ottawa

"You are now viewing," began the guide to a group of tourists of all races, colourfully undressed, "the Museum of Man of Canada, one of the provinces of the American imperial federation which, as you know, forms together with the Russian and Chinese empires part of our World Confederation. We begin our tour with historical exhibits that illustrate the evolution of this ancient colony from bilingual half-state to the enviable position of an autonomous province in our great empire."

One large space was devoted to the twentieth century, "the century of Canada," as the guide tactfully put it, fondly stroking a noble bust of Sir Wilfrid Laurier, "and the dawn of a still greater era."

In a transparent tube shaped like an ancient missile without head, a death mask of an old prime minister named "Dief" was moving in a kind of rebellious and shaking motion: a cavernous and trembling voice could be heard extolling the virtues of the ties with faithful England and of independence from the United States. "This grand old man pushed Canada towards its orgasmic fate of today by signing defence treaties concerning missiles with the future chiefs of our Western Empire." And the guide added, pointing to a polka-dotted bow tie around a head shaped like a Nobel peace prize medallion: "Only the heads misfired."

By far the greatest amount of space was occupied by exhibits about a later prime minister, the famed Sir Pierre Elliott Trudeau (with a warning on the floor: "Not to be confused with Pierre Berton, in the comic section downstairs"). A bigger-than-life-size bronze statue of his Apollonian body dominated the scene. The head was adorned with a crown of peeled grapes mingled with thorns intertwined in a B-B pattern. An

American maple leaf with a California rose hid what used to be hidden, while his feet stood firmly upon *fleurs de lys*, broken wheat stems and arrows. His muscular arms supported an MP chain encircling a throng of gagged Lilliputians labelled "Parliamentarians." All over his body, words flashed rapidly in a psychedelic blaze: "Parliament efficiency," "Universality," "Internationalism," "Individual Freedom," "Liberty in the bedroom," "Participation," "Kisses not deeds," etc. "He should have been a Greek god," mused the guide, "but he was born in a Mercedes." Quite near, a tiny old-fashioned rose swimming suit was draped upon a plush and dark synthetic velvet, with stroboscopic views of triple somersault dives by this athletic politician. Visitors of both sexes gasped with delight. "Sir Elliott," announced the guide solemnly, "is the father of our modern, democratic, efficient, participatory, universal and taboo-free empire. His output must be rated on a par with that of other great world thinkers: Mao, McLuhan and E.P. Taylor. He has been the apostle of close ties between individuals and between nations."

Further away, symbols of different religions were mixed in artistic disarray. "This was before ecumenism," eulogized the guide, "when there were WASPS, PAPISTS and ILOTS. Nowadays, everybody is reconciled to the new religion of no ties, no popes, no dogmas. And WAMPAP ("With as Much Pleasure as Possible") is preached every day without cost on your own live TV sets. Even ascetics, reactionary artists, philosophers and revolutionaries who have not yet achieved our scientific standards of perfect and universal happiness follow a mandatory, free and benevolent re-education program."

In front of a special niche reserved for books and authors were three huge columns of piled papers. "These are the collected works of Mackenzie King. Our computers have not yet been able to decipher his thoughts," the guide admitted, a little embarrassed. "Happy were those who believed without understanding, for they won elections." On electromagnetic tablets, busts of the Fathers of the first Confederation were interspersed with books on John A. Macdonald, the road to Confederation, etc. "These are the happiest of them all, perhaps," volunteered the guide. "What they longed·for has finally become a reality: the provinces of Canada have indeed be-

come municipalities. As for the distinguished author, he proph-
esied the rise and fall of the empire of the St. Lawrence,
little knowing that the New Romans, happily Anglo-Saxon,
would honour his memory."

On the floor was a depressed map which represented the
former western provinces. "People used to cultivate wheat in
this territory. Then a wise premier told them to stop it!
They did: two-thirds of humanity were dying of overeating.
So today we find there chemical protein factories for the underdeveloped countries. The western municipalities also contain
treeless areas for sun seekers and giant model villages for the
overflow of population from our poorer southern hemisphere.
They eat soya-derived proteins and government subsidies. This
is called regional planning and development, a promising innovation." Beyond a Rocky-curtain, a relief map of the old
province of British Columbia flashed on and off, with a superimposed sign: the American dollar upon the hammer and
sickle. "This paradoxical and self-satisfied region," continued
the guide, "was the laboratory of our modern empire: thesis,
antithesis, synthesis. What used to be spelled S-O-C-I-A-L —
C-R-E-D-I-T has now become simply M-O-N-E-Y."

At the other end of the hall was a fishing net in which
human small fry were caught. "The population of the old Mari-
time provinces," interpreted the guide, "has been diverted to
useful work somewhere else. This area has become a paradise for tourists who enjoy synthetic seafoods of uniform
quality; it's much better than those the fishermen used to
collect in the social security offices. Communications are still
poor here. However, the provincial government of Canada
has promised to build a magnetic causeway to Prince-Edward-
Island."

On a gold and platinum wall, a kaleidoscopic globule flash-
ing superimposed views of skyscrapers, industries, traffic and
air jams, words (T-O-R-O-N-T-O — O-N-T-A-R-I-O), etc.,
swelled with each new flash until it encompassed the whole
of old Ontario and territory on both sides of the provincial
border. A historic song explained this process of appropriation:
"Ontario, a place to stand, a place to grow, Ontari-ari-ari-o!!"
"This great imitation has finally made it in the new empire,"
proclaimed the guide. "Ottawa, where you are now, is a sub-

urb of this great intellectual and industrial heartland of our province. If it doesn't happen there, it doesn't happen!" Between the Ontario and Quebec exhibits, a knotty round column, pot bellied in the middle and even more bloated at the top, jutted from a collage of screaming titles cut from old Toronto newspapers. "This sculpture, called 'French Kiss,' is the work of Canus, a Toronto artist. It represents de Gaulle, the man who tried to be God and to divide what wars had united. He was not really important. His failure was."

A wall reserved for Quebec was illustrated with moving clowns, gesturing among *ceintures fléchées*, nuns and priests piously holding hands, traitors getting hanged, etc. A small clown with a huge crooked nose was distributing Greek gifts and free padlocks; another, with a vain and haughty mien, was surrounded by agitated valets trying vainly to build a toy house called "Maîtres chez nous"; two others, nearly carbon copies of one another, held wooden swords in one hand and popsicles in the other, and chanted "Egalité ou indépendance," both being routed by a bald fuming Q armed with a popgun. "These were the futile efforts of the Kebecq tribe before it finally understood, under Sir Elliott, that its individual members would be equal when they grew up to be like the others. Now, finally, they are equal North Americans." Then, showing the hugeness of Montreal on a map, the guide added: "After all, it is only thirty years since Montreal became officially what it had always been: one of the first North American English-speaking metropolitan cities. This shows the advantages of the infallible method Assimil."

To relieve the tired minds of the visitors, the exhibits closed on an Eth-Zoo. The guide said secretively: "This is the Pilot Ethnic Treasures Project of the Task Force of the National Reserves Ministry (PETPTFNRM; for short, PET)." Upper Canada Village was shown beside French Canada Village, or "Saint-Analphonse," with an old man in front of a decrepit schoolhouse teaching young children the ancient traditions and language of their tribe. A ram without horns looked on disinterestedly. "They used to be the first line of defence against the Americans. Obviously, they aren't needed any more. But this is a proof of our democratic respect towards minorities in this province: they are well kept." Just beyond, an electronic three-dimensional simulator of folk dances and songs revived the spirits of the tourists.

It was the end of the tour. The guide told his audience a new guide would conduct the visit through the next halls. "In this electronic age, our computers could easily handle the whole visit. However, the wise chiefs of our democratic and happy empire have thought fit to maintain a certain amount of human element . . . human element . . . human element. . . ." The guide turned rapidly away towards a small door on which was printed: "Repair Shop for Guides."

PART II. OBSESSIONS:
the world scene

J. L. GRANATSTEIN

43   **A World without War?**

GEORGE WOODCOCK

46   **Prophecies and Pontifications**

IAN DRUMMOND

53   **The Great Gold Crisis of 2018:**
The Gold Goes Ouest

DOROTHY FARMILOE

58   **Report of the Fact-finding**
Committee on Food

JAMES REANEY

59   **Supergenmot**

ADRIENNE CLARKSON

62   **Fable Class at the Company:**
The History of the Red-toed,
Hollow-chested Snackbuster

A. P. THORNTON

66   **Your World, and Welcome to It**
(the 33rd Earl of Chesterfield writes
to one of his sons)

overleaf "Inscape Detail" *by Harold Town*

Letter to Kyra (cont'd.)

However much your North America resembles Wallot's museum, if you are reading this section at all in 2020, Kyra, it follows that the nuclear obsession of most of our writers has not been realized. Our concern for global warfare, whether nuclear or biological, might appear quaint to you in the light of the technological threats that you may be confronting in 2020. We may have learned to live with the Bomb but the escalating weapons race between the superpowers and their competition to sell arms to the middle powers are preparing a mathematically certain disaster, as historian Jack Granatstein believes.

George Woodcock, anarchist, Orwell style, foresees a general advance of an enlightened Third World on the backs of the superpowers, by then declined and fallen. Gold, you may be amused to recall, was once a solvent for the international economy. Ian Drummond has written an economist's fable about the function of gold that underlines how much this accepted mythology greases the wheels of international finance. Dorothy Farmiloe's poem needs no commentary as a social statement on the implications of famine and overpopulation for the world.

You may well find James Reaney's short story still the most visionary of this section. Discovering the magic formula for energy is only one half of his vision. More intriguing is the recreation of earthly life by those who had tasted cosmic power and agreed not to play war again for real. Removing uncontrolled aggression instincts is also at the heart of A. P. Thornton's letter à la Earl of Chesterfield. Of all the global visions, this one by a historian of British imperialism is perhaps the most ominous, matched in that respect only by Adrienne's ultrapessimistic fairy tale of the destruction of human society.

A World without War?   J. L. GRANATSTEIN

Over the long run, it does not matter how small the probability of nuclear war is per unit time. It is mathematically demonstrable that, as time goes on, this probability approaches certainty.

This, you will agree, is a helluva way to begin an article in a collection devoted to utopian visions of the world fifty years from now. Granted that my proposition is more apocalyptic than utopian (for which humble apologies); unfortunately, the world today tends more to the horrific than to the beatific. One cannot be blamed for suspecting that the world of 2020 may be worse.

What grounds are there for being hopeful? Precious few. There is no real sign of approaching sanity in a world of insanity. Of course, you say, there is the nuclear nonproliferation treaty. Whoopee! But what use is that treaty in a world in which the ICBM, the ABM, the MIRV, MRV, FOBS and (best of all) CBW are proliferating? But man can put life on the moon, the eternal optimist says. Surely if we can reach the stars there is no limit to our ingenuity, no end to our resourcefulness, no task too great to be accomplished. The cynical/realistic answer is simple: What about the oppressed peoples of the Third World? What about the plight of the cities? What about the slums of New York, Toronto, Montreal, Vancouver? What about the pollution of the earth? If man is capable of achieving the grandiose, why can he not accomplish the merely prosaic — but far more important — task of ending inequality and suffering in his own world? Perhaps we can, but we are not.

How can one hold anything but apocalyptic views in this year 1970? The great conservative tide is beginning to sweep over our continent as a frightened America turns inward upon itself. The blacks, the yippies, the poor, the students — no one knows his place any more (those who have arrived maintain with set jaw and firm mien), and only force can restore the society and culture we know and love. Force will

be applied, let there be no doubt, in a fashion that will make
Chicago or Sir George Williams look like cakewalks. In all
probability, too, the *status quo ante* will be restored. This will
mean more money for defence and antiriot weaponry; this
will mean less and less spending on the problems of the
urban areas and on the rural poor. It will mean more strife,
more bloodshed, more of everything except peace. How can
one doubt that this will be the result when the United States
Army has already begun unleashing its public relations flack
with the pitch that after Vietnam (and when, oh when,
will *after* Vietnam begin?) the defence budget must be raised?
The shortages produced by the demands of the war will have
to be remedied. Of course, there have been attacks on the
Pentagon and on the widespread waste that characterizes any
military organization — even the "new" *Time* has taken
swipes at its erstwhile allies of the military-industrial complex — but these sallies will get nowhere in the face of presi-
dential stupidity, industrial cupidity and public susceptibility.
The war — any war — will go on until the next one starts.
    Still, honesty compels one to admit that there are occasional
flashes of sunshine on this dark and disturbing landscape. Oddly
enough, the nation of greatest hope at the moment is Canada.
The prime minister seems to have overcome the resistance
to change of the departments of National Defence and External Affairs. He appears to have cracked the shell of
imperviousness to ideas that seems to have been government issue to all fledgling soldiers and diplomats. He seems
to have altered the penchant for cement-like immobility that
has been the hallmark of Canadian policy since 1945, and
he seems to have injected some new ideas into the policy
process. It matters not a damn if these ideas are correct or
not — although they almost certainly are tending in the right
direction. What is important is that the ideological certainty,
the unswerving smugness so characteristic of the Ottawa brah-
mins has finally been shattered.
    And if it can happen to Canada, who is to say that es-
tablishments in other countries cannot be similarly overturned?
Until 1969 Canada had been the most loyal of satellites; perhaps our example will stimulate other defections in the Netherlands, in Norway, in Rumania. Trudeau's innovations in

foreign policy could be of enormous importance. If Canada can persuade others to follow her example, we could conceivably be on the threshold of a golden era in foreign policy. Conceivably. But one could wish that the direction of Canadian foreign policy were clearer than it is. Pearsonian internationalism appears to be dead and gone but, if it is slated to be replaced only with Trudeauvian isolationism, this will satisfy very few Canadians. The prime minister has the opportunity to turn our policy into new paths and towards the kinds of problems that must be solved if the world is to survive the next fifty years. The control of nuclear weapons is clearly the most pressing task, but there are other more prosaic questions. For example, how are we to control multinational corporations? That is an area in which Canadians will have to develop expertise soon, and our solutions should be useful to other countries such as Japan, Mexico, Brazil and most Western European states. If we can turn our hand to such tasks, if we can mobilize the smaller powers to work with us in the search for the solutions to these problems, we will merit the approbation of our peers.

Prophecies and Pontifications

GEORGE WOODCOCK

In the 1890s H. G. Wells made the point in one of his novels that, at the end of the Victorian era, the availability of cheap bicycles brought about a minor revolution in English life, not only in physical mobility but also in social definition. The bicycle defined the rising classes, the lower-middle-class clerks and the skilled workers, from the carriage-owning establishment and the impoverished unskilled.

Today in India, seventy years later, the bicycle is again a means of greater physical mobility and a symbol of social ascent. To own one means that a man has climbed out of the morass of deep poverty; that in his village he is among those carriers of black umbrellas who lord it over the less fortunate lingerers in chronic malnutrition and single-dhotied austerity; that his world has spread from a village into a district by virtue of two wheels; probably that his wife owns a sewing machine and is edging her way out of purdah. Over the past nine years I have watched the spread of the bicycle in rural India. In 1961 it was common in Delhi, the favoured transport of small government clerks but rare in the country districts. Today one still sees few bicycles in poor states like Kerala, where men either walk or travel by boat on the endless canals. But when one goes out of Delhi northwestward, the incidence of bicycles steadily increases. Moderately numerous in Haryana, they are almost universal in Punjab, the most developed region in India. Here there are towns like Ludhiana that have literally thousands of tiny workshops which assemble bicycles or make parts for them. In Ludhiana the Sikhs have in fact become so prosperous selling bicycles to the rest of northern India that a further stage in mobility and in the symbolism of social ascent is revealing itself; locally, bicycles are giving way to motor scooters.

When I think of the year 2020, it is this kind of time lapse that interests me. It has taken the most favoured parts of India more than seventy years to reach a stage attained in England in the 1890s, before the invention of the automobile. How far, I wonder, will this gap be telescoped in the next fifty years? For on its telescoping depends to a great extent the shape of the world we shall see in 2020. A future seen only in North American terms, a future that leaves out of account changes in the internal condition and international presence of major Asian countries is no future at all, but a wish-fulfilling mirage.

Of course, to imagine any future that will be less than tragic one has to make some massive assumptions of world-wide significance: that there will be no world-searing atomic catastrophe; that in certain areas which now excite enormous concern, man's sanity and his technological skills will have triumphed; that pollution will cease to build up in air and water; that the difference between birth and death rates will have narrowed; that a quarter of the world's population will no longer live in chronic malnutrition. And beyond these assumptions one must recognize as worldwide the changes we can read in the demographic probabilities for the next half century.

Today youth is numerically preponderant. In most countries the majority of the population is under twenty-five, and in many Asian countries, thanks to the dramatic reduction of infant mortality, it is less than twenty-one. The 1960s and 1970s are decades of the young, when everyone aspires to project a youthful image, when radical changes in social forms might conceivably be carried through on waves of youthful enthusiasm.

If, led away by the politics of withdrawal, the young have not lived up to their own promises by the 1980s, it will then be too late. The demographic situation will have changed irrevocably: the young of today will be entering middle age; the over-thirties will once again be moving into numerical ascendancy and the population will steadily age for several decades as the birth rate falls, until a new stability is reached about 2000. In the meantime, the accepted ideal will have shifted from the swinging youth of unisex ambiguity to the stable male of mature years; beards will be trimmed and Victorian, symbols of solid responsibility and paterfamilias resurgent. We shall face an interlude of social conservatism, even reaction, until new polarizations create new forces of revolt and begin once again to move society forward into change.

These forces of revolt will come from one expected and one

less expected direction. Paterfamilias resurgent will polarize the male-female rivalry, and the ensuing revolt of women will be much sharper in its impact and broader in its consequences than the present youth revolt. During the 1950s and 1960s the feminist cause steadily lost ground. The number of Canadian women MPs, for example, declined radically, and even among student activists the leaders have been patriarchs to a man, using the women mainly as bodies for demonstrations. Only countries like Ireland, Israel and India have in this period thrust up significant women leaders, and these have emerged from societies that still — in many ways — belong mentally to the age that produced the suffragettes. But by the 1990s everywhere, feminine resentment will have surfaced in a movement that will change sharply the composition of the power élite in most Western countries and even in some Eastern ones. (Note that I use the term *power élite*; in 2020 we shall still be crawling like snails unwillingly towards the anarchist millennium.)

The less expected revolt will be that of the old, or perhaps rather the elderly, those whom the shrinking demand for labour and the difficulty of coping with a rapidly changing technology will have rendered obsolete according to the values of the traditional work ethic. Growing quickly in numbers, infinitely better educated than the old of generations before, these people will demand that their capabilities be given means of fulfilment. It will be they, far more than the youth of the 1960s and 1970s, who will define in terms of actual daily life the revolution that takes place when we move not from a work society into a leisure society, but from a society where work is the price of a living to one where work, divorced from its necessary connection with commodity production, becomes a word to express any activity that satisfies a man's nature and distinguishes living from mere existence. We are nearer than many imagine to William Morris's dream of a society powered not by man's fear of starvation, but by his physical and aesthetic and intellectual joy in activities that only incidentally are socially valuable.

Yet for Canadians and Americans and Swedes to live in such a utopia without great changes in the have-not world would be as perilous as the situation of the graceful but defenceless Elois in Wells's *The Time Machine,* living by the work of the subterranean Morlocks who remotely share their human ancestry, but at the same time in perpetual danger from the predatory urges of those submerged half men.

Will the submerged half of real humanity move up out of Morlock darkness during the next fifty years? (Remember, as another demographic probability, that in 2020 the successors of the present malnourished millions will be even more numerous proportionately, since the decline in birth rate will continue to be inversely related to the increase of prosperity and sophistication.) And, if it does, will the rise be sufficient to obviate the chance of major conflict between the haves and the have-nots? These are central questions.

As Buckminster Fuller has shown in eloquent detail, there is no reason, given modern technology, why the world's poor should remain poor or mass starvation should recur. And the best act of all to give concrete form to such insights would be a fiat of the liberated imagination by which the economies of the United States, Russia, China and the major European powers were reoriented from war production to peace production aimed at the worldwide equalization of economic opportunity. I doubt if this will take place. What I do foresee through the 1970s and perhaps into the 1980s is a slow, steady increase in foreign aid that will eventually come to an end, because it has been too little and too late to prevent the turning away of the less developed countries and the creation of new forces in the have-not world that will generate from within the vigour needed for its transformation.

By 2020 the have-not peoples, inhabitants of all the petty little lands that arose in fervent patriotism out of the wreckage of old empires after 1947, will have grown wise to the folly of defending themselves against each other for the benefit of the large arms-producing countries, and will have become acutely intolerant of the narrow ways of 1970-vintage nationalism. The men shaping small- and middle-power politics in 2020 will have moved the world into patterns where regional and even subcontinental rather than national formations will counterbalance the surviving monolithic great powers, dinosaurs like Russia and China and the United States, sinking under the weight of the weaponry they will not relinquish and dare not use.

In the process, many currently acute political problems will be solved. The present alliance of Arab states — already a crude prototype of the future — will be rearranged to suit the real interests of Middle Eastern peoples. In this new context, technologically advanced Israel will cease to be the enemy and oil-enriched Iran will cease to be the outsider; indeed, both countries will play leading roles in the new formation, and power will shift away from Cairo and towards Teheran. On the opposite side of the world, a recognition of the identity of subcontinental interests will wash away the artificial frontiers imposed on Latin America by the warring interests of rival revolutionary chieftains in the early nineteenth century. A federation will emerge, sustained by its own adequate resources and equally independent of American imperialism and of the Cuban ideologues, who will survive — like the Albanians — in the isolation of a kind of Tibet of outdated revolutionary dogmas.

These regional federations of the future will often re-establish the boundaries of ancient empires, which possessed a great deal of geographical good sense. The new Europe emerging from the Common Market will correspond roughly to Barbarossa's Holy Roman Empire. The Middle Eastern grouping will be roughly coterminous with the empire which Darius ruled from Persepolis, and a Bosphorus alignment, reconciling Balkan-Greco-Turkish differences and recreating the core of the Byzantine empire, is a distinct possibility.

Most interesting, in view of the increasing importance of the Pacific Rim, will be the political reshaping of South and Southeast Asia. India and Pakistan face intense strains during the 1970s. Given the basic philosophies of both countries, these tensions are unlikely to end in Communist takeovers, but they will leave the generation of the 1980s with a growing conviction that neither country as it exists is politically viable, since each contains either too much (in the sense of disparate elements too closely linked) or too little (in the sense of a clearly defined geographical area insanely divided). We can expect a centrifugal process of dissolution which will result eventually in new unities. The Dravidian states of south India will draw away from the Hindi-speakers of Delhi and the North. Bengalis, whether Muslim or Hindu, will remember that they have more in common with each other than with Tamils

or Sindis, and Punjabis from Lahore and Amritsar, divided
by the passions of Partition in 1947 (seventy-three years ago
by 2020) will find the same. Thus, while regions *within* the
subcontinent will define themselves sharply, eventually they
will come together again in a confederation, including long-dis-
puted Kashmir as one of the constituents. This will recreate
the only unified India of the past, Queen Victoria's Raj.

Another direction in which traditional India may provide
a pointer for the world fifty years ahead is to be found in its
attitudes towards work. Traditionally in India, a man is expected to spend part of his life fulfilling a certain social or economic function, but there comes a point when work as we
conceive it is no longer required to make him respected and
when he does not feel the lack of it as a sign of inadequacy.
The politician, the man of affairs, the businessman, having
done his duty to his community and his family, retires with
enhanced prestige into the religious life where his past, including his caste, is no longer of significance. I am not suggesting
that in 2020 we will be learning from India how to become
sadhus. (I wonder how many Indians will be doing that fifty
years ahead.) But the knowledge will become universal
among us that· a worthy life is not based upon the prestige
of profit or of employment.

What else do I see of the future as the image fades in the
waters of fancy? Of the three obsolete great powers, China
— victim of dogmatic aridity — will have retreated into the
kind of paralyzing narcissism that rotted the Manchu empire;
the United States, having long since withdrawn from the shores
of Asia and left the China Seas to a resurgent Japan (master
again of Formosa and overlord of the Philippines), will be
recovering from the exhaustion of a quarter of a century of
bitter internal strife; Russia, once the pupils of Stalin have
died off, will loosen into a ramshackle empire where the subject peoples will have regained much of their independence, and
for this reason it will show a kind of submerged vitality denied
its two rivals.

As for Canada, we shall still be together, because the alternatives will always have seemed worse, and we shall have
found our appropriate place in a world of loose-working con-
federations. We shall have drawn power and independence

from our trading alliances with Japan and India and from a cultural rapprochement with the new Europe (once again the centre of artistic innovation and intellectual activity). But we shall still remember 1812, and the Americans will remain our dear enemies whose resurgence we shall welcome and fear. The moon? The planets? A dusty sickness in the minds of great powers from which mankind will recover when megalomania has ceased to be politically viable! Like Antaeus, we belong to the earth where evolution bred us. It will be good enough and large enough for a long time to come.

The Great Gold Crisis of 2018: The Gold Goes Ouest

IAN DRUMMOND

Years will pass before we can know all the details of the dramatic events which rocked the world's financial system two short years ago. Nevertheless, now that Raoul Sainfoin has fled to Reykjavik, the picture is becoming less opaque: we can begin to see beyond the bare outlines which blackened our visiprint outputs during those dramatic weeks. The emerging story is at least as bizarre as any we may have imagined during chemoeuphoria. And it is much more disquieting. One is not surprised to find that our political leaders were confused. But one is amazed — not to say alarmed — to find our financial Keepers, those technocorpsmen from whom all blessings must necessarily flow, confused about so elementary a matter as the nature of liquidity. Perceiving this, we may well feel a chill wind of disquiet in whose blast a stiff upper lip is hard to maintain. For when error so fundamental disports herself under the *proscaenium*, can chaos be far in the wings? When a witches' sabbath of misunderstanding is danced beneath the chancel arch, what hobgoblin may lurk leering in the clerestory? But to our tale.

Ever since the ancient times of St. Maynard Keynes and Blessed Robert Triffin, it has been vaguely perceived that countries could manage their affairs without the use of gold. Like theologians of other cults, the Keepers of the Financial Arcana have not been very successful in explaining the True Faith to the multitudes. But among themselves they have, one must admit, done rather better. The world has learned to expect that, when the archiflamens and archimandrites meet in solemn conclave at Basle, the world's financial wheels will be kept turning even though the theological communiqués may be unintelligible. While keeping the wheels turning, the Keepers have evolved, decade by decade, an international financial system whose complexity is rivalled only by the Talmud, the Soviet Managerial Handbook and the English Common Law.

But we can hardly blame them for this. The tangle keeps them more or less harmlessly employed. And it has certainly stitched a fair number of tears in the world's financial fabric.

Consider, for instance, that outbreak of competitive devaluation when the Bulgarian and Macedonian governments were fighting for the world market in attar of roses. Any economist could have told them — indeed, most of the world's economists *were* telling them — that the attar market is a classic case of perverse elasticities, where devaluation merely makes things worse. But only the Keepers of the Imf could convince the Macedonians and the Bulgarians. Or consider that long-continued and most unfortunate overvaluation of the Albanian lek. And do not forget the dreadful things which could have happened to the world's supply of new gold when the South African government proposed its policy of protective collaration. One can sympathize with that government's decision to weld a five-pound gold collar round the neck of every adult white serf. The blacks had laboured for so many generations in the mines that the gold had become a potent symbol for them. And certainly it was important to mark the whites with something nonremovable, and highly visible, so that they could not successfully colour themselves and pass for black. Hence, the South African government, pointing out that collaring was more humane than branding, properly ignored the pseudo-humanitarian supplications and imprecations from the North Atlantic Federation. But when the Imf pointed out that the program would absorb all of South Africa's gold production for a decade, the government reconsidered, and sensibly settled for iron.

The South African gold mattered, because the world had never completely accepted the synoptic and patristic truths with respect to the meaninglessness of gold. All central banks wanted at least a little to display on their balance sheets. Governments felt likewise about their foreign exchange reserves. And some countries were systematically building up their holdings, year after year. Of these, the most consistent and vigourous gold buyer was France.

The reader will remember that for many years the Sixteenth Republic has been stockpiling gold. For long it was thought in the Arcana that the reason was the Rueffian heresy, which

was known to have lingered long in Paris. But Sainfoin has
now told the world the true reason. Though Gallic, it is far
from base. Nor is it, in the abstract, foolish.

At intervals, ever since the 1960s, the buildings of Paris
have been washed. Grandeur and glory have required this.
Regrettably, it came to be noticed, the repeated cleanings were
gradually damaging the architectural monuments of the city.
The problem was not just a matter of mortar and woodwork,
which could be replaced; the stones themselves were beginning
to crumble. What could be done? To allow the noble façades
to engrime themselves once more would be to admit that in
technical prowess the French lagged behind the Anglo-Saxons
of the North Atlantic Federation. Emissaries were sent to the
politicians of the State of Quebec, but their suggestion —
aluminum foil cladding — was unacceptable. For a long and
anxious month of secret meetings, the cabinet debated the
application of transparent plastic mothballing. This, they finally
decided, was unworthy. For some time no alternative emerged.
But at length a young secretary, Charlotte de Gauloise, thought
of something which almost at once was accepted as national
policy. "Why not," she asked, "gold-plate them all?"

And so it was decided. Gold was to be accumulated and
cast into great panels which would, when enough had been
prepared, sheathe the façades of the City of Light. Meanwhile,
architects and artisans covertly measured, cast in plaster, sur-
veyed and schemed. A corps of workers was sworn to secrecy.
On the Normandy coast, long-abandoned submarine pens were
converted into workshops. The nation strained to increase its
balance-of-payments surplus. Large bond issues were floated
abroad, and the proceeds transferred to the shores of Normandy. France offered attractive terms to other countries
which sought safe storage for their bullion hoards. The European Confederates responded at once. And the North Atlantic Federation, its metallic security threatened by guerrilla
mutants in the Kentucky hills, was almost as eager to accept.

Slowly but steadily the auriferous work proceeded. Equally
steadily, but much less slowly, Raoul Sainfoin matured his
plan. An inspector of finances and a native of Cherbourg,
he had long schemed for Norman independence. Knowing
of the gold plan, he began to gather a band of zealots. As

the plot matured, the numbers grew. At length, on April 12, 2018, the Norman patriots rose in Cherbourg and seized the nearby submarine pens. With Sainfoin in command, they emptied the vaults and used the gold bars and castings to build a ten-foot wall round Cherbourg. The French, Sainfoin reasoned, would never dare to attack: to do so would destroy their most precious national asset — not only the gold itself, but the architectural castings which represented decades of work and national self-sacrifice. Paris would be obliged to recognize Norman independence.

For eight days, while the world waited, the French government debated. Sainfoin, who was in constant radio touch with them, claims that they never did decide anything — that what finally happened was an accident of some kind. Whatever the truth of this, no French politician will now take the blame for the events of April 20. Since April 13, the golden fortifications had been ringed with French troops, their laser cannons at the ready. At the stroke of noon, as the sun shone and the birds twittered, one of these fearsome weapons began to hurl its ray at the wall. In seconds a gaping hole had appeared and the gun was swinging in a widening arc, melting more and more of the blocks. Now more of the beams began to play and in less than fifteen minutes, the entire barricade had been converted into a river of metal. As its defenders fled screaming, the gold flowed seaward. Driven by the laser beams, it cut deep chasms in the landscape, burning on until, with a fearsome hiss and a cloud of steam, the molten gold plunged into the ocean and vanished. Only a few glittering puddles remained on the ravished earth. As Sainfoin found shelter in a peanut butter factory, whose extraterritoriality protected him, the French troops surged through the defenceless city. The Independent Duchy of Normandy was no more.

But the world's gold reserves also were no more. France had engrossed them all, then flushed them into the Atlantic Ocean. Hysterical finance ministers and Keepers took flight for Paris after gibbering to reporters in airport lounges. Exchanges and stock markets gyrated wildly all over the globe as a chillingly large flow of hot money surged from one financial centre to another. In one day the pound hit a fifty-year low and a fifty-year high, oscillating between twenty-five cents and ninety-seven cents. Goldmining shares sextupled in value. Even silver shares benefited, as financial pundits dreamed of bimetallism.

In Paris, the Keepers were met with an icy calm. It is true, the president said, that your gold is no longer in the submarine pens. But it is even more secure than before, for it now lies in a single immense ingot at the bottom of Cherbourg harbour. Who can get it now? Meanwhile, some Cambridge economists had formed a perambulatory colloquium to discuss the problem; their press release was, as might have been expected, iconoclastic. "Why do you care where the gold is?" they asked. "You know how much there is in that ingot, and you can earmark it and pass it from country to country and bank to bank — even count it in your foreign exchange reserves — whether it's in a vault, at the bottom of the English Channel or on the moon. Since the whole point of a gold reserve is that it can't be used for anything useful, what does it matter if the gold is more or less out of reach? It's as liquid there as ever it was."

But this obvious truth the Keepers could not accept. And so, as the world's troops massed on her frontiers, and as from the satellites the death rays were trained on the Elysée and the Louvre, the French capitulated. "Yes," they said, "we are very sorry, and we shall rescue your gold from the ocean. Also, as an indemnity for your distresses, we shall distribute our own gold among you once we get it all back."

It remains to be seen how successful they will be. Each month the dykes push farther into the English Channel. Each month the bathyspheres probe deeper. But the gold has sunk low into the craggy and splintered sea floor. Years of mining will be needed to retrieve it — even if the relevant ocean can all be enclosed and pumped away. The hopeful speak of spin-off benefits — better diving, better earth filling, better pumping . . . already housewives can buy Cherbourg Armour-plate Glass for their picture windows . . . already the offspring of the Sea-Deep Kelp Clipper can be found on suburban lawns. . . . Nevertheless, one wonders. Can this *really* be a prudent use of man's scarce talents?

Report of the Fact-finding Committee on Food

Gentlemen:
We meet this afternoon to study
ways and means of augmenting
the country's food supply.

The people are rebelling against
the Plankton Plan, and the latest
effort to transplant moss from Mars
has failed. This week General Motors
expropriated the last Ontario farm
but it was badly needed for
industrial expansion.

The subcommittee on natural
exploitation reports that toadstools
were found growing on the north slope
of the city dump; unfortunately,
they are of the nightshade variety.

You remember last year it was thought
that snakes and lizards might survive
in the city's sewer system, but that
experiment failed also. The food
picture, gentlemen, is not good.

However, on the bright side
of the ledger I can report
the euthanasia program has been
completely successful. All citizens
over thirty have been mercifully
eliminated. But there are still
a billion mouths to feed.

So, gentlemen, I have a modern
proposal: the poor we have always
with us and the children of the poor,
and those children, gentlemen,
are in plentiful supply. . . .

Supergenmot JAMES REANEY

April 3, 1969 – Kenneth McNaught has just written asking if I'd be interested in doing a Utopia article for the Forum's fiftieth anniversary issue. I'll start thinking now and see, by the time we leave the island, if anything is ready to bring – up to the surface.

July 2, 1969 – What came to the surface was/What you could see as happening a further fifty years on is . . . [fade out]

About the year 2000 A.D., an old math professor at Harvard (Ph.D., Tor.) discovered a formula which meant this: with a very little effort anybody could wrap themselves in light, go anywhere they wanted to, do anything with light they wanted to — energy, fuel, food, propulsion, etc. The formula involves such a very simple juxtaposition of materials available even to babies — I am about to write it down, but there is no need to. All my readers know about it and, as you well know, have good reason to forget it. Well, the old professor was killed shortly after his discovery in the Cafeteria Riots (some teacher was insolent with a waitress about a bolt in his salad); however, a group of Canadian and American businessmen bought the contents of his office, discovered the formula and were soon marketing its power under the acronym SUPERGENMOT. List just a few results:

1. Massive preconditioned "happiness."
2. Megalopolis out not just to Orangeville but — Saturn.
3. No one ever did, in government circles, explain why Betelgeuse disappeared, but a certain group of stockbrokers made a great deal of $ about that time. . . .
4. A huge BA sign on the moon.

Who broke this monopoly? A young lad rediscovered the formula, revealed it at a Boy Scout World Jamboree before anybody could stop him. The result of this was that everyone on earth learned the formula, learned the simple manipulation of light involved and left this planet as soon as they could. Anything to get away from SUPERGENMOT's "happiness." Results?

Moon badly damaged by youthful hot rodders in space.
A few stupid Canadians had to be pried loose from their
archaic twentieth century life patterns, had to be forced to
leave their mortgages, freeways and computers.

Problems at first, yes, but if there were a problem you
simply "lit" yourself to an uninhabited planet in the galaxy
and there were enough of these for this.

So — eventually no one lived here anymore and the con-
servation both of earth and the planetary system was suddenly
no longer a problem. Halley's comet slowly straightened its tail,
bent in an absurd experiment by McLaren's Advertising Agency; Neptune also slowly shed its polyethylene sheath (*vid.*
"Planet Art?" *ArtCan*, XXDCVII LX MXL, April 2012) and
the dodo swarmed again on that third planet out from the
sun. The last issue of the *Canadian Forum* came out (by this
time pronounced *Canuck Farm*): the world as we know it now
(August 1970, A.D.) had become a deserted ghost system,
manless apparently forever.

Suddenly rediscovered as a museum. Methane gas was
pumped back into Jupiter and the asteroids carefully counted.
Fifty new asteroids were flown in from Proxima Centauri.
Men came back to this galactic Williamsburg, both as tourists and curators and — actors. Dressed as in the old days,
moving through such dimly remembered but dearly beloved
pageants as World War III and the Indian Mutiny or the fall
of Babylon or the Crowe case. Slowly there grew up a colony
of people so devoted to earth that, although they knew the
formula and knew of the planet-for-each-delight thus available — they *stayed*. It had something to do with — *you knew
where you were.*

So, when the galaxy suddenly paranoided and almost nightly
another star fell — enfants terribles misusing the formulae —
the bored going amok — whole infinitudes revolting *against*
"happiness" and the ultimate "affluence" — you write the rest
of this sentence.

One a.m. earth dwellers realized that, as once before, they
were the only human beings alive — and alive, too, on the
planet that had "started it all." Systematically, *using* the formula, somebody or some organization had wiped out *all* the
people who knew the formula. *All* the people including itself

or themselves or himself. A huge asteroid missile obviously designed to slice the earth in half missed by fifty thousand miles (thank God the old math professor only got eighty percent in computer programming) and a later star-missile aimed at the sun only ripped the corona. But. . . .

Earth people kept themselves busy rehearsing the pageants. Whenever the men got bored or restless, World Wars I and II drubbed out their meanness. When the women felt a mystique coming on, the revival of a mediaeval witch hunt rid them of this friedan. Yes, even a rehearsal of SUPERGENMOT was occasionally needed to clear the air; through careful research a great deal of evil was avoided by — repeating the evils as a sort of museum game, although often it was hard to tell if the pageant evils were really game or for real. Odd things happened: *Edward III, II, I!* A copy of the *Canadian Forum* (by this time pronounced *Candid Frock*) printed backwards, or a lemur turning into a shrew turning into a small triceratops?!

Yes, when everyone had decided to be Cro-Magnon and to pretend they knew nothing about Euclid or McLuhan or tops or potatoes — an odd feeling would come about that perhaps this was exactly what the real Cro-Magnon man had been doing. For archaeologists had discovered in a supercave — a huge magic lantern apparatus (carbon dated to 20,000 B.C.) capable of projecting twenty prehistoric bison at a time. So . . . keep moving. Time for a plague, time for a social collapse, time for a Golden Age.

Re-enact. Re-enact. Perhaps even to such a minute extent that sometime in the very, very distant utopian future a piece of paper will be found, ink yet fresh, still gleaming saying:

April 3, 1969 – Kenneth McNaught has just written asking if I'd be interested in doing a. . . .

Fable Class at the Company: The History of the Red-toed, Hollow-chested Snackbuster

Once upon a time, dear little labour units of value, there existed in our universe a breed of animal known as the red-toed hollow-chested snackbuster. It resembled us in many respects, having four extensibles (somewhat longer and less specialized than ours), a nerve centre and a solid central mass designed for rudimentary processes such as energy conversion and a bizarre form of hazardous self-reproduction. Around this elemental base of functions, it had built a myth about itself that should stagger the rationality of all of you who are already five years old and have been trained to fulfil the specific needs of the Company.

In any case, the myth was built up over generations while the snackbuster pulled himself from the slime of his sloppy, disordered world. In the process, he gained those red toes through long, slow centuries of adaptation. With them he pulled himself out of the mud and clung to the rocks; with them he killed (yes, personally) those who blocked his progress. For with them he had pulled himself to an upright position and he wanted to maintain that dominance. Of course it all seems silly to us now, as we know that it is not necessary for the good of society that every one of us be upright; not all functions require it, and we have discarded it with a few exceptions. I, for instance, need it, because I am your fablemaker, but you, depending on your ability to produce for the Company, have been created by rational design and according to the Plan in various useful forms of curvature, cubage, et cetera.

The snackbuster's hollow chest was developed because this breed had a uniform speech capacity. Can you imagine the cacophony that resulted? With *everyone* able to speak? Only the total irrationality of these animals could have misled them to think that everyone was made to speak as well as listen. It was an extremely untidy and unjust situation, as they produced forty times their planet's weight in things called books, which were the unbridled overflow of the habit of speech. They had developed ways of transcribing speech so that all could understand it, as though everyone could interpret your individual work-order card. And they used this activity licentiously to propagate things called ideas, elaborate patterns of words with which they glorified themselves. The snackbuster began giving up killing and crawling out of the mud in order to devote all his time to ideas, and it is interesting to note that at this time the toes lost much of their redness.

Over a period of some sixty generations they were obsessed by the myth of Themselves. Using ideas, they developed such strange and ultimately self-destructive thoughts as the idea that they were the finest breed ever developed, that every one of them had the right (you will find this word defined in the central dictionary code bank if you get permission from me to see it) to do what every other one did. They became particularly obsessed with this latter idea, which was really an outgrowth of a larger thing which they called freedom. For the better part of half of their history they thought of nothing else; they fought wars and killed millions of themselves because, they said, each one of them must be free. Now I know those of you who have a laughter button are tempted to press it when you hear something like this, but I assure you that this was so.

They were divided into two sexes and one had been dominated for many generations because it was the reproductive one. Yes, that sex actually carried new ones within it, a wasteful and disgusting process to which these poor deluded animals hung on for so long because they felt it was personally enriching — a pathetic example of their native abhorrence for the rational uniformity and functionality that we have achieved. Gradually the carrying sex decided it wanted to give up the tedium of that activity and the dominant ones, deluded by their obsession with freedom for everybody, relieved them of the reproductive handicap.

It is curious to note that both the sexes came to resemble one another superficially; they lost lumps in one place and gained them in others. The dominant snackbusters seemed to lose their urge to kill and began to look for higher and higher places on the rock above the mud. They spent a great deal of time lying on the lower rocks, staring at the stars which they had only recently begun to conquer, while they jarred their already ineffective physical processes with various self-deluding and self-administered chemicals. They had not yet learned that only a planned, centrally organized administration of such potent things can be truly effective for the good of society as a whole. They became even more concerned with communicating their feelings (which had always been their biggest weakness). The din, as they all opened their nervous systems to one another, must have been aural pollution of the worst order for at least two generations.

Meanwhile, something parallel was going on. Even the stupidest of breeds (and this, as you can see from even a rough outline, was truly very stupid) has within it some enlightened beings who see what the shape of things must be. They started to realize that their breed was too inept to create a good society and they started (ever so gently at first) pointing out what horrors the idea of freedom had wrought — the death and destruction of millions; the useless, unproductive striving for the abstract (I hesitate to utter the word, it is so obscene); the futile myth making about unprovable feelings such as love, truth and beauty. They started by making the people who already had freedom feel guilty about what they had achieved; in this breed's dying years, guilt became a fetish and the unwitting forerunners of our new order learned over the years to use it well. They attacked the idea of freedom by showing that it meant injustice (an idea dear to those poor deluded beasts), knowing that when they offered seventy million filled rice bowls in the place of a sonnet, the guilty would choose the rice bowls. In other words, in the area of their greatest success and preoccupation, the red-toed, hollow-chested snackbusters were attacked directly. Because they lacked the confidence which is the mark of all successful and continuing order, they gradually deteriorated. The toes dropped off, the chest deflated: the snackbuster slid back into the mud. The stars disappeared and their planet was again mercifully silent.

I want to be very sure that you do not miss the point,

and think that they were victimized by the power of the Company. It was inevitable. A breed that could give up so easily what the force of its history had led it to strive for deserved its fate. For when the snackbusters came to fear that violence would result from the loss of their pathetic little order, they collapsed. No, my dear little perfectly functioning units, the red-toed, hollow-chested snackbusters were doomed. No one destroyed them; they destroyed themselves.

Your World, and Welcome to It (the 33rd Earl of Chesterfield writes to one of his sons)

A.P. THORNTON

October 22, 2020

My dear boy,

My secretary has advised me that a missive of yours was by error commingled with the mound of correspondence which my ninety-ninth birthday has evoked from a host of duns and well-wishers. As I sit here in the evening of a full but rewarding day, I can observe from my windows a collection of natives, some of them Albanians, some of them British, some of them doubtless an admixture of both, folding away the marquees that had been erected in my park to celebrate the occasion — one which Her Majesty deigned to irradiate with her gracious presence (she still looks remarkably young, though she is, of course, five years my junior). I hear their laughter as they at once busy themselves with this task and disport themselves with uncoloured balloons, and I am reminded how far we have come since the days when a cry of *Pinkos!* or, *Pales!* would assuredly have been the prelude to their lynching or burning, *tableaux vivants* which were always an expected feature of the *fêtes champêtres* of my youth.

That your letter should have been so long mislaid is by your own doing, since you directed it via the postal services in what you call "Ottawa." Surely even the authorities of your Baffinland Force must have learned that all capital cities, ever since the 1990 gathering of the International Garment Workers' Union set fire to Paris, are designated Zion, plus the appropriate zip code number: thus, "Jerusalem" is Zion Zip One, "Washington" Zion Zip Two, and so on. (Ottawa, you should note, is Zion Zip Forty.) Moreover, the note of peevish rancour that permeates your letter might well spoil my day, did I permit it to do so. For it is assuredly by no wish of mine that you have immured yourself in what you describe as a condition of "irrelevance." Your devoted wrongheadedness, in which you favour your mother (my fifth wife, I surmise), has ere now worked vastly to your own discomfiture. From the day when you first resolved to enrol yourself in the Styoodint Moovemint — ignoring all my warnings, which proved to be entirely well founded, that the Mattoors (or Thirties) would one day put that *claque* utterly to the sword — you have most perfectly succeeded either in isolating yourself from or in misreading every trend of the present era in the history of humankind.

You adhered to "the Libberals," even while they were being pertinaciously rounded up, in everyone's best interest, in three a.m. vans. You insisted on proselytizing the works of Mau and Marks long after every person of substance had forgotten who precisely these persons may have been. In your time you have picketed Cuban embassies for expropriating industrial combinations belonging to the citizens of the United States, and have protested the right of the Bantu to congregate in societies of none but their own kind. It is not for nothing that the Greeks and the Turks, two tribes of the Levant who do not belong on the island of Cyprus, have erected a statue to you there as champion of their distinctive but now forgotten causes. You have contrived not merely to be expelled with ignominy from England and Russia, but to be publicly degraded in Thailand as well. I recollect that it was to my guests at my own dinner table that you elected to announce your amazed discovery, arrived at while passing your post-doctoral year on a peregrination to the continent of Africa, that the rich should live so well but the poor — so poorly. For years you railed at the Panamericans for seeking to subjugate the Panasians, and at the Panafricans for seeking to subjugate both, heedless of the susceptibilities of all. And all this has been, I must ask, to what end? As one of your brothers remarked to me shortly after he had been made responsible for a country the name of which I cannot at this moment recall, you live now not only with none of your best friends — Jews — but with no friends at all.

Nor can I but find your comments on the issue of civil

rights other than totally ill judged. If your commanding officer does not keep you informed of the affairs of the day, I suppose I must take it upon myself to do so, although heaven bears witness I have sufficient calls on my time. Know, then, that two decades since, the League of Black Women Who Combine a Chinese Education with an English Accent issued an edict which proscribed forever both majorities and minorities, on the ground that these were patently antidemocratic. Your antediluvian diatribes against discrimination thus have no reference to a situation wherein marriages between persons of the same race are declared not only misguided by the Cegenation Society but actively hostile to the interests of the stockholders of Posterity Inc. — a corporation which, as surely must have penetrated even to your benighted igloo, has the indefeasible constitutional right to decide what is and what is not valid for the future. You would have been the better apprised of this had you chosen years ago to accept my offer to elect you to the board of direction of my own joint-stock venture, on whose prosperity my fame and peerage chiefly depend. But no, you insisted on shunning all proceedings of the SunTan Cartel, and in your fatuity took no part in its celebrated and crucial decision whether to opt for the black shade or the yellow, the Nwars or the Joans.

You ask, apparently expecting an answer, what has become of the hopes and ideals with which I myself once faced the world. You are confusing me with someone else: possibly with one of your uncles, or some unhappy lover of your mother's. I early resolved never to be taken either at a disadvantage or by surprise; and you are living proof of this, since even your own career as lackbrain and wittold has but slightly shaken my natural affection for you. It was not in my gift to discover an answer; sufficient to encompass the questions. The world in which I grew to maturity was populated with persons and panaceas strange in the extreme. The doctrine of balance had few practitioners. There were those who with all solemnity averred their determination to create a New Order, a Free World and a Great Society. Others no whit less assured announced that since mankind was already doomed, the most prudent course was to exclude themselves from all of its affairs, and the better to effect this they clouded their mind and their vision with opiates of differing potencies. There were yet others, who inclined to classify themselves as Lopsiders or the Left, who asserted that everyone could be educated to share their curious views on everything, including themselves. Some were convinced that an absence of years denoted the presence of wisdom, that whatever was difficult was wicked and that what one did not believe in was unlikely to exist. Others, proclaiming that the poor would always be with us, took steps to ensure the success of this prophecy by placing an interdict on whatever mechanick contrivances promised to reduce the number of births within any given year. And everywhere persons who proscribed all pleasure were seriously engaged with persons who proscribed all else.

Since men of learning were not required by this society — or, to borrow a cant phrase of the time which you still employ, not "relevant" to it — they took ship to the South Seas where, under the cognomen of Beachcombers, they remain to this day. Philosophers were anyway become indistinguishable from grammarians, while the craft of the dramatist had been overlaid by the art of him who knew best how to titillate the town with exhibitions of naked females. Painters and poets and composers, a tribe which for centuries past had been relied upon to enliven or at the least render endurable the more sombre scenes of the human comedy, were nowhere to be found — and indeed no whisper of their whereabouts has ever yet penetrated to a society that would still be very ready to patronize them, even to the extent of making them rich. Polite letters as a vocation had been usurped by the denizens of Grub Street, persons from whose raking cynicisms one was hardly safe even within one's own *salon*, did it happen to house a cathode-tube container. Men who granted themselves the name of medium, but whose message was minimally spiritual, abounded on all sides and in every profession.

Since the domestick scene was thus made the stage for internecine strife, where the loudest huckster commanded the raptest attention, it will not surprise even you to learn that in the great world of affairs the same condition prevailed, the atmosphere being one of suspicion tinged with ˙fear and of hatred tempered only by dislike. Small nations who were known clandestinely to have assembled, with the aid of foreign manuals, a single weapon of a lethal destructive capacity were able extensively to press upon the policies and statecraft of great nations, whole provinces of whose territory had been set aside as warehouses for stocks and piles of weapons even more effective. Every chancellery took its public action in the name of interests and principles which for fifty years or more had not enjoyed the slightest positive life or content. The shortage of accurate histories of their own time, due as I indicated to the retirement of the wise and honest to Polymicromelanesia, contributed to the fears with which statesmen and nations confronted one another: thus, no one was certain that those with whom he now locked in quarrel had not been his former comrades in arms. There were, for example, Americans who continued to assume that the masters of the Russian peoples were Communists. There were Russians who did not cease to plan for the downfall of capitalism, Chinese who dreaded that the foreign devils would reintroduce a mandarin class among them, Africans who supposed that Indians were multiracial in their political outlook and Indians who were similarly misled concerning the Africans. Complication everywhere reigned. Not only did the Arab and the Jew, both of these the scions of a race old enough to consider more deeply, take a diametrically differing view of an identical problem, there were even two tribes of Germans — each oppositely oriented, but neither (fortunately) inflamed by a cause. Lopsiders of all nations continued to believe that in the day of their triumph the State, being no longer necessary, would wither away. Their opponents the Hardheads, while in the meantime assiduously promoting associations of the ILL [International Lion-Lambs] in every zionzip, also looked forward to the time when socialism would everywhere hold sway, since thereafter they themselves would be kept fully employed in the tasks of controlling its manifold operations.

From time to time, a few seers of private means — the occasional Swedish baron, or some inevitable nephew of a Greek shipowner — warned the world that it could not safely continue so to comport itself, if indeed it could be said that it was comporting itself at all. And assuredly disaster would have struck, had it not been for the genius for organization which was my own to command, and for which I have been so signally fêted this very day. (I see through the dusk that the Albanians have now composed themselves to sleep in my pleasaunce: the British, a sterner race, have gone hunting for women in the nearby villages.) The first of December is, as you know, an international holiday — but, crouched in your subterranean shelter, your eyes narrowed on a periscope which reveals only a waste of ice and snow, have you ever asked yourself why? Perpend. That was the day when, within the antiseptic chambers of my SunTan Cartel, a drunken Scottish fellow, a counterjumper with only one degree but a plausible tongue, dropped from a bench a glass vessel that contained a culture of the preparation which had already brought a considerable degree of racial peace to the world by making everyone the same hue. The culture exploded with a loud report; and the Pictish jackanapes, whose interest in things of the mind had not totally evaporated even within the fumes that enveloped his own, proceeded to analyze the residue. Before he died that rogue was to own castles in Spain, the seacoasts of Bohemia, compounds in Johannesburg and palaces in Notting Hill Gate — for it was from that same dish that the AA or anti-aggression pill was evolved which made an end, once for all, of violence as a context in which the affairs of the world were conducted. Bronzed, yellowed and disaggressed, the men who inhabit the globe which you see today — or *would* see, could you be pried loose from its Arctic extremities — are those whose prosperity and harmony is a monument to my own foresight and indeed to my habit of remaining unsurprised.

It is true that the Celtic tosspot did, in a letter to me shortly before his death (he fell from a police launch into New York harbour, I have never been certain why), suggest that perhaps every seven years everyone should cease to take his AA pill, so that his natural instincts might have sabbatical scope. He believed that a lottery should be held towards the close of the sixth year, in order to ascertain which nation or people should become the recipient of international hatred in the seventh. I need hardly tell you that the details of this project were forthwith locked in my strongbox, and will not be investigated until after I am departed: I have, I trust, a sufficient sense of morality.

One moral that emerges is that a life spent in the service of the community, such as my own, is of higher worth than one such as yours. I shall not pretend that a world such as I have both experienced and described is one with which any man of taste and sensibility would prefer to be associated. But, although I myself endured much from a parent whose principal pleasure was to issue homilies at stated intervals, I should fail in my own duty did I not urge upon you that the coat must be cut according to the cloth, and that spirit no less than skill must attend the hand of the tailor. For your part you appear to believe that honour can best be preserved when frozen. I exhort you therefore once more to return to the world such as it is, and such as the sagacity of your forebears, who include myself, have made it.

I am enclosing an apple from one of my orchards. Contemplate this. I of course cannot tell in what condition it may find itself when it reaches you, but you will please to accept it not only in compliment to its own sturdy self-confidence but in the knowledge also that a keen interest in your welfare is still retained by

Your entirely obedient servant,
CHESTERFIELD

PART III.   REALITIES:
the social fabric

CHRISTINA NEWMAN
77   **Some People, Places and Attitudes that Won't Appear in My Next Paradise**

HARRY G. JOHNSON
81   **The Economic Future of Sex**

ROBERT FULFORD
85   **The Future of Death**

JOHN T. McLEOD
88   **Looking Back on IIIth**

EUGENE FORSEY
94   **Trade Unions in 2020?**

DONALD MacDONALD
94   **The Future of Unionism**

HUGH HOOD
103 **Places I've Never Been**

overleaf "Smoke—Flag Down" *by Harold Town*

Letter to Kyra (*cont'd.*)

By now, Kyra, you may be feeling from your 2020 vantage point that, if global or continental disaster was all that occupied their creative mind, the entire Canadian intellectual establishment of 1970 was totally deranged. This section should reassure you. "Realities" is a group of un-far-out visions, based firmly on the concrete here and now of 1970. Christina Newman, a journalist, has described her female utopia as what she doesn't like in the current unequal status of women. No suffragettes, thank you, but no condescending either. What Harry Johnson, an economist of international renown, shares with Newman is a fascination with the evolution of the sexes over the next fifty years. In his view affluence will change the social role of sex much faster than eloquence. As the wages of wifery fall behind the economic attraction of a female career, woman will be freer both of the obligation to get married and the social pressures imprisoning her as full-time babysitter and housekeeper.

The reality of death as a complex social institution may be as hard to manipulate as woman's status. For Robert Fulford, currently editor of the monthly Saturday Night, it's as simple as lifting the taboo on death. The restraint on the individual's right to order his own death is out of step with our other powers of self-control in birth and life.

Another obvious reality needing rationalization is health care, already the third largest industry in North America. According to Jack McLeod, who has just completed four years' study on the healing arts, the treatment of "illth" must be coordinated as an integrated part of the social process.

Putting trade unions after death and health isn't so much a political as it is an editorial comment. It's interesting that Eugene Forsey, a retired labour movement organizer, and Donald MacDonald, president of the Canadian Labour Congress, are both so steeped in the reality of past and present that their projection to 2020 is simply a continuation of today's concerns about wage *negotiations. No thought is given to the possibility of industrial democracy – of workers' participation in management's creative decisions at the local, national or international level. From conservatism to despair there is but a short step. You will live to see if the failure to involve the working man, whether "blue" or "white" collar, in the decisions that affect his professional environment will indeed spark the forces of class war, increasing violence and greater social alienation that are depicted by Hugh Hood's nightmarish short story of the lone man retreating to the north.*

Some People, Places and Attitudes that Won't Appear in My Next Paradise

CHRISTINA NEWMAN

When you get right down to it — staring at the blank paper, plumbing the depths of the even blanker imagination, reviving forgotten fantasies left over from world-beating yapfests in college common rooms — it soon becomes obvious that the postulation of a paradise for women of my age and general persuasion is pretty bloody difficult, if not to say impossible.

For I belong to that nameless generation of the fifties, that uncommitted company of the cool who were born in the years just before the Second World War: educated in the expectation of equality, confronted by the realities of domesticity and the double standard, too young to have been gulled into believing in the feminine mystique (as was the generation of the forties for whom happiness was supposedly a man, four children on three levels, Birks sterling, real pearls and a grand slam at the Victoria College Alumnae annual bridge) but too old and oh! shameful admission, too liberal to be affected by the Sisters, Unite-against-the-Capitalist-Imperialist-Phallic-Society! militancy of the new women's liberation movements.

If you add to the uncertainties of my whole generation my own specific experience — too many dues paid to feminism in the form of five years spent on a women's magazine writing such mind blowers as Why Can't We Treat Married Women Like People? and Working Wives Are Here To Stay! — you realize that it would be paradise enough for me if by 2020 A.D. people had simply stopped talking about women as though we were a national problem like the Indians and the surplus of wheat.

In brief, it's far easier to describe what my utopia won't be like than what it will and to say that everything will be groovy half a century from now if:

— All women's organizations, including women's institutes, women's press clubs, associations of women electors, wo-

men's Christian temperance unions and all Old Girls
associations everywhere (as well as all schools that produce Old Girls) either have ceased to exist or have
amalgamated with similar men's groups so that the Elks
and the Eastern Stars, the Shriners and the Daughters of
Empire will lie down together like the lion and the lamb,
donning their fezzes and reciting their creeds in bliss-
ful asexual community.

— Betty Friedan and her ladies of NOW are all sleeping
securely underground in some corner of Westchester
County, happy in the knowledge they were lowered there
by female gravediggers earning union scale; New Fem-
inist Abigail Rockefeller is clipping coupons in the
First National City Bank of New York, having long
since abandoned the karate chop, test tube babies and
Freedom Now!; Pierre Elliott Trudeau and Julia
Verlyn LaMarsh belong to the same branch of Swingles
International; the quintessential New Woman, Baby
Jane Holzer, has married the quintessential New Man,
Andy Warhol, and Lionel Tiger is spending his declin-
ing days in a leatherbound chair in the McGill Faculty
Club, cackling occasionally and murmuring constantly,
"Males bond . . . males bond . . . males bond."

— No one ever says "She thinks like a man," "She's
a person in her own right" or "A toast to the
ladies — God bless 'em," or talks about penis envy,
castration complexes, momism and a confusion of roles,
or uses such phrases as "my better half" or such words
as poetess, sculptress, authoress and housewife. (It's a
funny thing about the word *housewife*. I've seen it
turn sweet and reasonable women into sullen shrews.
A famous Canadian writer-editor not very long ago in-
terrupted a dinner-table conversation about inflation he
was having with my husband to say kindly to me, "Aren't
you complaining about the price of chops like every
other housewife in the country?" I wanted to shout,
"Listen, I'm no housewife — I'll admit to being a hundred other things: schemer, dreamer, sloth, wife, lover,
mother, sometime journalist, one-time correspondent,
part-time char, lapsed Presbyterian, disenchanted hu-

manist. But not a housewife. Never!" I didn't do it
though. I figured it would show a confusion of roles.)
— No dear friend of mine — and no dear enemy either —
will ever be found in my living room complaining that she
isn't getting ahead in journalism/academe/television/poli-
tics "Just because I don't have b---s." (Come to think
of it, in a well-ordered paradise it will not be necessary
to print balls as "b---s.") Instead, women will be able
and willing to admit that in this best of all possible meri-
tocracies, they aren't getting ahead because they're
chronically lazy, hopelessly ill educated, secretly disin-
terested or victims of a widespread prejudice against
people over five-foot eight.
— Publishers have abandoned forever magazines devoted
exclusively to fashion, food, royalty and your child and
no serious newspaper editor thinks that in publishing a
whole section page of cooking and marketing trivia he's
taken care of the interests of his female readers. This
will mean that I'll have to give up collecting dimwitted
headlines like "Whom Will Prince Charles Marry?"
"Don't Be Fooled about Italian Onions" and "Spend
the Summer under a Big Black Sailor," a line which
appeared once years ago in a fashion spread about
hats and is still one of the four sentences I mutter to
myself when I'm in total despair. (The other three sentences come out of *Paradise Lost,* madam, so hold your
snotty remarks.)
    Lest this appear entirely negative, I'll finish in solemnity
by stating that I do have a few positive and not entirely improbable ideas about what the next fifty years ideally will
bring to women. I hope that by 2020 A.D. women will not
have to consider choosing *between* being wives/mothers and
career women; that it will be possible and seem natural for
them to be both (or one or the other) without feeling guilty
or unfeminine; that employers and educators will provide
courses and jobs so that girls can get married early, work or
learn part time while their children are young, without the
worry and hardship such arrangements now impose, and return
full time to work later if they want to; that we will have a
society which, as Bruno Bettelheim said, "can afford to ac-

commodate itself to the real intellectual and emotional needs of people, not just to the demands of economy and efficiency or of ancient prejudices"; a society in which women aren't and don't even feel like an oppressed minority, a society in which they are truly equal to men. But not, of course, the same.

The Economic Future of Sex

An economist looking ahead fifty years, in the confident optimism born of the past twenty-five, is bound to concentrate on the prospect of ever-increasing affluence. With increasing affluence will come increasingly the problems of affluence, the external diseconomies as economists call them: congestion, pollution and a growing scarcity value of privacy. But we may hope that prosperity and technological progress will find tolerable solutions to these problems, or at least pessimistically expect man to get accustomed to living in conditions of squalid opulence. The predominant effect of increasing affluence should be to expand the range of human freedom, both by increasing the means people have at their disposal to display and develop their personalities through the exercise of choice among alternative modes of living, and by increasing, through more extensive and intensive education, the capacity of people to make such choices intelligently.

Among the many dimensions of freedom, it is particularly interesting to speculate on what rising affluence may do to increase the freedom of relations between the sexes and to alter the institutions of marriage and related modes of living. Such speculation is facilitated by a plethora of evidence offered by contemporary society, some of it conflicting.

In the past, rising affluence has exercised conflicting pressures on the typical (by whom I mean middle-class) woman. On the one hand, the transition from an industrial technology to which most humans contributed little more than brute force to one in which the human contribution is based on manual dexterity, literacy and specialist knowledge has done much to give women more economic equality with men. The influence of this in freeing women from the obligation to get married and stay married in order to live respectably has been reinforced by the general rise in real wages, which has enabled women to live decently even on relatively low incomes. In addition, the upward trend of real wages has made the career of wife decreasingly attractive to the intelligent woman, since it has meant that she has had personally to assume the roles of cook, nanny, maid, skivvy and coachman — all of whom could previously be hired at a low wage rate — albeit with the aid of electric power and all sorts of labour-saving equipment. On the other hand, however, for a variety of reasons too complex to enter into here, the affluent society has been both making early marriage an increasingly viable economic proposition and putting social pressure on girls (and boys) to marry. Hence the paradox of more freedom in the choice whether or not to marry, and less use of that freedom — but more use of the freedom to abandon a marriage that is proving unsatisfactory.

Much of the willingness of women to succumb to the pressure and temptation to get married, one suspects, can be accounted for by two factors. One is the fear of pregnancy and the ignominy of desertion. Modern technologies of contraception and the probable eventual legalization and social sanction of abortion will remove that reason and, indeed, put women in a position of mastery over men with regard to the mysteries of sex. The other is the anachronistic social emphasis on the prime function of women as being the bearing and rearing of children. This emphasis should yield to the gradual recognition, first, that a woman who marries at the now-customary age and bears the normal number of children with the normal accurate control over timing will emerge from the child-rearing function a physically young woman with twenty-odd years of active and useful life ahead of her, so that she had better plan a career to return to rather than become a bore to her ex-children and her husband; and second, that the general improvements in female health and longevity and in medical knowledge mean that a woman can fairly safely count on being able to postpone the bearing of children — if that is her ultimate desire — until her forties, while in the meantime she builds up a career of her own. AID available on a commercial basis will enable her to do this without the need for a husband or a lover.

The result is likely to be a profound change in both the actuality of sexual freedom for women and the institution of marriage as traditionally understood. Women will probably assume the dominant selecting role and the associated freedom of fickleness in sexual adventure; men who cannot stand the pace will simply have to get married in self-defence. Women who wish to have babies will gradually learn that they do not require legal husbands for the purpose, providing they are affluent; that the role of the father in child rearing is both problematically useful and short lived in duration, given the specialization of participation in modern society on the one hand and the expanding social responsibilities of the education system on the other; and that the male role in child rearing is probably better performed by a variety of males interested in a woman as a feminine personality rather than as a legal spouse. Women who like running households, including the provision of any range of services that males may require, will probably come to appreciate that this career may be more successfully and profitably pursued as a purely commercial operation than as a career presumptively based on love for a single individual — and carrying the obligation to bear and rear his children.

The increase in sexual freedom and the erosion of the institution of marriage that are likely to accompany the progress of affluence should have some interesting effects on the architectural appearance of our cities. The suburb is now the domain of the family with children, the city the bleak repository of the as-yet-unmarried, the childless couple and the affluent elderly-but-unretired. Affluence and greater sexual freedom are likely on the one hand to move some of the single and childlessly married who like village life out to the suburbs, which will accordingly blossom with appropriate one- and two-person dwelling units, and on the other hand to move many of the married-with-children-but-still-with-it back into the cities, where crèches, kindergartens and higher-quality formal schools will have to be built to absorb the jettisoned burden of parental responsibility for child rearing.

Finally, increasing sexual freedom is likely to mean the social legitimation of homosexuality for both sexes. Once childbearing has become a completely scientifically controllable process, it can be divorced from sexual relations, which can become a matter of intimate communication between personalities regardless of sex. But, paradoxically, there will probably

be considerably less homosexual practice than heretofore, because homosexual inclinations are so closely associated with
the sharp differentiation of the social roles of men and women
that has characterized the pre-affluent society and the family
as traditionally organized.

The Future of Death   ROBERT FULFORD

The twentieth century has managed, at least in a few developed regions, to achieve a comparatively objective view of birth.
Slowly, the birth of a child has become, for parents, not
something to fear or pray for but something to manage; it has
become for the first time not an arbitrary act of an unpredictable God but rather the result of a decision made, on
however shaky grounds, by human beings acting for themselves. In the twenty-first century, it seems reasonable to hope,
our culture will develop a similarly cool view of death. Death,
like birth, will become at least partially controlled, subject to
the decision of each individual.

This will require a major adjustment in our culture's attitude
to death, and the adjustment will come only when we realize
how badly we need it, how badly we have so far mismanaged
the act of dying. For surely it is one of the worst scandals
of our way of life that we spend much of our lives trying
desperately to ignore the fact of death, trying to deny that
it is the most concrete fact of life. We hide discussion of it
from our children (as the Victorians hid discussion of sex);
an interest in death we regard as "morbid," which is another
way of saying neurotic. We even try to make death unfashion-
able, as if that would cause it to go away — consider the dusty
antique style of hearses, of funeral parlours, of funeral
wreaths and funeral prose: we may live in the twentieth century,
but stylistically we die in the nineteenth. We are all involved
in an attempt to distance death, to make it something "other."

The result is that an honest death is close to a cultural im-
possibility. A poet or hero, penetrating the cultural fog, may
manage to "make a good death"; a madman (socially so
regarded) may make a decisive death. But the process of ignoring and denying death brings most of us unwillingly to
our ends; we are dragged kicking and screaming into the
grave, as if death were an imposition — as if, indeed, it
were a surprise. We spend fortunes, both as individuals and
as a society, on adding months or years to the lives of rusted-

out men and women who are no longer in a position to do anything for themselves or others. Surely civilized life in our time offers few more distressing spectacles than the sordid conspiracy between anxious relatives and self-enriching doctors-to-the-old, the union of neurotic guilt and ill-used science. At some point society must recoil from all this and say: No, there must be a better way.

The better way is what we call suicide. As the next century will no doubt discover, the way to control death is to kill yourself. This is already possible, of course, and is no doubt the procedure followed by a few far-sighted and courageous individuals — indeed, one imagines there have been such deaths for thousands of years. But for most of us suicide is impossible because our culture tells us it is unthinkable. Priest and psychiatrist and man-in-the-street, they all *know*, in their bones, that suicide is taboo. Someone who attempts suicide is in most modern societies a criminal and in all of them a mental patient, automatically. The result is that those persons who are not remarkably individualistic, who are mere creatures of their culture — that is to say, almost all of us — are afraid of the idea of suicide. We may have lost the religions that condemned suicide, we may have abandoned all ideas of heaven and hell, but still we believe the suicide is a deranged person.

We have no right to make such a judgment, of course, and the chances are we shall shortly cease to do so. The idea of euthanasia, or mercy killing, has been playing around the edges of our culture for decades, but it is only a small step and a rather feeble, perhaps misguided one. Euthanasia, as we have so far discussed it, postulates a patient so ill that he has long since lost his dignity as well as his will to live; so far gone, in fact, that an all-wise doctor (briefly substituting for a forgetful God) must make the patient's death decision for him. Euthanasia, in short, may be a way to reduce pain and increase the efficiency of medical practice; it is not a way to dignify the life of the individual, and that is what we need.

The way to do that is to spread through our culture — providing, first of all, a sound philosophical base — the idea that suicide, or death decision, is a reasonable course of action which may be taken under certain circumstances by an individual who is sound of mind and body.

One imagines that this will happen within half a century. One imagines a society in which death pills (quick and reliable) will be as available as, say, birth control pills are now. One imagines people openly discussing their deaths, deciding reasonably and honestly the point at which their lives should finish. In 1970 a willed death, at whatever advanced age, is still considered a confession of failure or madness; in 2020 it may well be considered an affirmation of success — "I have succeeded in my life, I have pleased myself and others, I have decided on many thousands of days *not* to take my life; now I realize there is nothing ahead for me but boredom and sickness; I have had enough, I am satisfied, I am ready to go." One imagines a dignified leave taking, the individual putting his affairs in order, saying goodbye to his friends, gathering his children around him, finally taking his pill. One imagines those close to him being left with an image not of screaming pain and squalid helplessness but of clear, clean finality: death finally controlled and finally robbed of much of its horror.

By the year 2020, possibly, it will not be unusual for one free individual to ask another: "How do you want to die? Where? When? With whom?" In the next fifty years a transformation of the style of death may indeed be the most profound change in our way of life.

Looking Back on Illth   JOHN T. MCLEOD

"Your generation of students has so little historical perspective. You're so impatient with the follies of our forefathers, but you scarcely understand them. It's true that today's health care system, in 2020, remains imperfect — your radical zeal for improvement is laudable — but you must try to appreciate how far we've come in only fifty years. Consider, for example, that back in 1970 it was more difficult to get one-stop service for your body than for your car."

"You're kidding us, professor."

"Not at all. There were elaborate clinics offering on-the-spot diagnosis, repair and advice on preventive measures for automobiles, but not for people. By 1970 almost every major industry and service in the economy was organized and coordinated except health care, even though it had become the third largest industry in North America. Physicians remained the last rugged individualist entrepreneurs (apart from farmers) in the technological society, and made a fetish of something called 'solo practice' in the name of "independence.' Sick people had to trot all over town, to general practitioners, to specialists, to radiologists, often spending a week in an expensive hospital for tests, then back to specialists, not to mention separate trips to physiotherapists, dentists and pharmacists, and frequently there were long waits for appointments. Medical records as well as patients had to be shuffled about. Healers often possessed great skill and dedication, but you could scarcely say the system was geared to the convenience of patients, never mind economy or efficiency."

"It doesn't sound as though it were an integrated 'system' at all."

"Right. By 1970, many students of the health sciences began to complain that medicine was a 'cottage industry' or a 'push-cart industry.' House calls were virtually unknown, and many people had great difficulty in finding a family physician at all. Then too, approximately one person in five suffered from

some form of mental illness, but psychotherapy was neglected
and facilities were primitive."

"That's hard to believe."

"I know it is. In fact, I want to devote the remainder of
this seminar to a historical discussion of the origins of the
present health system which evolved from the Dark Ages of
IIIth. Please refrain from snickering as I describe what will
seem to you the more incredible aspects of health care in the
sordid sixties and the silly seventies of the twentieth century,
but feel free to ask questions as I go along.

"Until the 1980s there was very little 'health' care as we
know it today, since most physicians were taught only illness
care or curative procedures, and the shortage of medical personnel plus their burden of paperwork meant that they had too
little time available for anything else. In other words, there
was little attention paid to preventive procedures and environmental control. The urgency was for cures only; the social
causes of disease were neglected. You can read the reports
of innumerable task forces and royal commissions on health
care from the 1960s and '70s and find scarcely any mention
of such primary causes of illness as poverty and diet, bad
housing or the air and water pollution of the increasingly nox-
ious industrial environment. Small wonder that doctors were
busy. In direct contrast to today, for example, marijuana was
illegal, but cigarette smoking was not only legal, it was widely
advertised. . . ."

"Excuse me, professor, but what was a 'doctor'?"

"Ah, well, I forgot your unfamiliarity with the old general
term. Fifty years ago there were hardly any doctors of clinical
psychology or manipulative therapy or pharmacy, not to mention doctors of preventive medicine and of environmental engineering. Physicians tried to keep the title 'doctor' highly
exclusive. Even specialists in dentistry were not usually admitted to practice in hospitals.

"The medical doctors tried to keep health care very much
to themselves, then wondered why they were overworked. They
organized themselves into tight professional associations rather
like medieval guilds. Initially the government gave them a
monopoly, for the purpose of maintaining high standards of
practice to protect the public. Physicians did this very well,

on the whole. But then they also used their professional colleges, like most monopolists, to protect their own somewhat narrow interests, often to the detriment of the public interest. Once public representation was added to the composition of the colleges, there were fewer abuses of professional power.

"But for a long time the physicians' guilds and professional associations spent remarkable quantities of energy and resources trying to do two things: to combat public regulation and financing of health care, and to prevent or inhibit nonmedical health scientists from participating fully in the provision of health care."

"They failed in both purposes, I suppose?"

"Inevitably, since politically and technologically they were on the defensive. There was something to be said for the physicians' position, but they stated it badly, went about their purposes rather negatively and failed to lead."

"Why did the physicians have such a sharp quarrel with the state?"

"Most professions did, including the lawyers and the economists and the dentists, once the public came to realize the enormous power that was wielded by the 'private governments' of the various technological guilds, but medicine was an early and special case; medicine's struggle with government tended to set the pattern for the relationships of other professions with the state.

"The physicians were worried, often with some reason, about bureaucratic control by the state. Several factors weighed heavily. There were economic fears of reduced incomes and a shift from fee-for-service payment to salaries. Professional traditions are always prized, and doctors feared a loss of their traditional freedoms and independence. Much of this fear was based on antique theorizing concerning an artificial separation between 'public' and 'private.' Anything public was thought to diminish freedom. It was a quaint idea, particularly since physicians were educated in public schools at enormous public expense, obtained their initial monopolistic powers and licences to practise by delegation from the state, received most of their research funds from the public treasury and depended even more than the rest of us on hospitals which were financed by the public. But most people in the collectivized society took a long time to realize that skills and technology, particularly those involving essential services, could never remain 'private.' Both private and public interests were inextricably intermingled. Necessarily, the interests of patients and society had to come first."

"Professor, how did doctors ever acquire such narrow social views?"

"It was largely as a result of capitalist (rather than post-industrial) ideas, and the shortcomings of professional education. If I may exaggerate to make a point, in their schools doctors were taught to memorize rather than to think in the abstract, especially where social questions were concerned, and until the computer with its memory bank was added to medical practice, the physician's memory was his principal tool. Furthermore, physicians were taught to be solo practitioners, like corner grocers. An integrated health delivery system emerged only later. Doctors were trained to be highly skilled technicians but were largely innocent of the humanities and social sciences, and consequently were rather remote from the rapidly changing society. Even the schools of public hygiene and preventive medicine were usually hived off and kept separate from medical schools."

"Before you get launched onto educational problems, what about the conflict between physicians and the other health sciences?"

"That also involved education. You see, the combined multidiscipline schools of health sciences developed only gradually. Absurd as it may sound to us, medical social workers, optometrists, psychologists and others were trained separately and outside of medical schools in most parts of North America until the end of the 1970s. This limited the quality of their training and also limited the physician's understanding of the utility of other disciplines as part of a health team."

"Is that why doctors were so slow to delegate various functions to other types of health practitioners?"

"Partly that, but there were also other factors. There were real dangers involved in delegation, since the training of other practitioners tended to be narrow. Then too, it was difficult for physicians to delegate functions when they were not entirely sure what their own functions were.

"As I've said, some physicians honestly tried to do almost everything. However, there weren't enough of them, and there was too much to learn . . . the explosion of knowledge overcame them. Doctors were partly natural scientists, but certain specialists in chemistry and biology were better at that; they were partly social scientists, notably where mental health was concerned, but their training in that sphere was woefully inadequate; they were partly magician-priests (or at least their patients expected them to be), but various quacks and faith healers had more time to specialize in that line. Certain fringe healers, by the way, possessed sincerity and insight, and often effected cures when the doctor could not. Still, most of these cultists were either dangerous or ignorant or both. For a time in the twentieth century, more money was spent on quackery than on medical research.

"But once physicians began to think hard about their functions, a structuralist approach was developed, the application of information theory to the structure of health care. The physician, of course, dealt mainly in information, and the transmission of that information often broke down between the general practitioner and the specialist, the specialist and the laboratory technicians, the nurses, other therapists and the hospital staff, as well as between the physician and the patient. Once people began to think of health care in terms of information flows, the roles of various practitioners became clearer, computers could be utilized widely and the structure of the system was quickly altered. Delegation of functions was facilitated; development of various allied health professions flourished in truly interdisciplinary schools of health sciences; planning became more effective and more attention could be paid to the creation of an improved health care delivery system."

"Didn't people realize that the delivery system is as much a part of health technology as transplant operations?"

"It took some time for that realization to take hold. Once it did, reform of professional health education was quickened not only by the integration of paramedical personnel, but by change in medical education. Problems of the delivery system, together with preventive and environmental medicine, found their way into the curriculum.

"Previously, most doctors had become specialists and the shortage of family physicians was acute, but the improved delivery system eased their load and economized their time, making the role of the family physician more attractive. The new generalist physician became the chief and the integrator of health care.

"And he was educated differently. Earlier, medical students were taught almost exclusively by specialists and their training took place almost entirely inside hospitals, where the most common illnesses were seldom seen. Someone once observed that teaching doctors exclusively in hospitals was like educating foresters only in lumberyards. By 1980, a medical student was taught by general family physicians as well as by medical and nonmedical specialists. His training took place side by side with nurse practitioners, medical assistants and the whole range of professional therapists and technicians, the complete health team.

"Schools of health sciences moved out of the hospitals into the community and took charge of the total health needs of a specific population. Community health clinics were established, providing all aspects of care from dentistry to psychotherapy to family planning services, not omitting well-baby care and public health education. Patients' associations played active roles in running the clinics as cooperatives, and specialists in preventive medicine and environmental engineering worked with their communities to produce more satisfactory environments."

"Yes, we know about the fights over the establishment of group practices, community health clinics, consumer panels and pollution control. But what about the background of computer diagnosis, the test-tube-babies battle, genetic engineering and the breakthroughs in religious psychotherapy and medical research?"

"Ah, those are even longer stories. Anyway, I must cut this seminar short and trot over to the clinic. I'm suffering from a severe upper respiratory infection and otolaryngolic congestion . . . what they used to call, in the twentieth century, a common cold."

Trade Unions in 2020?   EUGENE FORSEY

The editors suggested I should attempt this subject. But, as has happened with several things I have been asked to do in the last few months, it seems to me that I have few qualifications for the task and serious disqualifications. I am not the seventh son of a seventh son. I do not possess the second sight. I am not a Marxist, nor a social science fiction writer. I have long considered it one of God's greatest mercies that the future is hidden from us. If it were not, life would surely be unbearable.

As if this were not enough, I have been buried for nearly six years in the nineteenth century, working on Canadian trade union history from 1812 to 1902, and have, accordingly, about as much knowledge of contemporary affairs, let alone trends, as Rip Van Winkle. I have managed to keep track,

The Future of Unionism   DONALD MacDONALD

While prognostication is always a perilous practice, there are some recent trends in the labour movement that do appear to be with us to stay. These developments undoubtedly will have an impact on the shape of labour in the future and, on that basis, we may safely predict some of the changes that are likely to occur in the trade union movement by the year 2020.

The first of these is the change that is occurring in industry itself through increasing technology. For years, there has been a great deal of speculation about what technology is doing to industry and to the human beings employed therein. As a movement, labour has no desire to slow down or stop the use of every human and scientific resource to increase production for the well-being of all. But the trade union movement is concerned about what happens to the people who

to some extent, of constitutional developments and of the French-English, Quebec-the-rest-of-us business, but no more. To cap it all, my intense dislike of most of what I see about me when I do return, blinking, to the twentieth century, and my apprehension of what I think I can discern of the shape of things to come, leaves me with neither appetite nor aptitude for this task.

But to an old *Forum* hand like me, an invitation to contribute to a fiftieth anniversary book is a royal command, and as the invitation specifically insists on some kind of look into the future, have at it I must. So I shall suggest what seem to me certain possibilities.

First, will unions still be here in 2020? Unless freedom in any recognizable form is utterly extinguished, I think they will. In any society I can imagine, there will still be employers and employed; they will still have differing interests and the employed will still need representatives to look after their interests.

THE FUTURE OF UNIONISM

make this expansion of technology possible, namely, the workers themselves. We hope that increased technology will result in an abundance of productive and consumer goods; that this abundance will be distributed equitably, and that the workers who produce it will benefit from shorter hours of work and more leisure.

We are also concerned that constructive, creative leisure-time activities be available to workers, including participation as citizens in the democratic processes of government. We think we can safely predict that by the year 2020 a much shorter work week will prevail — to specify exactly how many hours at this stage would be folly — and that people will be taught through formal and informal institutions to use their leisure more productively. We are concerned that now, in the age of the forty-hour week, many workers are using their leisure time by working at second jobs, a practice known as "moonlighting," sometimes at tasks they find unpleasant and

If the unions are still here, will they be seeking the same ends as now? Again, I think so. Gompers' statement of union aims, "More, more, more," still holds, and is likely to hold. If the pressure of population on increasingly scarce resources becomes severe enough, "More, more, more" may be transformed into resistance to "Less, less, less." But the struggle, even then, will still be essentially the same: to keep rather than to get for the workers as large a share of the collective product as possible.

Will any unions which may exist in 2020 use the same methods as now? Collective bargaining? Surely, yes. Political pressure (what the Webbs called "the method of legal enactment"), in one form or another, again yes. Collective bargaining, indispensable though it is, can never be enough. It must be buttressed by laws which protect the unions' freedom and by the whole apparatus of a welfare state, though a welfare state of perhaps a very different kind from what we have now.

DONALD MacDONALD

certainly far from creative. Almost invariably, the reason they moonlight is that their living costs exceed their earnings from their regular employment.

Another current change that will continue is the tremendous growth of conglomerates. The word *conglomerate*, which recently has come into everyday use, aptly describes the rapidly growing phenomenon of octopus-like corporations with tentacles extending often to the most remote parts of the world. Entire companies, which may employ thousands of people and be extremely impressive enterprises in their own right, suddenly become minor parts of an enormous, complex corporate structure with its head office perhaps thousands of miles away and its interests spread around the world amongst scores of completely different enterprises and industries.

The result is that a great many workers in many countries of the world don't really know exactly for whom they are working. Certainly they get their pay cheques from a specific

What about strikes? I am inclined to think that in essential industries and services, strikes may give place to what might be called participatory compulsory arbitration. Already, in such services as the railways, free collective bargaining scarcely exists. There is an elaborate ritual dance whose final figure is sometimes a short strike. But everyone knows that no government will tolerate a prolonged railway strike, so the dance goes on under the shadow of a possible *ad hoc* compulsory arbitration. The day may come when unions in such industries will decide that they have more to gain by helping to devise machinery, of which they will be a part, for joint determination of wages and working conditions by mutually accepted standards, without a stoppage of work which accomplishes little except loss of wages to the workers concerned and disruption to the economy generally.

And if anyone says, "Hmm! We notice he waited till he was safely retired from the union movement to say that," my answer is, "No, he did not. He said exactly the same, several

---

THE FUTURE OF UNIONISM

---

company, but the ownership and the effective control of that company are often lost in a maze of corporate structures. Decisions that vitally affect the lives and welfare of workers and their families are commonly made in boardrooms thousands of miles away, by financiers who have never seen the plant where these people work and who, in any event, may regard it as a relatively insignificant part of the conglomerate's operations.

In the face of the development of conglomerates, there is a growing need for a broad international trade unionism, a need that is far greater than at any time in history. Thus, as conglomerates increase, we can predict that unions will become more global in their structures and in their policies. More and more, they will consolidate their strength and their resources with others in the same industries in which they are organized.

To offset the power of these conglomerates, unions have al-

years before, publicly, at a conference sponsored by the Canadian Labour Congress."

After all, opposition to compulsory arbitration has not always been part of the Canadian trade union faith. On the contrary, the Trades and Labour Congress of Canada repeatedly pronounced in favour of compulsory arbitration, and from 1898 to 1902 included it in its "Platform of Principles."

And how will "essential industries and services" be defined? Ah! There's the rub! It will depend on the state of technology, and on the relative strength of the various pushes and pulls in society.

Will unions get bigger? Almost certainly, yes. Is there any escape from bigness in our world or any world likely to develop from it (assuming atomic war does not wipe out most of the human race)? The overmastering problem already is to find some way of at least mitigating the impersonality which bigness inevitably tends to bring with it. How successful any organization will be in doing this, who can even guess?

DONALD MacDONALD

ready begun to consolidate more and more of their operations. For example, within industries we see the growth of joint councils whereby unions within the same industry can meet and compare problems and sometimes agree on bargaining goals. From this there sometimes follows actual coordinated bargaining, in which the unions involved do sit as one entity face-to-face with management.

Finally, sometimes these steps lead to organizational unity — to mergers among unions — so that instead of several small unions in an industry, we have one or two large unions facing the growing strength of management. An example of this trend occurred recently when the International Federation of Chemical and General Workers Unions negotiated an agreement with one giant employer on behalf of several unions that are members of the federation.

As this trend to internationalism develops, the year 2020 may also see international trade union secretariats, such as the

Will Canadian unions break away from American? I should say that will depend entirely on Canadian workers' judgment of the relative advantages of international and purely Canadian unions, and *that* will depend partly on the performance of each kind of union.

All this sounds a good deal like "the mixture as before," though with some changes in the proportion of the ingredients. Quite. The deepest impression left on me by my study of the first ninety years of Canadian unionism is the astonishing degree to which unions in the nineteenth century resembled unions now. There were, of course, immense differences of size, of organization, of affiliation, of legal rights and disabilities. But in aims, demands, methods, arguments, and in the aims, demands, methods and arguments of employer resistance, it is the sameness, not the differences, which stands out. In dispute after dispute, one has only to change dates and proper names, and the tale might have come out of yesterday's newspaper. Even big percentage increases are nothing new:

THE FUTURE OF UNIONISM

Transport Workers' Federation, the Food and Drink Workers' International, the International Federation of Chemical and General Workers and the International Metal Workers, playing an increasing role in collective bargaining and in trade union activity generally.

Of this we can be certain, whatever political processes within the trade union movement bring the change about, the labour movement of 2020 will be much more international than that of today. This will occur not because the unions of any one country are in a dominant position within the trade union movement itself, but as a consequence of the structural change of industry resulting from the growth of conglomerates. It is a truism often repeated that the kind of trade unions a country has often results from the kind of industry that it has. So, too, with world industry and world trade unionism.

One other current trend in organized labour; not only in Canada but in many parts of the world, makes another pre-

there are instances a century ago, and there was a notable instance in the great telegraphers' strike of 1883 (the first nation-wide strike in Canada, and the only genuinely continent-wide, international strike North America has had), when the *average* increase demanded was twenty-seven percent, and the increase for the lowest-paid employees was ninety percent or more (plus shorter hours). Even the demand for wage parity with the Americans is nothing new: the Toronto printers struck for parity with New York City in 1836! (They lost.)

So my guess is that there will be unions in 2020, and that they will be essentially the same sort of organizations as now. Disappointing? Unimaginative? Elderly? Well, you were warned!

DONALD MacDONALD

diction quite safe: that is, that unions in the public sphere of employment likely will dominate the trade union movement by the year 2020. The trade unions began as, and for many long years remained an institution rooted among so-called blue-collar workers. But within the past decade a significant change has been taking place, the end of which is not in sight. Government employees, among others, have begun to transform what once were commonly known as staff associations into genuine agencies for collective bargaining.

This emergence of government employees as trade unionists is being accompanied by a very considerable transformation of the Canadian labour force from one which was, until recently, largely dominated by the manual worker into one that is becoming increasingly typical of the clerical, the technical and the professional worker.

Another very safe prediction for the future is that more and more professional people will turn to collective bargaining. This has already been happening. Nurses, teachers, engineers and many other categories of employees not normally associated with the trade union movement are developing means of bargaining collectively with their employers. There is every reason to believe that these people will become part of a trade union movement which will represent most people in collective bargaining, whether blue-collar worker, white-collar worker or so-called professional person. Professionals who work as the hired hands of salary-paying employers are becoming more and more aware that their situation in relation to their employer is no different from that of the blue-collar worker or the factory hand. They, too, will become trade unionists in the contemporary sense of the word.

We can also safely predict an expansion in the labour movement's involvement with such community problems as housing, poverty and discrimination. From their origins, unions have been concerned with the living as well as the occupational environment of workers and their families. In the future, more and more of the union movement's energies will be devoted to applying labour's organizational skill to the needs of slum dwellers, exploited tenants, consumer groups, community and neighbourhood organizations, and to helping the poor, the underprivileged and other social minorities organize for self-help.

As a pilot project, the Canadian Labour Congress has had a community-development worker active on Indian reserves in the Kenora, Ontario, region for more than a year. He is trying to help with the development of local leadership among the residents of the reserves, and has achieved considerable success. We see this project as showing organized labour the way to helping urban social minorities in similar ways. Labour's future programs will extend even further beyond collective bargaining and administering collective agreements.

With more professionals, more white-collar employees and more public servants taking leading roles in the trade union movement, we can see changes in its relationships with employers and with public authorities. But whatever the interests and personalities of the leaders of the labour movement in 2020, its primary functions will still be much the same as they

are today: collective bargaining, working for fair labour legislation and working for social legislation that will benefit not
just a privileged minority, but all the people of Canada.

Places I've Never Been   HUGH HOOD

Seems late September. A man comes out from behind the general store at the landing carrying a white fibreglass canoe with a paddle clamped under the thwarts. Sets it down beside two eighty-pound rucksacks, food in one, camp equipment in the other, right at the shore. Waiting for sunrise for luck, lifting one rucksack into the bow, the other between the thwarts, packing them down low. At daybreak the storekeeper comes onto his porch, jingling his keyring. "All set?" "Yes." "You pack good, never saw such a man to pack, what do you do, number things as you put them in?" "I like to know where everything is. I'll need chocolate first." "She's mighty light, eh?" "Not too light, you know how to handle her. Had her moulded to order, got to keep your centre of gravity where it belongs. I'll go now. I'll be in there pretty late in the year, look here." Finger running over the grid on the survey map. "I'll be here, on the bay, make a note of the reference, will you? Just about 243/355. If I'm not out before the ice, ask the Aerial Survey to take a look, right here by the point, OK? I could always walk in over the ice." "I'll do that, all right." "I'll be going, then." Bow into the water, rocking the canoe lengthwise to check the trim. "Looks fine." Gives her a shove, only getting the one boot wet, swings well inboard on his knees, unhooks his paddle trailing it in the still water, moving the blade — strangely long narrow blade — like a rudder, checking his control. On his haunches. Takes a long pull, shoulder muscles well into it, and the canoe shoots ahead like a guided missile over water like smooth silver foil. Gray light in clearing mist, Milk Lake, yes, Milk Lake, milky, takes a second pull, wake narrow behind, stroke stroke two hundred yards out settles into it, the whole back crawling with serpentine muscle, wake shore falls behind, nothing to see but milk, sun higher but not warm yet, at about three miles begin to feel, ah yes, feel the slope, no wind, but the slope of the bottom tilting the whole surface gently gently feel it begin to slide under the canoe, feel it tilt and sideslip left, still no north shore,

should be in sight in fifty strokes, timed it often, there ahead
line long low, grass trees grass, closing on the north shore and
the current begins to run now, change hands, stop, watch the
bow come round as I coast . . . round . . . water begins to
ripple under the bow, stroke now and again now and rest, feel
the current, off on the right the first of the grass islands, sliding
by, feel her pick it up and move. Sunlight now, coming into the
river and sliding down west; the power of it. Both shores visible
and closing into the river and away down. And down. Water
crinkling. Faster now. Try steering. All right. Grassislands gray
green gold tangling swirling running alongside, now full white
sunlight. Try steering. Ride it. RIDE IT. Shores closing. Now
it begins, hear that. One mile. Rockledge now both shores,
current faster, start stroking, rocks in the water, don't hole
her, stroke, half a mile, hear that. Get ready, get ready, mist
and spray in seconds . . . there we are . . . quarter mile
. . . it's like re-entry, got to find that keyhole. OK NOW
STROKE. Canoe up on its heel like a riderless horse. Watch
that spur, stroke, fishtail my blade and in we go and into
quiet water and landing high up onto pebbles pineneedles sand,
to the right two hundred yards west high cloud of spray and a
hundred-foot drop over the falls.

Six miles climbing, mile there and back repeated three
times, up into the forest, then a steep descent past the falls.
Food. Camping stuff. Last the canoe. There'll only be four
miles of it coming back, and dozens of empty cans neatly
buried in a filled-in latrine. Coming up on final portage, canoe
on back and sweat in my eyes, almost fall on pineneedles
over rock, grab a juniper root, could have been dangerous.
And down to shore and another hour's paddling to a still cove,
nobody else coming here this year, not alone, not with that
portage, haul the canoe well up on shore and moor her to a
tamarack, carrying supplies up a hundred feet from shore to
a flat natural rectangle open among trees, looking for traces
of two years back, none, none more recent, nobody knows
this place. Get at tent fittings, spade, hatchet, drive long
sharp shining point of metal pole through tentbottom grommet
deep into soil, telescope pole up and out through ridgepole
lock and into peak, crawl babylike into tentsack and sitting
up in darkgreendark drive long sharp second point through

tentbottom, raise ridgepole and lock in place, walk bent but erect from tent, peg and guy it full up, leaving slight slack for raintautness. Hang lantern. Tentheater at rear. Unroll down-stuffed bloody expensive sleeping bag, then check to see that the fall of the ground runs away under the floor to drain it. Trench out drain around tent perimeter with good deep channel running down northwest to gully and shore. Silent so far but now stand, speak: "I'll eat that Crispy-Crunch." I eat it slowly, take a smoke and make sure it's out. Coming up to noon. Two things: fireplace, latrine. I spade out a two-foot circular hole which, lined with rock and hung with metal grid, is coffeemaker, lightbringer, heartwarmer. Two quick cups, hunger coming now, so I work my way down into the gully and there dig latrine and garbage pit, making it deep and clean, a crime to befoul this place. Take a long piss. Find fallen tree and trim it for first fire, cooking bacon and speaking for second time this trip. "That's good, oh, that's good," bacon, biscuits, more coffee, a fast trip out and a good morning's work, who would think, back in the city, so much could be done in this place by a man alone? In the afternoon I go with gun, rod, a mile west for a first look around, might be three weeks till the weather breaks and a week more before the freeze. More work on the fireplace in late daylight, and in twilight frying canned luncheon meat. Tie back flaps over plastic windows for early sun next day, in underwear and flannel shirt slide into sleeping bag manchild in wombweary, face to banked fire. Rain begins in the night as

I SLEEP

in darkness loitering under deep shadow at dockside early April night. Empty street of rough cobblestones split by dis-used tramtracks, silence, then a mile away the sound of a car coming slowly, red flasher revolving. Into doorway. Noth-ing to hear but the faint squeak of tires over stone, the patrol car stops on the corner and I/he steps well back into shadow in the doorway, padlock bumping between the shoul-derblades, softly clinking. The squadcar's motor idles, thrum-ming, and the radio squawks noisily over static, seconds pass, car door opens and policeman gets out, flashlight in one hand, other hand on gun, *"pas mal. Y'en était d'autres."* and walks

down the sloping alley towards the water crunch crunch
crunch over pebbles on cement passing close enough to touch.
He swings the light over the bollards, racked life preservers,
mooring lines, and in the striped black/gray sky clouds part
and moonlight streaks water in the slip. The man in the doorway watches tensely and begins to ease his way from the
shelter of the doorway into deeper shadow along the side of the
shed noiselessly as the beam of light swings right then left
crossing the dock in front of him, swings away irresolute, man
moves a bit quicker into darkness but now catches his heel
in a curving tramline and falls, hands coming down, whack, onto
sharp gravel, he stifles a cry and the cop shouts, "*Qui es?
Arrêtez-là. Au secours.*" turns on his heel and peers into
blackness, "*Je tire . . .*" and hears pounding running footsteps
receding along the quayside, runs to the patrol car and leaps
in, car picking up speed as he slams the door, swooshing off to
the other end of the loading shed.

Double back, didn't see me. Our man stops where he stood
before, straightens his necktie and smooths black thick hair
graying at sides, steps jauntily out under the street lamp, let-
ting it show him clear and immediate to any observer, walk-
ing briskly off, heels tap-tap-tapping, only sound along the
street. Not many lamps along here so he is in darkness mostly, passing from one small circle of light to the next, cloud cover
closed again and the moon invisible. He comes now to the
wide main road along the wharves, paved with heavy wide
slabs to take the weight of the trucks, can watch the length
of it in the darkness. Three blocks east the road is split in half
by a rail spur which curves out of the dockside, along the
road, then north between warehouses into an enormous open
door like a yawning mouth.

Crossing the wide uneven roadway three blocks down is a
girl in a white raincoat. She is carrying a cheap suitcase
lashed round with cord, and picks her way warily over the
cracks and holes in the paving stones. There are never any
cars at this hour so she takes her time about reaching the
sidewalk. Twice she stops and lifts her left foot, running a finger around the inside of her shoe. Seems footsore. Seems to
sense that she is being watched and lifts her head nervously
like a fearful small animal, vixen or doe. The watcher

closes in on her, sliding from doorway to alley entry. Now
he can see her clearly and it is maybe the young Anouk
Aimée who straightens her beret and puts her foot down
on the uneven paving. She has come up tonight from Amqui,
riding a slow rocking train all day, half nauseated by the
unaired stink of the coach, to arrive in *Gare Centrale* an
hour before. What is she doing down here by the docks, miles
from the station, lugging her suitcase first in one hand, then in
the other? Is it the old Simenon tale of the girl from the country, will she end on a slab as thick and cracked at the edges
as these paving stones? He follows closely now, feels in his
pocket for his papers — they are there in a thick wad. If I
only had a gun, he thinks, I can't do anything without a gun.
Then he remembers the bilious tang of nausea he has always
felt at the sight of a gun, and knows that it isn't a gun that
he needs.

Peeks at the girl round a corner and sees at the end of
the street a small restaurant and bar, open twenty-four hours
a day, like a lighthouse in the middle of nothing. Determined
now, and sure of her pace, the girl walks quickly, staring
straight ahead towards the restaurant, and he forgets about
concealment and moves along behind her. She is at the door,
hand on the latch, opens it and a puff of noisy chatter
and music billows out onto the quiet street. She goes in.

Restaurant windows steamy with heat and moisture from the
kitchen, strung with cheap checked curtaining below the letter-
ing: RESTAURANT MARIO: METS ITALIENS BOISSONS LEGALES.
She is at the cash register making some enquiry of a
slatternly hard-faced woman of forty-five in a black silk
dress who leans against the counter. The woman nods her
head to one side and the girl goes through the door marked
Femmes.

As he comes in he sees a party of four at a table around
the corner in the dining room stop talking, lift their heads
and give him a long look, four pairs of hostile male eyes.
Next to the toilets there's an opening into a kind of office, no
door but a curtain made of strings of beads, behind it a sickly
pink light from under a paper lampshade. He can see through
the beaded curtain and spots the boss at once, in striped shirt,
sleeves rolled up and secured by springy metal bands around

the biceps. Curly abundant oily hair, thick neck, coarse black
sideburns and a heavy moustache. Where's the girl?

He sits at a small table next to the window and the woman
in black comes over to him unwillingly. *"Je prends un Molson,
un smoked meat, lean, café, crème, pas de sucre."* Where is
she? Left by another way? Drugged and unconscious on a
sagging sofa under that pink light in the office? Through the
window he sees the patrol car roll quietly up the street and
park directly beside him; they are coming in. He pours his beer
quickly into the glass, swallows some mouthfuls and takes
the empty bottle by the neck as the cops come in and the
lights go out.

FUNLAND

oom-pah-pah oom-pah-pah oom-pah-pah Over the Waves on
steam calliope, vapour whistling through holes and blending
with the music, the carnival crowded with summer-Saturday-
night pleasure seekers oom-pah-pah, pap pap pap from the
shooting gallery. "Get your Red Hots, get your Red Hots."
"We've got a lucky winner here folks, step in here Madam,
your choice between a giant Panda, a chromium-plated Roto-
Broil, and an automatic electric alarm clock." "Hurry, hurry,
hurry, see the shortest skirts on the Midway, the next show
starts in ten minutes, come on in and see the swinging
girls from Carnaby Street." Clanking of the engine under the
old Ferris Wheel as we swing to the top and stop, sitting together in the swaying seat arms round each other nobody else
on the wheel. "Why isn't there anybody else on the wheel,
do you think they've spotted us? Look down!" On the ground
the operator pulls a long lever and the leather drive-bands
engage the motor, the wheel lurches forward, then we hang
rocking over space. The operator climbs onto a little platform over the motor and starts to climb across the beams of
the frame, something in his hand. "He's got a gun," "no,
it's an oil-can." "Why doesn't he let others on?" she whispers,
digging her fingers into my shoulder. "He's just making a repair." "A repair? I think it's been sabotaged; we're caught
up here like sitting ducks. How are we going to get down?
We shouldn't have come." "Yes we should, it's the best way

to get a view of the whole place, look over there, that's the Fortune Teller's tent, can you see where the back door is?" "No, just a bunch of tents crowded together." "We won't go in there if there's no way out; we don't want to get trapped." "We're trapped here." "No we're not, they haven't caught on to us yet." "I wouldn't have come with you if I'd known what you were carrying; have you still got them?" "Yes." "Where?" "Never mind where; it's better you don't know. Ah, now we're moving; they can't get at us while the wheel's moving."

Whirling down to the ground I see them standing in the middle of the roadway by the weight guesser's stand, looking around. They glance at the Ferris Wheel and as we come over the top I holler "Whoopee" and wave my arms and as the wheel brings us back down I grab her and kiss her, then whisper in her ear, "Kiss back, we're out on a date; they don't know yet you're with me." Put my hand on her breast, feeling the cheap gauzy fabric of her blouse, hug her tight. She kicks her legs out and wriggles. "Got them fooled, I think, they're moving away." The wheel slows and the attendant unhooks the safety bar in front of us. I take her hand and we jump off and run down the exit ramp and along the road to the booths and games.

Black diamonds on red diamonds on white spinning 28, 46, 62, 18, click click click click slower click ... click ... WHEEL OF FORTUNE stops on 32 and somebody shoves a red vinyl handbag into her hands, "your prize, Lady," and a man, apparently drunk, in a tattered clown suit, black with red diamonds and puffball pompoms, staggers between us, his face painted dead white with large greasy red spots on either cheek, carrying a bundle of long thin sticks with balloons floating above them, turns his head and looks into our faces. "At the shooting gallery. Ask for two dollars worth of tickets, go on!" We stumble arm-in-arm past the french-fries booth, the crowd pushes behind us and the sound of the shooting gallery grows pap-pap-pap-pap-pap. An eight-year-old girl, alone in the crowd, looks up at us and turns to follow as we work past her in the crush, follows us as we work our way to the counter.

"Two dollars worth of tickets, please."

All the noise stops

little girl silently licks her candy apple and gives a sniff, wipes her free hand across her nose, sniffs again. The crowd draws back and we take up our guns and look at the targets: clay pigeons, ducks on an endlessly revolving chain, pink piggies, we fire, fire again, the crowd surges in around us and the music and hollering starts up again. "Way to shoot, Mister." "Oh, I can shoot all right, don't kid yourself." She's banging away at the ducks, hits, misses, hits, a gong rings again and again. "The lady wins a prize, what's your pick, Lady?" He doesn't really let her pick; he shoves the big stuffed bear into her arms and goes to listen to a dissatisfied customer further along the counter. "Hey, that was my target; you gave her my prize," and we scramble away into the crowd. "It's so big," she says laughing "I can hardly hold it, it's so heavy." "A heavy teddy bear? Let me see. He palmed it on you, didn't let you pick. Sure it's heavy, too heavy, I can feel a lump in the back. Come on, let's go where it's quiet, and open it."

"Mister, hey Mister," narrow white face, cheap suit, "Mister, they gave your girlfriend my prize."

"Beat it."

"Mister it's mine, I'll pay you for it."

"Go win one of your own."

"No it's that one I want you gotta give it to me Mister."

"Come on," she says.

He puts his hand on my arm and I can feel his hand shake. "There'll be trouble, Mister."

"For who?" I give him a push and he grabs me and behind him I can see three of them looking around. I pass the bear to her, "Run," and I hit the little guy and he falls. Police whistles somewhere. He looks up at me, propped on his elbow, "Aw Mister," whistles everywhere and we run towards the tents and down an alley, tripping over guyropes into a kind of closed-in runway between two tents. "There's a zipper in the fur on the back; open it quick!" "I can't, it's sticking, they're coming." "In here." We slide in under a tentflap and stand side-by-side in the semidarkness looking at the light in the crystal softly glowing, barely illuminating the edge of the table, a ring of pale light, beside the table a shadowy gypsy woman, head in a kerchief, wrinkled, face like a religious carving. Shuffles towards us with a paper in her hands. She says, "It's the bottling company, here's the organization paper." She's no gypsy, she's a disguised person, and that's the hit, the bottling plant by the railroad tracks, strikebound for seventeen months, policed round the clock by city cops and a huge private army of so-called security officers, show windows boarded over and smaller panes taped across, no trucks in the garage for months because of slashed tires. That's where it is. She says, "Take the paper to Jean-Marc."

"I'll have to walk it. I'm being watched."

"Then you'd better go alone. Leave the girl here, I'll look after her."

"Who are you? How do I know I can trust you?"

"Funland," she says, *"Funland!* Doesn't that mean anything to you?"

"You've got it right, I'd better be going." The girl kisses me in the darkness and starts to cry. "I'll be all right, I'll hitch a ride."

"Don't take the first ride you're offered or the second, and remember, *Funland!*"

Plenty of patrol cars around so I don't try to hitch a ride, just hop on the back of a farmer's truck at a stoplight for a ride to the city limits, can walk from there. Corner of Greenwood and Willowdale I slide into an apartment house doorway to look around. Down the block, well away from the street lamps, are four men who suddenly split up and walk away in pairs in either direction. I get out of my doorway and around the side of the building to the *ruelle* and along in the dark, feeling other people near me in the blackness, Christ, a hand on my shoulder. "Shut up, it's me, Helwig. The others are up in the apartment with Jean-Marc. Have you got it?" "Yes, but how . . . ." "Over the roofs, come on. Can't reach the bugger, let me get on your back." Helwig is bigger than me, damn near breaks my back to grab the ladder leading to the fire escape. Up we go. "Pull it up; they'll spot it." On the roof, tripped against a TV aerial. "Watch yourself, they'll hear, come on." At the edge of the roof, twenty feet across to the next building. Helwig lowers

a plank over the gap. "They'll see us crossing from the street."
"No, they've gone to the corner." "I can't walk across that,
I'll fall." "Run, you can do it." I hold my breath and run to
his shadow. "Jesus!" Drop through the skylight to the hall
outside Jean-Marc's door, into bright light behind heavy cur-
tains, smoke, to hand him the papers. "Right, it's time, we've
got a fast car in the garage, we'll have to break out quick.
They're waiting for us at the plant. Remember now, we've
got to shake them soon as we come out of the alley so they
won't know where we're headed. Out the north end fast
and along to Rockland and across the overpass, got that?"
"Me?" "Sure, you're driving, you're the best wheelman, here
we go now, make it sharp." Down to the garage, there's the
car, slide the door up and six of us pile in. It's a very hot
Rover TC4, goes like hell, WHAM bursts out of the alley, right,
then left onto Plantagenet, right again heading for de Vimy,
left, LOST THEM LOST THEM, hey, we can't go up Rockland,
it's one-way south. "You're going to start a riot and you're
worried about the traffic detail?" "No." "Then go, for
Christ's sake." Cars swerve around us and drivers scream an-
grily as we come north and around and up the ramp. BAR-
RICADE. Right through it; on top of the overpass we see fire
in the sky; coming down we see the roadblock. "Hang on!"
I swerve left, almost kill a cop who steps in front of us waving
a signal lamp, sideswipe the concrete rail, bounce past a fire
truck and a pile of hose north to where the turn is. They've
got a police line here where we test them, coming at them
full speed, at the last second they break and scatter, we're
through and into the middle of the strikers, piling out of the
car. Shout goes up, "Jean-Marc, Jean-Marc." By the railroad
fence they've got a stolen Railway Express truck with Molotov
cocktails in it and other stuff and we move in a solid wall to
close in on the building. Start throwing firebombs, crash
against the white wall and black smoke rushes up the wall,
smearing and dirtying. Shouting.

"*Solidarité révolutionnaire.*"

"Students and workers."

"Black action."

"*Impérialisme anglophone.*"

Got a rock in my hand and throw it, first one to throw a

rock. It soars up and smashes a second-floor window. Anybody inside? "Hey, is anybody in there?" "Security guards maybe." "We don't want to burn them alive." "Let them run, the scabs, it's their fault." "No murders though." Dozens of sirens, a line of cops linked arm in arm moving down from the north, firetrucks behind them with the hoses, in the centre that goddam riot-control armoured car. "Get that tank. Strikebreakers, Cossacks. Get that tank." Oil-filled bottles whizzing through the air, bursting against the armoured car, red-orange then white fire around it, in fifteen seconds the crew jumps out to run, one man on fire rolls on the ground and the cops blanket him and stifle the flame. He screams. Screams from all sides. "Murderers. Thugs. Fascist shit. Tools. Lackeys." The building is on fire now; suddenly the cops part and the firemen come with the hoses, the ultra-high-pressure jets. Right beside me a guy takes the force of the jet high on his chest, you hear the air go out of his lungs in one gasp; he falls as the firemen play the jets back and forth. I'm on my knees beside him, his eyeballs rolled back into his head; he's trying to get air and his chest heaves; he rolls and twitches as the air begins to come, then I'm hit by the pressure jet on the hipbone, it's like being pounded by a heavy balk of timber. I lift my head and see we're in the middle of no-man's land with firemen and cops up there, strikers and workers by the tracks. I get up and get my arms under the guy, he's getting his breath and groaning, I haul him away to our side, soaking wet and my hip bruised stiff. No shooting yet, no gas, but the cops are putting on respirators. I stumble backwards and a voice hollers, "Look where you're going, you'll put us off the air." It's the TV crew from Channel Six, one of them talks to me. "Want to be interviewed, want to say something? Be on TV?" "No, I don't want to be on TV because I'm carrying an injured man, I'm being chased by a hundred policemen, my face is dirty so nobody would recognize me, besides I don't want to be a celebrity, you bastards stick your noses in every place, ruining everything that's decent. Take that bloody microphone away from my face. This has nothing to do with you. You dirty everything, give it a bad smell, some of us will get hurt here, there'll be blood and pain, but nobody will touch you and your cameras because you own all of us, you run us, you think you

can't be touched because you're the camera eye. Shit on you."
"You're out of your mind, Mac, look at the monitor, you're
on Candid Camera." "I am, am I? Liars, cheats, sellouts,
fuck off, how do you like that? Fuck off! (picture goes
blank) ha, that got them." A commercial comes on the screen
for Ford cars, with cute little animated ducks and a stupid
hunter. Then thirty seconds about somebody with midriff bulge
who needs a long-line bra. Then the weather report. Then I
drag the heavy limp man past the TV truck to the ranks of
the strikers, where he lies on the ground, chest heaving.

Confrontation. Thirty feet apart two solid lines, they have
clubs, respirators, gas, we have rocks and baseball bats . . .
if they loose off that gas . . . here it comes over the ground in
a whooshing puff into our lines, you can feel small drops of
condensation from the dirty stuff. Hurts the eyes like hell.
MOVE ON THEM. We go forward and they start swinging with
the *matraques* shoulder crushing, bone splintering, duck, Jesus
they're big bastards and

VERY LOUD NOISE

BLACK

cold in here towards morning, gray light in rain, fire out,
light that tent heater. Christ, my head, I sure pulled the plug
on that TV crew, my face in the middle of the screen, black,
like seeing yourself from outside in a nightmare. Rain, light the
heater take off the chill turn off the TV so all I can see
is the light from the crystal ball, that wooden-faced gypsy,
where did she go with my girl? What girl? My girl in the raincoat Anouk Michèle Marie-Josée Danièle dead in the morgue
everyone where's that gypsy? WHEEL OF FORTUNE with clown
face red diamonds black diamonds white ground Milk Lake
. . . ah . . . yes, milk haze and afterwards the freeze, who'll
come and get me after the freeze? I shouldn't have come alone,
you're useless alone. I can walk on water all right . . . if it's
frozen. Like Général de Gaulle. Politics, there's no getting away
from it oom-pah-pah oom-pah-pah oom-pah-pah roaring from
the falls spray from teargas rain on the tent heels tapping metallic on cement in the empty street in darkness feet going away
follow follow fall away follow way tap tap tap tap tap taptap
. . . taptap . . . tap-tap . . . tap . . . . . . ta

PART IV. REALITIES:
the political loom

ROBERT STANFIELD
119 Man and Government

MICHEL BRUNET
**123 Quand un historien se mêle de lire
dans la boule de cristal**

RAMSAY COOK
128 No More Fun and Games

WALTER L. GORDON
132 The Future Politician

THOMAS A. HOCKIN
**136 The Shape of Government and
Politics in Canada in 2020: Some Speculations**

ABRAHAM ROTSTEIN
141 The Great Moral Addiction

overleaf "Ego Screen" by Harold Town

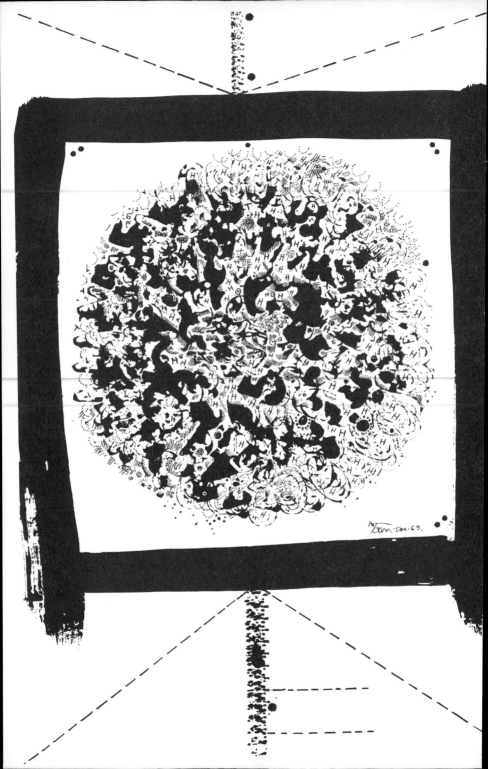

Letter to Kyra (cont'd.)

Is our political choice going to be between the firing line on the streets and escape to some private northland as Hugh Hood implies? This isn't the feeling of this section's authors. Their political realities envisage with some optimism the outcome of the next fifty years.

Robert Stanfield, the leader of the federal Conservative party and so of the official opposition, poses the traditional question of how man can order his society in a world of conflict. Will this view that we must strengthen the party system read in 2020 like political art nouveau to you, in fashion again after so many decades? Michel Brunet, as doyen of the Quebec school of nationalist historians, is directing his crystal gaze at what appears in 1970 to be a reasonable time horizon: épanouissement for a socialist Quebec in a freely restructured federation and a de-imperialized North America. It's hard to anticipate what will be the reaction of No More Fun and Games (a Women's Liberation movement magazine) to Ramsay Cook's article – or, for that matter, what yours will be. Will your feminine sensitivity be outraged? Will this picture of Parliament with the genders changed still appear as far off a counterutopia as the current Parliament without women?

For my generation, Walter Gordon was a breath of hope. As Finance minister he had the courage to deal with the problem of American control and force the Liberals to confront the issue of our vanishing national independence. Here he is pleading for both more expertise yet more mobility in politics, so that the socially committed can spend a stage of their career in active politics without having to feel wedded to Parliament for life.

Prediction has never been the forte of political science, despite the profession's label. Tom Hockin goes as far as political scientists venture with his consideration of the consequences of some observable trends in Canada's political structures. The spectre of a growing public sector *has haunted the minds of democrats for over a century. It is interesting that, at a time when the whole nature of "participatory democracy" is being challenged, Hockin returns to the elected politician organized in parties as the means to make public policy respond to individual needs.*

That these needs will be endlessly expanding is the implication of Abraham Rotstein's essay that foresees no end to the discovery of new sources of oppression.

Man and Government

ROBERT STANFIELD

The last fifty years have established Man the Scientist and
Man the Technician. We have been to the moon, and doubtless
will go beyond. The next half century will test our capacity
as Man in Society. Our challenge will not be so much to make
new discoveries — we know we can do that, and we shall —
but rather to make good use of the tools and the resources
which our discoveries provide.

The basic question is whether we can live together, in a
way that benefits us all. Of course, that has always been the
question, but it will be our fortune to face it. We simply cannot
avoid it. The meaning of living in a global village — or a
Spaceship Earth — is that we no longer have myths or ignorance or distance to keep men separate. When war can destroy
us all, we have lost the luxury of uniting against our neighbours. When communications media portray African starvation to Canadian housewives and Canadian wealth to
Asian slum dwellers, our differing standards become an in-
cendiary affront. Science and technology have made it impossible for men to live apart, but they have not demonstrated
how men can live together — or even if we can.

The basic challenge of the next half century is a political
and an institutional challenge: to work out a satisfactory arrangement by which different men, with different individual
goals, can live together. As Canadians who believe in what
we call democracy and as realists who recognize that most
people in the world now know enough about self-determination
that they won't long accept subjugation, we would add the
requirement that this arrangement not be totalitarian.

We must be frank, and recognize that there is no certainty
we will succeed. Indeed, there is an alarming amount of evidence to suggest we might fail. It is, for instance, difficult to
cite many examples of the introduction of régimes of genuine
self-government in this century. Yet, in the same period, countries with traditions of self-government have suffered intense
attacks upon their representative institutions, occasionally by
critics who offer anarchy as an alternative.

There is a temptation to assume that our scientific and technological accomplishments will make government easier. I wish that were so; I fear it is not. In fact, the effect may be the opposite. We can expect an expansion in the degree of information available to the individual citizen and in his desire to participate. That might make government more representative, but it will also make it more complex. On quite another level, the responsibility of government has been extended by scientific and technological advances to embrace economic management, exploration of space and other problems which literally were not contemplated earlier. So the agenda of government grows while the consensus on which government can draw becomes less firm.

None of this is meant to minimize scientific and technological accomplishment. I assume science and technology now have — as certainly they have earned — a momentum of their own. With appropriate public support and direction, the march of discovery and technological improvement will continue. I have little doubt that, by the year 2020, we will have developed the technological capacity to overcome such manageable disorders as poverty, ignorance, inequality and disease, just as we now have the technological capacity to stop pollution or to produce enough food for most of the hungry. The question remains whether we can organize ourselves to use that capacity. At the least, our scientific and technological advance, awesome though it is, is no assurance of the millennium. All science and technology can provide is the means and the opportunity to build a better world. There is no guarantee that men will build it.

Nor is it a guarantee for men simply to want to use these new tools to resolve our old problems. That kind of commitment is essential, of course, but even if it comes, we still will need a method to make the commitment work. We will need political institutions which provide order and allow action, yet protect freedom and variety. If it has been difficult in the past to maintain such institutions — and demonstrably, it has been — it will be so much more difficult in the future as to constitute the most serious single challenge to mankind.

We seem to face an irony that, as man becomes more accomplished, he becomes less governable. For example, modern society requires men to have specialized knowledge, yet this requirement could create separate enclaves of specialists, increasingly unable to communicate their own goals or to comprehend the goals or situations of others. Individuals today have more information and more incentive to form and express their views; consensus is therefore more difficult and the instruments of consensus are edged into disrepute. The extension of education, opportunity and mobility relentlessly erodes the authority of faith and family and the other integrating agencies which traditionally have reminded man that he is part of something larger than himself. We are perhaps developing a respect for individuality, but at the cost of a sense of community.

A totalitarian régime would resolve that irony by fiat, subjugating the individual to the community. That is not acceptable to us. But neither can we simply accept the irony. We cannot hope to make the difficult collective decisions which the next fifty years will require if each of us insists on the luxury of going his own way. In my view, we have found only one means by which a free society can reconcile the requirements of individual choice and collective action. It is to develop institutions with enough flexibility to encompass and integrate the whole community, and individuals with enough flexibility — and modesty — to admit that their views need not always prevail.

I believe the Western democracies have devised the institutions, if we can only summon the patience and resolution to make them work. Our party system and the parliamentary or congressional institutions it makes possible offer the only known prospect of progressive and stable self-government. The party and parliamentary systems, of course, have faults, and must constantly be reformed, particularly to involve many more Canadians in political activity in a meaningful way. It is obviously essential to ensure that our political parties be relevant, and be felt to be relevant. But they alone allow the essential but often contradictory elements of order and freedom to exist together. They alone allow the integration of a disparate community, and yet the preservation of its vital individual parts.

These same requirements — of stability, yet variety; action, yet consent — are as necessary internationally as they are within any single state. While we are all still groping for the most effective forms of instruments of international government, it is clear that these same elements must be reconciled.

Naturally, then, I am concerned by the evidence that citizens of the democracies are becoming increasingly impatient with their political institutions. It is not only in Canada that the cry for the reform of Parliament is more widespread than the understanding of the role of Parliament. We are not the only country where support for the party system declines because individuals educated to be independent consider political parties to be confining. Membership in a party requires the individual to accept some views of others in return for the opportunity to assert successfully some views of his own.

That is also, of course, the difficulty of membership in society, but men have the illusion they can opt out of the party system without consequence.

It would be the final, and perhaps the fatal irony if those countries which are most advanced in education, technology and self-government should carelessly destroy the only institutions which give us a chance to extend self-government or even to survive to enjoy our technology.

Let me be clear that I do not extol these institutions because they are traditional, or because they have been criticized, or because they are ours. I believe they offer the best response we have to the most urgent challenge we face. If we cannot make them work, we have gone to the moon in vain.

Indeed, I suspect we will find that going to the moon was relatively easy.

Quand un historien se mêle de lire dans la boule de cristal

MICHEL BRUNET

Chargé d'étudier et de décrire le passé, l'historien est très souvent invité à prédire l'avenir. Comment expliquer ce paradoxe? Celui-ci m'apparaît comme un hommage rendu à l'historien. Ses contemporains en viennent spontanément à la conclusion que sa connaissance de l'histoire vécue le place dans une situation privilégiée pour expliquer le présent et y découvrir des lignes de force susceptibles de préparer les lendemains qui chanteront et ceux qui décevront.

Je prends donc le risque de répondre à l'invitation du Canadian Forum. En fait, je ne manifeste aucun courage particulier en rédigeant mes prophéties puisque je serai mort et enterré lorsque la première heure de l'année 2020 sonnera à la tour du Parlement d'Ottawa. Le gouvernement fédéral existera donc encore? Je le suppose. A la condition bien entendu – c'est mon hypothèse de départ – que l'Amérique du Nord ne soit pas anéantie, avec le reste de l'humanité, sous une pluie d'engins nucléaires.

Au cours du demi-siècle qui prend fin en 2020, le Canada s'est profondément transformé. On peut même dire qu'un nouveau pays, habité par des citoyens bien différents de leurs pères et de leurs grands-pères reconnus pour leur manque d'imagination, a pris naissance. L'Expo 67, qui fut le véritable premier laboratoire de ce canadianisme du XXIᵉ siècle, avait jeté les germes précurseurs de la révolution que vient d'accomplir le Canada. Le printemps de 1968, où un politicien traditionnel maquillé en prophète fit une apparition météorique dans le firmament politique, avait laissé momentanément croire qu'une moisson miraculeuse s'ensuivrait. Des millions de citoyens canadiens furent cruellement déçus lorsqu'ils découvrirent qu'ils avaient été victimes d'un mirage.

Néanmoins, cette amère déception joua à la fois le rôle d'un catalyseur et d'un démarreur. Les Canadiens de toutes les régions du pays se sentirent personnellement lésés et provoqués. Habitués de vivre à la remorque des grandes puissances — France, Grande-Bretagne et Etats-Unis — qui les avaient tou-

jours maintenus en tutelle, ils avaient longtemps cru qu'ils ne
pouvaient rien créer, qu'ils étaient condamnés à demeurer de
vulgaires imitateurs, de serviles entremetteurs, de mesquins
pique-assiettes. Soudainement, comme s'ils avaient été soulevés
par un dégoût profond d'eux-mêmes et scandalisés par la con-
duite irresponsable des générations précédentes, ils prirent la
ferme résolution de sortir des sentiers battus, de risquer le
tout pour le tout. L'époque des demi-mesures, des compromis
à la petite semaine, des marchandages de maquignons avait pris
fin. Le Canada ne voulait plus être un pays entretenu. Il avait
honte de s'être prostitué.

La contestation globale d'un passé sans grandeur, d'un
présent dépourvu d'idéal et d'un avenir symbolisé par la carte
de crédit *American Express* partit d'abord des milieux étudiants.
La jeunesse ouvrière se joignit bientôt à eux en forçant le
syndicalisme à ne plus s'identifier avec la société d'opulence.
La population rurale découvrit également qu'elle était solidaire
des étudiants et des ouvriers. Conscients de leur force numérique
puisque les moins de trente ans formaient plus de la moitié de
la population, les jeunes organisèrent un nouveau mouvement
politique qui s'appela le Parti de la Révolution permanente.
Leurs parents et leurs aînés, reconnaissant les échecs qu'ils
avaient accumulés et incapables de défendre un ordre écono-
mico-social dont ils pouvaient difficilement se glorifier,
acceptèrent en bonne partie — les uns avec enthousiasme, les
autres avec fatalisme — leur leadership. En moins de dix ans,
le Parti de la Révolution permanente réussit à influencer la
législation adoptée à tous les niveaux de l'administration
publique, depuis les conseils municipaux jusqu'au Parlement
fédéral.

L'évolution de la politique américaine favorisa la renaissance
canadienne. En effet, forcés de s'attaquer résolument à la
solution de leurs problèmes intérieurs, les Etats-Unis aban-
donnèrent leur ancienne échelle de valeurs devenue depuis
longtemps désuète. Après avoir mis fin à la guerre criminelle
et coûteuse du Vietnam et évacué leurs bases militaires à
l'étranger, ils renoncèrent à tout impérialisme. L'U.R.S.S. se
vit obligée d'en faire autant. Tous les peuples de la terre avaient
enfin la liberté de se donner les institutions politiques, écono-
miques et sociales qui répondaient à leurs besoins. Les Nations-

Unies, grâce à la collaboration de tous les pays disposant d'un surplus économique, constituèrent un Fonds mondial de Développement au bénéfice des pays sous-équipés. Tous les Etats s'étaient entendus pour adopter une politique de désar mement graduel et le Conseil de Sécurité des Nations-Unis avait reçu l'ordre de procéder à la destruction de tous les engins nucléaires et des autres armes de destruction massive. Une force de police internationale se chargeait de maintenir l'ordre dans les régions souffrant encore d'instabilité politique.

La société américaine, assagie par les lourdes épreuves que lui avaient imposées l'aventure vietnamienne, la révolte des noirs et des autres groupes défavorisés, la contestation de la jeunesse et l'indignation de la masse des citoyens qui n'acceptaient plus de se taire, avait enfin découvert que le capitalisme et l'entreprise dite libre étaient devenus, au cours de la deuxième moitié du XXᵉ siècle, une vaste mystification destinée à tromper les faibles et à servir les forts. En renouant avec la tradition révolutionnaire de l'époque de la Déclaration de l'Indépendance et de Thomas Paine, le peuple américain mobilisa toutes ses ressources humaines et matérielles pour corriger les injustices et les abus qui avaient conduit la plus grande puissance du monde au bord du chaos. L'audace que manifestèrent les Etats-Unis en s'engageant résolument dans la voie du socialisme et de la planification marquait la fin d'une époque dans l'histoire de l'humanité. La "Grande Société" n'était plus un slogan électoral mais un programme d'action à l'échelle mondiale.

Au Canada, le Parti de la Révolution permanente avait résolu les problèmes constitutionnels en créant une nouvelle Confédération canadienne composée de cinq Etats régionaux: Terre-Neuve (unissant les anciennes provinces de Terre-Neuve, de l'Ile-du-Prince-Edouard, de la Nouvelle-Ecosse et du Nouveau-Brunswick), Québec, Ontario, Manitoba (réunissant le Manitoba, la Saskatchewan et l'Alberta) et Vancouver (l'ancienne Colombie britannique). Le Québec était reconnu comme le territoire national de la population francophone de la Confédération canadienne. Les citoyens francophones des autres Etats régionaux qui refusaient de s'intégrer à la population anglophone avaient reçu des indemnités de déplacement leur permettant de venir s'établir au Québec. Le même avantage avait été offert aux habitants anglophones du Québec qui

préféraient émigrer. Cependant, Montréal conserve toujours un
certain nombre d'institutions d'enseignement bilingues depuis
l'école primaire jusqu'à l'université. Ottawa et Hull forment un
district fédéral bilingue. Québec est appelé à devenir un Etat
français et le reste du pays continue à demeurer anglais.

En adoptant cette solution qui s'inspirait de celle en vigueur
dans la Confédération helvétique, le Parti de la Révolution
permanente avait fait preuve de réalisme. Le bilinguisme *from
coast to coast* qu'avaient recommandé certains esprits utopiques
n'avait pas donné satisfaction aux Québécois qui réclamaient le
droit de vivre en français sur leur territoire national et avait
soulevé le mécontentement des habitants des autres régions du
pays. La nouvelle constitution de la Confédération canadienne
reconnaissait également le droit à la sécession de chaque Etat
régional. Cette clause avait rassuré les Québécois qui procla-
maient depuis plus d'une génération leur droit à l'autodéter-
mination. En acceptant, à la suite d'un référendum, de s'associer
à une union canadienne complètement rénovée, ils avaient posé
un geste réfléchi d'hommes libres. Pour la première fois depuis
la Conquête, les Canadiens français du Québec avaient eux-
mêmes choisi leur destinée comme groupe distinct en Amérique
du Nord. Cette option politique prise en toute lucidité, après de
longues discussions à l'intérieur même du Québec et à la suite
de négociations laborieuses avec le Canada anglais, les avait
enfin libérés d'un traumatisme séculaire. Ils en avaient récolté
un nouveau capital psychologique et se savaient dorénavant
engagés dans une entreprise collective où ils jouaient un rôle de
partenaires égaux avec les autres membres de la Confédération
canadienne.

Le pays jouit d'une prospérité équilibrée dont bénéficient
toutes les régions. Une Commission du Plan et des Finances
publiques, que régissent les cinq Etats régionaux et le gouvernement confédéral, veille au développement harmonieux de
tout le territoire canadien et au partage équitable des ressources
disponibles pour le bien-être de la population. Chaque citoyen a
droit à un revenu annuel garanti. Toutes les entreprises autrefois
contrôlées par le capitalisme américain sont devenues graduelle-
ment la propriété collective des habitants du Canada. Le
gouvernement des Etats-Unis, en abandonnant toutes ses bases
militaires, avait également prévu le retrait planifié des capitaux

américains investis à l'étranger. Cette opération de désengage-
ment économique s'était réalisée sous l'autorité du Fonds
mondial de Développement auquel tous les pays participaient.
Au début de l'an 2020, on peut dire que le Canada se prépare
à entrer dans une autre étape de sa révolution permanente.
Ayant réglé les problèmes les plus pressants — relations inter-
ethniques, réaménagement constitutionnel, structuration des
régions, décentralisation administrative et planification socio-
économique, pollution de l'air et de l'eau, partage moins injuste
de la prospérité, rationalisation du développement urbain,
expansion des services de recherches — les dirigeants de la
Confédération canadienne sont maintenant en mesure de relever
le défi que pose la civilisation des loisirs. La semaine de travail
sera prochainement réduite à vingt-quatre heures et les vacances
annuelles varieront entre six et dix-huit semaines. Le Parti de
la Révolution permanente et le Parti du Progrès révolutionnaire,
qui sollicitent tous deux les suffrages des électeurs, ont préparé
des programmes audacieux. Ceux-ci ont pour but de créer un
nouvel homme qui aura appris à se dominer lui-même parce
qu'il a substitué à la loi de la jungle celle de la coopération
fraternelle entre les Etats, les nations et les groupes culturels
pour bâtir un monde soumis aux impératifs de la justice . . .

*Je dois abandonner cette belle vision. Le bulletin de nou-
velles que me transmet la radio, me rappelant brutalement à
la réalité quotidienne, ne parle que de scandales financiers, de
crise monétaire, de chômage, de familles vivant dans la misère,
de coups d'Etat, de génocides en Afrique et en Asie, de grèves,
d'émeutes et de menaces de guerre. L'an 2020 n'est pas pour
demain.*

No More Fun and Games ROSEMARY COOK

Ottawa, July 1, 2020 (Our own Co-respondent)

Rather than celebrating Canada's national holiday today, our elected participators stayed close to their Telex machines awaiting the results of the four-party negotiations that have been taking place during the past twenty-four hours. It is hoped that these discussions will end the long debate, described by some as "a stupid fillybuster" and by others as a "last-ditch defence of democracy," over new proposals to reform the rules of the national participatory democracy centre in Ottawa. The Conservative government, led by Renée Lévesque, has been attempting to win approval for a rule which would permit the government to establish an annual IQ test for members of the opposition.

The opposition parties, not unpredictably, have insisted strenuously that the test be applied to both sides of the House. It is rumoured that the prime minister has allowed her House leader, Melinda Watkins, to offer a compromise: the test would be applied to all members except those who hold office under the Crown. (Queen Elizabeth's unexpected longevity has ensured that this hoary institution has so far remained untouched by the revolution.) One opposition spokesman, Cynthia Gonick of the *Créditistes*, has leaked word that a counterproposal has been advanced by the NDP leader, Marcella Faribault. This would make party leaders an exception to the IQ rule. This may well prove acceptable to Prime Minister Lévesque, whose aides have made no effort to disguise their interest in the IQs of several cabinet ministers.

The marathon debate over the new rules climaxed a tumultuous session of the participatory democracy centre. The new government has now ended its first year of office (the first government elected on the new, segregated voters' list) with some notable achievements to its credit. First there is the Official Languages Act abolishing the masculine gender from the French language. The act brought bitter attacks from some western Liberals, led by Harriet Crowe, who held that the measure discriminated against several minority groups whose languages retained both genders. It was also denounced as a plot to force central Canadian genders upon westerners. The prime minister struck back, claiming that such fears resulted from misleading editorial comment by the male-dominated newspapers of the country. A task force to examine this problem, headed by Lubovina Zink, is expected to be announced after this session's participation is adjourned.

A second measure, which absorbed many weeks of debate, was the new Omnibus Bill amending the Criminal Code. The most controversial sections of the bill prohibit marriage and heterosexual relations. The NDP, though insisting that the measure failed to go far enough, gave it reluctant support. Charlotte Taylor, the Liberal leader, with accustomed logic demanded a free vote on free love, but in the end supported the government. This came as a surprise only to those who remain unaware that the Liberal leader is now surrounded by a group of highly liberated urban intellectuals who are attempting to change their leader's image. It is rumoured that a trip to Denmark will form Charlotte Taylor's summer agenda. (Her forthcoming book, *The Petting of Politics,* may prove a revelation.) The Liberal leader was not, however, able to carry all of her party with her in supporting the Omnibus Bill. A large splinter group, led by Pierrette Trudeau, joined the *Créditistes* in denouncing the proposal as an attempt to put the state into the bedrooms of the nation — a condition Mlle. Trudeau rejected in her bestseller, *Feminism and the Female Canadians.* This view is said to be shared by the Canadian Council of Prioresses and numerous Protestant clergywomen.

It was this debate, more than anything else, which convinced the government that Bill 29-C should be rammed through the House. Its acceptance, so the opposition claims, will allow the government to limit debate to those members whose IQ falls below 100. The prime minister insists that, in fact, this represents no limitation at all. "That remark," the opposition leader retorted, "is just another example of the prime minister's determination to replace participatory democracy with priest-essential government."

Nevertheless, the prime minister is reportedly convinced that she must have this new rule since next session the government intends to introduce its highly controversial, and long-awaited, Canada Development Corporation. (It is rumoured that it will be codirected by the well-endowed financier, Gisella Grégoire, and the philosopher Georgina Grant, author of the influential *Lament for a Gender: The Defeat of Canadian Masculinism.*) The goal of the CDC, it is understood, will not be to buy back control of Canadian males. These, the recently disbanded Royal Commission on Females, Males and other Sexual Groups made plain, have already fallen into the hands of the Americans. Instead, the corporation will concentrate on channelling Canadian energies into future deviations. Moreover, it will act as a state agency governing relations with foreign countries — "a sort of publicly owned whore house," a high-ranking Ottawa mandarine has sneered. (The civil service is obviously still dominated by celibate continentalists.)

A second subject which is expected to provoke widespread controversy is the forthcoming white paper on taxation. This policy statement is widely expected to propose a human capital gains tax, the effect of which will be to wipe out the last vestiges of the nuclear family. So, too, it will suggest the termination of depletion allowances granted to the few remaining fathers of extended families. The opposition is building its attack on the argument that the measure will destroy incentive without giving any real stimulus to those sections of the population whose productivity has already disappeared. Murmurings have already been heard that the measure will prove what many have long believed: a libertarian leader has taken control of the Conservative party.

Clearly, then, much depends on the outcome of today's all-party negotiations. One imponderable weighs in the balance. This is the prime minister's long-standing engagement to open this year's Couchiching Conference. This year's theme is "Has Technology Made Woman Obsolete, Too?" The prime minister's prereleased speech is composed of readings from, and comments upon, the recently rediscovered classic history of the Couchiching affair, *In Praise of Older Women.*

Word has just come from the Parliamentary Powder Room

(made obsolete by the revolution, and slated for transformation into the Judy Lamarsh Fitness Forum) that the negotiations
have failed. "Another abortion," was the prime minister's comment. "Contraception will be imposed at once." The
gathered crowd outside looked from woman to man, and from
man to woman; but already it was impossible to say which was
which.

The Future Politician   WALTER L. GORDON

Politicians, like everyone else, must learn their trade and, therefore, soon become professionals. This does not mean that to succeed in public life Canadians will need to enter politics at a tender age and before they have acquired experience elsewhere. There should always be opportunities for men and women who have made their marks in business, in the trade union movement, in the professions or in other occupations, to switch to politics in middle life. But having done so, the newcomers will have to learn all they can about their new occupation: it is not a field for dilettantes.

Any consideration about the nature of Canadian society fifty years from now must be based on certain premises; *viz*:

— That somehow a major war will be avoided, a war in which nuclear weapons, chemicals, germs or nerve gases might very well be used. Those who are as concerned as I am about the attitudes and aims of the military-industrial complex in the U.S.A., and of the Russian and Chinese dictatorships may be forced to accept this premise with considerable scepticism.

— That there will not be another world depression as extreme in its effect or as long in its duration as the one experienced in the 1930s. This I believe to be a not unreasonable assumption.

— That at least for the next half century, the United States will continue to be by far the strongest power on earth. There are some who see signs of civil war between the blacks and whites and the almost immediate break-up of the American Empire. While I do not underestimate the danger of very serious racial conflict, I see no good reason for believing the United States will lose its present position in the world in the foreseeable future.

— That Canada, fifty years from now, will still be a united, independent state. This presupposes that Quebec will remain in Confederation. It presupposes also that we shall take steps to regain and to maintain a greater measure of economic independence than we have at present. For if we lose our economic independence, we shall lose our political independence also. I am less certain about this premise than I could wish to be.

Now, on the basis of these premises — whether or not we are able to accept them without reservations — what will Canadian society be like fifty years from now, and will there be a place in it for the newcomer to politics?

Many present trends are likely to continue. For example, a still larger proportion of the population will live in our cities and metropolitan areas and a smaller proportion on the farms. Canadians as a whole will become increasingly affluent with a shorter work week and more leisure time.

As it becomes ever more impossible for any one individual to comprehend all fields of knowledge, despite the increasing use of factual data banks and computers, the present trend towards specialization in the professions and in industry will continue.

We can expect more monopoly or oligopoly in industry and commerce, which in turn will call for more countervailing checks and more direction by the state. Inevitably, there will be a greater measure of government intervention in our lives. This does not mean that rhetorical references of a nostalgic character about the free workings of the market place will cease, only that they will become even less relevant than they are today. Nor does it mean a victory for democratic social-ism. On the contrary, with increasing affluence, Canadians probably will become more conservative and even less in-clined than they are at present to upset the existing order.

Again, while I deplore it, I expect that in the future little toleration will be shown for those who are unwilling to con-form. Those few Canadians who may be prepared to protest against outmoded policies or against abuses of fundamental human rights will need to be encouraged and protected. Such people are always badly needed, but probably this will be even more true in fifty years than it is today.

The discrepancies in the incomes of people in different oc-cupations and professions should be narrowed. I see no rea-son why university teachers, for example, should not aspire to the wage scales enjoyed by members of the building trades!

We may hope there will be changes in some of our existing
priorities, with less emphasis on defence and more on the
alleviation of poverty, both at home and abroad. In the United
States, this would mean less emphasis on government expendi-
tures on arms and exploring outer space, and more attention
to improving conditions in the cities and making people's lives
pleasanter and more worth while.

There should be less difference in the social structures of
the industrialized nations of the West and East: in the West,
more government intervention; in Eastern Europe and Russia,
more freedom, let us hope.

Finally, fashions will change from time to time, but it is
not possible to predict the exact position of the pendulum in
the specific year 2020. Will there be more hair or less? Will
it be easier to distinguish between boys and girls? Will skirts
be shorter than they are today? Will there be greater freedom
in individual behaviour, or a reaction in favour of a more
Victorian code in both attitudes and conduct? The only prediction I am prepared to make with any confidence is that I shall
not be there to see.

In the Canada of the future, more people with initiative
and ideas should be able to move from one occupation, including
that of politics, to another as is quite customary in the United
States. Surely some Canadian university teachers of economics
or business administration, for example, could make a go of
things in finance or industry. Surely, despite the trend to
specialization, many members of our large industrial and
commercial bureaucracies would find themselves quite at home
in the civil service. It is hardly conceivable that an experienced
university president could not be equally successful in the
realm of politics. And at least one of Canada's ex-prime ministers would have been a smash hit in vaudeville if his true
vocation had been recognized.

Times are changing much more rapidly than was the case
a few generations ago. There was a period when "personal
survival" was a sufficient goal in itself for aspiring politicians.
Mackenzie King is perhaps the patron saint of the members of
this school. More recent examples might include Paul Martin, John Diefenbaker and George McIlraith. But in the future,
Canadians may wish to change their public idols more fre-

quently than was once the case. They may even prefer to have them younger and a bit more photogenic and exciting in appearance. Trudeaumania may have been a precursor of what lies in store.

We shall always need more humour in our daily lives and more people with a ready wit. This is particularly true in politics. When I was a member of the House of Commons, the wits — Mike Pearson, Gene Whelan, Harry Hays, Joe Greene, Tommy Douglas, and sometimes Gordon Fairweather — were in a small minority. We shall need more of them in future. In addition, it will be important to encourage people who favour new ideas and new approaches to become involved in politics for a time. Most politicians and most civil servants, like most people everywhere, tend to resist change on principle. Why rock the boat if it isn't absolutely necessary? We can only hope that in an age of increasing affluence and conformity, there will be a few who are not satisfied with the *status quo* and who are prepared to do battle with the establishments who defend it. We shall need innovators in the future as we have done in the past. Let us hope that such people will be sought out and persuaded that a few years in public life can be worth while.

The Shape of Government and Politics in Canada in 2020: Some Speculations

THOMAS A. HOCKIN

One peculiar idiosyncrasy of this generation of Canadians is our tendency to think that Canada is on the threshold of many important, even revolutionary political changes. Nothing very striking has actually happened to Canadian politics yet, but to many, the portents of change seem irrepressible. Most likely it was the torrent of serious Centennial feature articles that has left us awash in this sea of ruminations about "Canada at the Crossroads" in almost every political context.

Even with this acknowledged, however, I think that incipient disenchantment with our political parties and with Parliament will probably produce some important political transformations in the next fifty years. In two other vital contexts of Canadian political culture — the evolution of federalism and the growth of government — important transformations likely will sweep away the bench marks of the present no matter how strong or weak is popular dissatisfaction.

Our present jurisdictional and bicultural notions of federalism will be important in the next five decades but they may be utterly transformed by Canada's immigration patterns. At present a rigourous enforcement of the "educational and skills" standards of the Immigration Act discourages a great deal of nonwhite immigration into Canada. But this will not work forever as the educational achievements of nonwhite peoples — of black Americans, for example — improve in the immediate few decades. Since it is doubtful that the Canadian public would support new racist immigration legislation, the immigration mix into Canada in the future will be vastly altered, especially if the deployment of domed living centres and weather-controlled environments makes our harsh climate less a deterrent to immigration from southern countries.

This development will test the depth of Canadian federalist beliefs. Does the Canadian concept of federalism include *only* 1) a devolution of some power to ten provinces and 2) a recognition of the necessities outlined in the first two Bi-Bi Commission reports? We make much of our federalist creed but the root value of federalism should be more profound than a mere acknowledgment of provincial rights and of bilingualism. If Canadians are to be said to hold anything that could be called a truly "federalist" attitude in the year 2020, it will be necessary to admit far more cultural and racial diversity than is dreamed of in the current arid jurisdictional and financial wranglings over the constitution. To be truly federalist, Canada will have to believe in diversity, encourage tolerance and stimulate an openness to different peoples and life styles.

This may be made easier by the elimination of vast islands of discrimination and inequity in the private sector simply because the private sector will be smaller and less private. To predict that the public sector will grow and the private diminish is simply to recognize that the whole fabric of our mixed economy is now undergoing profound changes that make government activity in many cases a matter not of ideological debate but of structural inevitability. Just as the importation of cash into feudal society subverted, then dissolved the traditional ties and relationships of that society, the accelerating insinuation of science and technology into business enterprise promises fundamentally to alter the shape of Canada's economy. Much is made about the increase in leisure that will be brought by automation as a result of improvements in science and technology. Other alterations, however, will prove to be far more striking by the year 2020. As Robert Heilbroner and others have noted, technology tends to create new social problems that require public controls to correct or forestall. We already have in Canada a vast network of government agencies which try to cope with the social repercussions of the automobile, the airplane, drugs, pollution, nuclear energy and even advertising. This proliferation of public control agencies will continue. On a broader level in our post-Keynesian economy, however, we have a mind-boggling patchwork of government-inspired indulgences, protections and compensations. This patchwork may become so internally contradictory and discriminatory that broad reforms far more comprehensive than those of the Carter Commission or "guaranteed annual incomes" will be necessary.

Directly or indirectly, government will also become the employer of probably well over two-thirds of the Canadian labour force in fifty years. Many people in the private sector today wonder what will happen to all those who will be rendered unemployed as cybernetics and automation invade still further mechanized and unmechanized work. In fact, by the end of the next half century there may not be a great increase in unemployment or in leisure time since many new areas of employment will open up in the reconstruction of cities, the provision of education for all age groups, the improvement of health and cultural facilities, the counselling of the young and the aged, the beautification of the environment. However, as Heilbroner, John Kenneth Galbraith, Carl Kaysen and others have been saying for over ten years, the incursion of technology will push the frontiers of work into a new range of jobs whose common denominator is that they require *public* action and *public* funds for their initiation and support. And this is what will make government such a major employer before too long.

This assimilation of activities by government will, of course, open up a new set of challenges if the rights of individuals are to be protected against an increasingly vast set of governmental bureaucracies and if the political process and the governmental process will not continue to open ever-increasing distances between each other. To embarrass your opponent, to create controversy simply to keep public attention on yourself and your party, to win at the "game of politics" with only tangential regard to creative and efficient public policies are all manifestations of the pursuit of politics for its own sake. The efficient but insensitive production of public policies by civil-servant-dominated cabinets with little or no regard for certain regional, economic or cultural abilities to absorb or support policies is, on the other hand, an example of government for its own sake. Today the House of Commons is becoming ever so slightly a forum (especially in its committees) not simply for political jousting but for producing creative public policy. Departments of government have even been challenged by the Senate and the House as sources of input into public policy in the last three years.

At one level, however, the gulf between politics and government will grow ever wider as specialization, technology and complexity increase. The House of Commons in 2020 will probably look superficially like the Bundestag in Bonn today. It will meet as a whole only infrequently — one or two months a year — for certain major "debates" — all before television — and for giving formal approval to legislation. The real contact between politics and government will be maintained by the MPs on continuing task forces, commissions (no longer called Royal) and scrutiny committees manned by outside experts, civil servants, ministers and junior ministers (as in Sweden today).

But what about the future of our political parties? Political observers from David Hume to the present have noted that political parties continue to exist long after the principles which originally animated them are forgotten: most of the principles of our contemporary Liberal and Conservative parties are virtually unrecognizable from the days of Macdonald and Brown. So the parties of fifty years hence will no doubt bear but faint resemblance to contemporary parties. Some parties may die. Some will be born. If national political parties fifty years from now are going to reflect the most basic political concerns facing the country, then I would suggest that although economic disparities and federalism (in its more comprehensive form) will still be vital national issues, they will be less important than the impending clash of values between those concerned with quantity and efficiency and those concerned with the quality of life.

One cannot predict that we will necessarily have a "technological" political party and a "humanist" political party, but this is quite possible. (It is more likely, however, that the technological-humanist split will reside within each of the major parties since the search for a majority will dictate that a majority party be hospitable to both groups of vested interests.) As economic inequalities continue to decrease, more Canadians will have a vested interest not in increasing their income or possessions but in finding a pleasant, stimulating and humane pattern of life. This may involve a decline in the pride of ownership and a rise in the value of community organization. It will change the nature of universities, cultural centres and entertainment. Those with a vested interest in a "humanist" political position — broadly conceived — will include a minority interested in cultural or intellectual refinement and a majority interested in recreational forms of culture. Those with an interest in the values of technological and economic growth will include vast numbers of people who share many of the aspirations and pleasures involved in the pace, atmosphere, services and products that result from rapid technological and economic growth.

Once broker parties deal with both sets of values, the distinction between both sets may become blurred in terms of public policy. But it would be idle to suggest that there will be no meaningful differences. Like all major political parties, what will distinguish them from each other or distinguish the warring camps within each party will be the life styles and attitudes of their supporters as much as their policy platforms.

This development may produce the kind of "creative politics" so many people are demanding today, or it may produce a deep, even intolerant ideological split across the whole country. One thing is certain, however. If political attitudes and values start to coalesce around both of these poles, by the year 2020 we may have found cause to hope that the people's elected representatives may regain much of the moral and policy-making authority that has drifted, in the last fifty years, to the public servants.

And this development alone would help to make political participation a far more respectable enterprise than it seems to be today to many people.

The Great Moral Addiction ABRAHAM ROTSTEIN

In the Age of Aquarius morality becomes a mind-expanding drug. What the future holds is increasing moral addiction as we are continually turned on by human oppression we have yet to "discover"– highly original sins leaping out at us in psychedelic revelations. Our grandchildren looking back will envy our present pagan innocence. This is how they will see it.

The midsixties provided the first clues. Wars on poverty and racism were suddenly placed on the establishment agenda. Although they were sins as old as mankind itself, they were suddenly "discovered" and attacked with varying blends of utopianism and empty gestures. A fierce intolerance prevailed, at least among some portions of the "progressive" population. "High time" said the socialists, who have overheated consciences anyway. But it was curious nevertheless that poverty and racism should generate such public passions as they accelerated out of nowhere into headlines.

Women's liberation sent out its first crackling signals at the end of the sixties, but we hardly got off as easily here as with the token poverty programs. First it was a matter of social perspective. Marxism had had a clear monopoly on oppression theory for one hundred years. All oppression had been reduced to a function of class and ownership of property. It was a tortuous exercise to tie it all together, but somehow it was convincing if you didn't press the matter. Obviously the upper classes were richer and more powerful — ergo the lower classes (and everybody else) were exploited.

What threw this conveniently simple theory into chaos was the women's revolt — this time for real equality, not just votes. The Lysistrata legend, dormant over two millennia, suddenly came alive. Pursued to its logical conclusion this newly discovered oppression absolutely shattered a class analysis; it cut across every grouping and refinement of Marxist sociology. Not capitalism but *men* were the oppressors.

With enormous social strain, all basic institutions were recast. Women moved rapidly ahead in the factories and offices.

The nuclear family was reshaped by communal apartment buildings and dining rooms; day nurseries sprang up everywhere
and men shifted to half-time jobs to take on their share of the
remaining family responsibilities. It made hay of the old debate between private and public sector. The new debate was
about the *communal* sector (i.e., where men-women equality
prevailed): how were society's resources to be redirected to
make it effective? The women never looked back.

The Pied Piper of Hamelin had his own rebirth. The ambivalence of society to the young had reached intolerable limits.
Youth was exploited first in myth, the ideal background for
the projection of liberal fantasies. One example was the great
success (who can now remember it?) of the musical *Hair*,
where the ideal of youth became the rear-view fantasy world
of the middle class — but enjoyed only vicariously somewhere
in the early life of mankind. The fantasy ideals were unattain-
able — excluded by a barrier as relentless as death — the
clock could not be turned back.

The darker side suddenly became clear as well. The uni
versities were youth reservations to confine the unemployable.
The public and high school curricula were ritualized *rites de
passage*, attenuated initiation ceremonies whose pain lay in
the rote learning and the rote discipline. Drug laws became
the instrument for waves of prosecution of young people. The
atavistic puritanism of society claimed its own retribution for
the new sexual freedom of the young.

Action began with mass festivals such as Woodstock. Soon
it dawned on the young and on everyone else that they could
and would build their own "free" societies. They simply walked out of the high schools and universities, created their own
educational programs and built youth enclaves and cultures.
Adults were excluded.

The revolt of the old was also a revolt from the impoverished reservation. They opted to rejoin society. Whole quar-
ters of cities contained senior citizens' apartment blocks —
but only the air of death stalked those communities. Pitiful
pensions were the immediate rallying point — but the overt ex-
clusion from human community was the heart of the matter.
The exploitation issue was put forward as an "interest-rate"
problem. Investment of a lifetime of labour had added to a

capital base from which society as a whole was reaping the rewards. But the aged had been excluded from the long-term benefits of their labours. They were viewed moreover as a "charge" on society rather than as its benefactors. They storm- ed legislatures and created civil chaos until society readmit- ted them once again to life and to community.

The nonarticulate but the most cruelly and inhumanly ex- ploited were the animals. Half in jest, the slogan arose — "Animals are people, too." The cruelty of breeding for slaugh- ter gradually hit home, the bloodlust of the hunt, the carnage and sadism of the annual decimation of the seals in North America, the thin façade of fishing as a sport, zoos as concen- tration camps.

Injustice, cruelty, exploitation of animals were denounced in turn by militant groups from all of society. The dumb animals found their supporters mainly among those who had been educated into an ecological conscience in the battle of the environment. A nature that was wounded and partly destroyed gave great impetus to the care of its living beings. Vegetarian- ism received a new and enormous advocacy.

After the animals had been freed — in overtones reminis- cent of Abraham Lincoln's speeches on slavery — a power- ful and disembodied craving for social justice was left with no new worlds to conquer.

The five decades were a golden age for the discovery of invisible oppression. We have touched on the major groups, but we could also mention the renaissance of the neighbour hoods, the militancy of the unmarried and the eradication of the deadly rooming houses, the revival of the ethnicity of the immigrant generations, the revolt of the handicapped and the maimed, democratic upheaval not only in industrial plants but in prisons and mental institutions.

The historians of the 2010s looked back on the first half of the twentieth century with stupefaction — how could we have lived in such oblivion to universal oppression?

But it was no simple matter, once the last pockets of oppres- sion had been routed, to find an antidote to the Great Moral Addiction.

PART V. HOPES:

canada, true north and free

WILLIAM THOMPSON
149 **2020 Hindsight**

WILLIAM NICHOLLS
158 **Canada – World Melting Pot**

GREGORY BAUM
161 **A New Renaissance?**

HERMANN REBEL
165 **2020 Visions of an Electric Mutant German Historian Guitar Player Berkeley Expatriate Prophet**

JOHN McCUAIG
170 **Software and the Imploding Spastic Inevitable (home hints for 2020)**

overleaf "Easter" by Harold Town

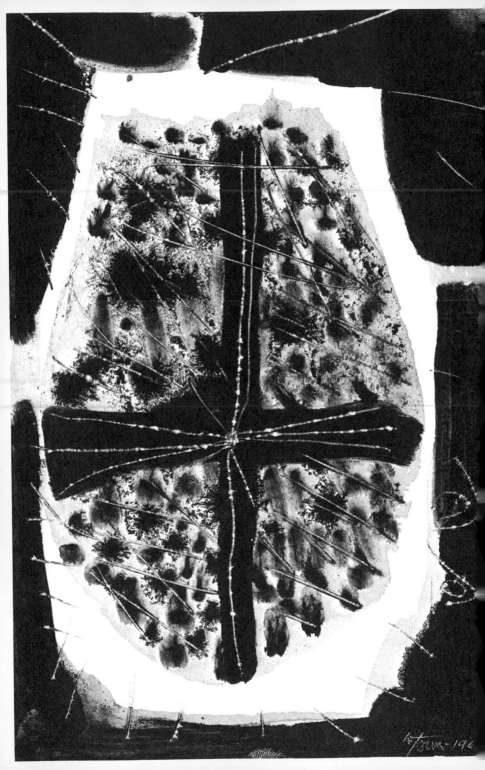

Letter to Kyra (*cont'd.*)

Not everyone who is thinking of the shape of the Canada to come is as apprehensive about our political future as is Abraham Rotstein. In this section you will find some of the more adventurous projections that offset the obsessions of parts I and II.

It is very unlikely that these articles could have been written five or ten years ago when the Canadian psyche was still submerged in its long-standing dependency and inferiority. In recent years a combination of the outrageous American war in Asia, the outburst of racial civil war at home and the evident social disintegration of the American cities has made Canadians suddenly aware of the intrinsic value of their own society and of the need to "close the 49th parallel" to Americanization. This renascent Canadian nationalism is not restricted to third-generation citizens. In many cases it is recent immigrants from the United States who are more sensitized to the American time bomb and Canada's promise. William Thompson, for instance, projects in the northern youth reserves this hope for the blossoming of a new human culture and a new art after the anticipated American apocalypse. William Nicholls has an analogous utopia based on the large-scale influx of the world's Asian communities. As a scholar of comparative religion Nicholls sees Canada taking the lead in developing a culture of new spiritual capacities that make life in the technologically advanced society an instrument for individual and social liberation. For Gregory Baum, an equally avant-garde but Catholic theologian, a religious renaissance based on revolutionary discoveries of extrasensory communications could have a socially explosive impact on human behaviour and relations. There's no point giving a linear interpretation to nonlinear thinking. The hopes that burn in Hermann Rebel's electric historian's poem take on a McLuhanesque dimension when read with John McCuaig's "home hints for 2020."

2020 Hindsight   William Thompson

Now that Apocalypse is over we can look back with wonder
at the unimaginable events that turned Canada into one of the
centres of planetary civilization favoured by the Directorate.
Since we have been altogether too serious about the past, it
may be worth recalling for a laugh the way the twenty-first
century was envisioned fifty years ago. Back in 1967 before
the Industrial Dark Ages began, everyone thought that the
year 2000 would bring the millennium to the United States.
A rash of books was published predicting (in fact, celebrating) the triumph of technocratic liberalism all over the world.
Now as the archivist leafs through the charts and graphs for
the extrapolated GNPs of the major powers in 2000 A.D., he is
astonished at their naïveté. The experts were moving headlong
into disaster and yet had no sense of where they were going;
the student of the twentieth century can find more sense in
the works of the poets, mystics and writers of what was then
called science fiction. The vatic nerves of the powerless tingled
with an uneasiness and caution that the busy minds of the
powerful ignored, and only they could sense that they were
hanging at the edge of history.

No one dreamed in 1967 that man's whole view of history,
nature, self and civilization was about to be turned upside
down: all the surprises were thought to be behind him in the
Copernican revolution during the Renaissance and in the Dar-
winian revolution of the nineteenth century. History, it was
felt, had finally achieved its ultimate form in the hands of the
liberal experts: with the experts in charge of man's destiny,
all problems would be solved by the problem solvers and
there would be progress and increasing GNPs forever. It is easy
to mock the arrogant stupidity of our twentieth century ancestors, but it is too easy. What separates us from them is
an abyss of events that no one in his right mind would have
been able to predict (which is, no doubt, one reason why
those who were not in their right minds actually did predict the
darkness to come). If we feel superior to their ignorance, we

should remember that the men of the twentieth century also felt superior to "the primitives" they placed at the beginning of their pseudohistory. They were so wrapped up in a historical myth that it was fitting that the new knowledge of man's mythic history should open up the ground beneath their confidently placed feet. And then, before they had a chance to gain their bearings, the five-dimensional biophysics touched the confusions of the old technological world view with a devastatingly elegant simplicity it could not survive.

In the twentieth century, man thought he was the product of the chance events of junk colliding in an insignificant corner of infinite space. The inevitable correlate of this world view was a compensatory megalomania in which man regarded the entire universe as his own underdeveloped Fourth World. The scientific base for this ideology began to give way in the 1970s as the theory of superconductors furnished models for the way biological fields behaved in consciousness-resonant single quantum states. A. N. Whitehead was prophetic in this, but the bridge between solid-state physics and biology provided specific content for his philosophic structures. This new Whiteheadian science was profoundly unsettling for the old culture of technology but, by the seventies, that culture was beginning to collapse far more dramatically in the field than in the laboratory. The nerve-gas leakages in Colorado, the nuclear-wastes accidents in Oregon and Washington, the salinization of the soil in the Midwest, the death of the California forests, the disruption of the eastern Atlantic weather system by the American Army Corps of Engineers, the horrendous famines from colossal overpopulation, the continental pollution, the bombing cults, the disintegration of urban life, the general panic and madness: all of these converged to make the 1970s and 1980s a time in which the old reality died a very violent death indeed.

Precisely because the United States was the triumph of the era of the industrial nation-state, it became the greatest victim of the exploding internal contradictions of that system. Caught in a double bind in which the more successful were its American-based multinational corporations, the more exhausted were its dollars, the United States learned with the collapse of the International Monetary Fund that you cannot do a planet's business on a nation's currency. And it was precisely because Canada was midway between America and the underdeveloped Third World that it stumbled into the right position in which to encounter the apocalypse of the seventies. With a surplus of food and water, with spaces as vast as its population was small, Canada entered the Industrial Dark Ages in one of the strongest possible conditions.

There was a time when the United States looked as if it were going to make the transition from industrial nation-state to scientific planetary civilization, but the wrenching cultural change terrified the industrial lower-middle class into holding on tight to the past. And then the war in Vietnam was brought home to America with a vengeance. Like a body in which there are so many white corpuscles that they begin to attack the organism itself, the military and police forces in America destroyed the very values they were supposed to protect. The country that loudly screamed its denial of Marxist materialism yet sought a technological answer for every human problem. The answer to the riot was the invention of an antiriot technology. One would have thought that the failure of the bombing of North Vietnam in the sixties would have taught the Americans a lesson on the limits of technology, but it did not. With the fall of Southeast Asia in the election year of 1972, the Democratic-Republican consensus led by President Nixon disintegrated. The United States withdrew to Fortress America where the newly elected right-wing extremist government sought its revenge upon the leftists who had encouraged the enemy to hold on, and so were "responsible for the first war America ever lost." In defeat America went home, but not without making a point to the Third World — and tragically, again it was a technological point. With consummate display of instrumental precision, the United States used tactical nuclear weapons "to remove surgically" China's nuclear capacity. A point was made to the Third World, and it was a point they were not likely to forget: once again the white race had used nuclear weapons upon Orientals.

It was a catastrophe, and I suppose one could say that, from the law of karma, what followed in North America was retribution for the enslavement of the Negroes, the genocidal elimination of the Indians, the concentration-camp imprison-

ment of the Japanese-Americans and the nuclear attacks on
Japan and China. The Second American Civil War, of course,
broke down Canada's friendly relationship with the States. The
right-wing American government was eager to tap Canadian
resources of fuel and water on the one hand and the antigovern-
ment American sanctuary for deserters and emigré intellectuals on the other. But the more imperialistic the American
government became, the more the American protest movement made Canadian sovereignty an internal domestic issue
of the civil conflict. Had the ecological disasters not come
when they did, it is more than likely that the protest movement would have been as futile as the protest against the elimination of the Indians. The tactical nuclear strike against China
signalled the cracking of a fault that went throughout American
history, from King Philip's War to Vietnam. It was a complete
disaster, but it was also the end of the union of science and
nationalism.

As the scientists began to detect "the planetary damage"
brought about by so small a nuclear strike, they realized that
the human race could not possibly survive if it continued on
its present course. With smaller nations developing a nuclear
capacity and with the American reactionary government firmly in the hands of the engineers and military technologists,
it became clear to the pure scientists that nationalism was
bringing about the death of the human race. The United States
and the Soviet Union had always tried to keep science sub-
servient to nationalism through police-enforced secrecy because
both countries understood that, if the planet's knowledge were
invested in a close, international scientific fraternity, that fraternity would be stronger than the nation-state. Eventually,
however, nothing could be done to keep the scientists apart;
the very weapons they created in isolation from one another
only forced them closer together in disarmament talks.

It was through these disarmament channels that the first
meetings of "the Hidden College" began. As one disaster
after another hit the earth, it became unmistakably clear
that something very radical had to be done. The something
was very radical indeed: overnight the structure of human
civilization changed as the scientists effected a palace *coup*
on the planet. In a state of panic and exhaustion brought

on by the disasters, the people had no other alternative but to look up to their saviours who promised "to keep the life-support systems of Spaceship Earth working at the price of absolute scientific control over environments and populations." The multinational corporations, of course, gave their immediate support to the Directorate; the days of "the great powers" were over and the days of planetary civilization were at hand, but for bourgeois, industrial and democratic man, it was the end of much of the freedom and alienation that he would look back on with nostalgia.

As it had happened before in history, the old forms, stripped of their power, were free for artistic use. Like candles used in an elegant electric home, the old nation-state took on a new humanistic and artistic life in the midst of scientific planetary civilization. And no country shone more brilliantly in the seventies and eighties than Canada. When America fell back into a lower-middle-class reaction, Canada began to attract thousands of intellectuals from Europe and America. Since Canada did not have to carry the burden of a mammoth defence budget and since the consciousness of the wilderness was a strong part of the national ethos, Canadian scientists took the lead in the vital ecological sciences. As one solution after another began to appear, the Canadian phenomenon gained momentum and America lost to Canada what she had gained from Europe in the thirties and forties.

Why Canada did not fall in behind the extremist American government is really a test case in the supremacy of ideology over economics. For all intents and purposes Canada was technologically and culturally indistinguishable from the United States — except that south of the border there was despair and hysteria; north, there was still hope. Perhaps something of Canada's conservative nineteenth century heritage helped it avoid the excesses of an unbridled technological hedonism but, from whatever source, it was the ineffable confidence that Canada could do something that enabled the unexpected to happen.

Canada's *genius loci* was the tory-radical, an example of a tradition that was never able to take hold, for all the efforts of Boston, in the mass society of the United States. And yet disaster was close for a while, even in Canada. As early as 1968, just as the American intellectual exodus was becoming visible, the Liberals mounted a fairly successful campaign to lead Canada into the American technocratic dead end. Mastering the media techniques of American advertising, the Liberals were able to take a bald, homely, forty-eight-year-old bachelor and turn him into the "charismatic" leader of a "swinging new Canada." Behind the media images a whole new army of technocrats was trying to create Canadian versions of Americans like McNamara, Bundy, Rostow and Kissinger. And as progress and technocratic development were being sold by exploiting Canadians' self-conscious stodgy self-image, Victorian Toronto began to chase after a combination of the worst qualities of New York and Los Angeles. By 1970 it looked as if Toronto were going to be a warehouse of high-rise apartments in which human beings were filed away in habitational envelopes addressed to *anomie*. But, fortunately, the reaction to Trudeau's technocratic manipulations set in and the New Democratic party emerged as a totally novel historical consensus of antitechnocratic tories and New Left professionals and students.

Few people would have thought in 1968 that a tory-radical coalition was possible, but it was precisely in its nineteenth century heritage that Canada had the sense not to become so unwitting a victim of its own technology as the United States had been. Lacking the energy and rush of American power and historicist dreams, Canada was free to take a slower, more human perspective on technology. America had always been subject to Faustian intoxications with its own aerospace thaumaturgy. Between city-states and provinces, corridors and federations, Canada found just the right kind of flexible, multistructured government appropriate to the age of transition. Whereas the planetary Directorate had to suppress American and Russian national power, that very suppression gave Canada the space in which to become the country it never had been as a colony of Britain or a branch plant of America.

But antique nationalism and the even more antique city-state polity were not the only forms of nativistic movements within planetary civilization. During the late seventies the Canadian Indian renaissance, stimulated by new archaeological discoveries, began in earnest and brought a whole new revolution in man's consciousness of the mind's relationship with nature. The first expression of this revolution came in the Indian movement of "architecture without architects." The proliferation of high-rise filing cabinets generated a great longing for other forms of life and the North began to seem no more uninhabitable than Toronto. Youth groups, with the artistic discovery of the Indian, were able to persuade the NDP government to turn the North over to them and not to the "developers." Since the era of ecological disasters in the seventies had created all sorts of youth task forces, it was rather easy for the young to convince the government they had helped to elect that, since the future belonged to them, why not give them the part of it adults weren't using anyway.

The opening of the Youth Civilization of the North came at a fortunate moment, for by the eighties North American institutions were so out of tune with the life cycle that the universities had become little more than youth reserves on the one hand and informational merchandising centres on the other. Children at eleven knew more and were more physically developed than the sixteen-year-olds of 1920, yet adults had the same educational containers for them. The adults, of course, worked with all the old assumptions of citizens of an industrial middle-class democracy; they couldn't see that their children were not going to take over the shop so much as return to the mythic soil and become the superstitious peasants of a new hierarchical civilization. Once the young were up in the North creating the Alternative Civilization, the universities ceased to be the exciting places they once had been. The radical Left revolution in the seventies had begun the process, for when all "undemocratic standards" were eliminated by the academic liberals, the schools became openly the youth reserves they always had been in secret. Once the adolescents had their way, though, they found that, as a youth reserve, a university left something to be desired. It became painfully clear that their former allies, the liberal grown-ups, were vampires trying to keep from growing old by sucking the youth out of them. Because the new mythic and Pythagorean science of the seventies had been too imaginative for the bureaucracies of the technocratic centres, geniuses had long since abandoned them to their bureaucratic fate and walked out to build the

Ionas and Lindisfarnes appropriate to the Industrial Dark Ages. Just as once before the ecclesiastical hierarchy had been eclipsed by the university, so in the eighties the university hierarchy was eclipsed by the small Pythagorean institutes, ashrams and youth communities. In all, the effect of the Indian, Pythagorean and youth movements of the eighties and the planetary religious movement of the nineties was to bring about a whole new rhythm, for individuals, of growing in time.

Today, from incarnation to age seven, *Homo ludens* rules, and the individual in the *kibbutz* develops in polymorphously sensuous ways. But, as each thing generates its opposite, the period from seven to fourteen is the age of *Homo faber*. The natural tendencies of latency are encouraged and intensified as the child begins to delight in facts and information gathering. By fourteen the child has mastered calculus, basic science and the native, scientific and religious languages. To our ancestors in 1970, he would be ready for university, but we realize that, on the contrary, he is ready for the Youth Civilization of the North. Once again, *Homo ludens* replaces *Homo faber* and from fourteen to twenty-one the adolescent realizes himself in the androgynous and polymorphous growth and development of play. After a surfeit of sensory awakening, eroticism and embodied consciousness, the individual is free to return to the university-cities of the South. From twenty-one to twenty-eight the adult may move through the willingly accepted routines of B.A., M.A., Ph.D., or he may turn away from the intellect for the forms of self-realization offered in the craft and industrial guilds. Then from twenty-eight to thirty-five, *Homo ludens* returns again and the chosen few may move to the childbearing *kibbutzim*. With the return of *Homo faber* at thirty-five, those who wish to do so are free to begin the study for a whole new career. All is in rhythm now: for the many there are the craft and industrial guilds; for the few there is science; for the elect, there are the Mysteries and, "because there is no equality, there is love and justice for all." Everything is in its place and all our institutions, from incarnation to apotheosis, are guided by the Directorate.

With the planetary crisis fading in our memories, mankind

seems to be lowering its vistas. No doubt it is a normal reaction, and perhaps that is why the nations are striving to fight against it in a general cultural awakening. The United States seems to have recovered from its defeats and is now trying to regain the lustre that Canada took away from it. Canadians would do well to think of the American awakening as we settle into our villages, where we may talk of planets and extraterrestrials, but walk to work and play. Now, in the year 2020, the Dionysian period of expansion and wild transformation is over and the period of Apollonian consolidation is firmly upon us. *Now* it almost seems as if it would have been worth living in those great and tragic days of an entire epoch but only half a century ago.

Canada —
World Melting Pot

In the early years of the twenty-first century Canada began
to experience fully the transformation of its culture brought
about by the massive immigration from Asia that had begun
in the 1980s. The population of the northland was by the
year 2000 almost wholly of Japanese, Chinese and Indian origin. In the second decade of the twenty-first century, the population of Canada overtook that of the United States; although
Canada has still not acquired the technological resources of
its southern neighbour, this is largely due to the ecological
self-restraint its people began to practise somewhat sooner
than the Americans, partly as a result of their predominantly
Asian cultural heritage. Technology was necessary to open up
the resources of the northland, but the great cities of the
North left their environment unsullied from the first in a way
that the old cities of the southern strip managed to achieve only
under the strictest regulation and at the cost of profound changes
in their traditional way of life. By 2005, Canada managed
to establish an oxygen balance once more, after a period in
which it had been under constant censure from the United
Nations for overconsumption and underforestation.

Canada is drawing ahead of other advanced industrial nations in the unremitting struggle to reclaim man's environment from the disastrous effects of the uncontrolled exploitation practised throughout the twentieth century. The rash of
local atomic wars, first between Israel and Egypt, then between
South and central Africa during the seventies, had resulted in so
sharp an increase in infant mortality all over the world that
a working disarmament agreement between the major powers
was at last laboriously achieved in the nineties. Canada, like
other nations, contributed a contingent to the Nuclear Inspec-
tion and Enforcement Branch of the World Peace Force.

After the knife-edge struggles of the previous fifty years,
when man tried to gain control of his own explosive expansion
in population and technology and to achieve a high level of
comfort for a world population stabilized at about three times

what it was in 1970, a new world culture has begun to emerge, building on the spiritual foundations laid in the last century by the convergence of all man's religious traditions on North American soil. The mixed population of Canada provided a kind of spiritual pressure cooker for a new synthesis unmatched in more racially homogeneous areas. From the nineties on, Canadians have been aware that their heritage is as much Hindu and Buddhist as it is Jewish and Christian, and the pragmatic North American background has transformed all these traditions into methods of self-liberation rather than systems of belief and institutional life.

From India, Canadians learned the idea of living life in successive stages in which different aims are dominant. The average Canadian now spends his or her teens in learning to love sexually, his twenties in work, his thirties in political leadership and the rest of his life in artistic creation or in meditation. The old, not the young, are once more the cultural leaders, and the unprecedentedly rich achievements of Canadian art and literature have grown from the seedbed of meditation and contemplation so widely practised by the young as well as the mature. Self-liberation is the most highly prized option open to man, and even those who become fixated at the immature stage of power seeking, which is characteristic of people in their thirties, have to pay lip-service to the cultural ideal of the sage who postpones his own final liberation in order to set his fellow man free. A succession of prime ministers of Asian origin has established a new ethos, that the politician must be a detached guru who leaves contemplation for the service of his people only with the greatest reluctance.

But the art of government, which has been raised to such levels in Canada that three out of five of the last general secretaries of the United Nations have been Chinese-Canadians, owes more to the Confucian tradition and to the practice of consulting the I Ching systematically whenever an important decision has to be made. The original I Ching has now been associated with a computerized library of its own past answers which combines memory and the "chance element" so effectively that no practical problem need be tackled without effective guidance.

Japanese Canadians have for several decades led the world

in the prestigious science of ecotechnology, and Canadian-designed controlled environments enjoy world leadership. The great Zen revival in Japan in the first years of the twenty-first century was initiated by Canadian roshis, trained in the religious studies departments of our universities, who returned to Japan with the new simplified and accelerated methods that Canadian research had discovered.

Though Canada had profited by the influx of Asian citizens to so great an extent that a new Confederation was symbolically entered into in 1995, her older population is still highly esteemed. The revival of indigenous Indian culture began about the time of New Confederation under the sympathetic stimulus of Chinese and Japanese Canadians, but French and English culture has been even more challenged and stimulated by the new environment. For a time, French-speaking Chinese in northern Quebec seized the leadership of television production, but Francophones of European descent more recently have re-established Montreal as the film and television centre of the country.

Jewish Canadians adapted perhaps more quickly than anyone else to the new possibilities, and the Chinese, Japanese and Sanskrit editions of the Talmud now have an even wider circulation than the original. Canadian public law is largely based on computerized responses of rabbis to problems of justice raised in interpersonal and intercommunity relations. And the WASP minority has discovered a remarkable capacity for solving administrative problems. Lacking the creative powers of political leadership manifested by Chinese Canadians, the WASPS still prove indispensable in the middle echelons, and their Protestant Christian heritage makes them the most zealous for the social rights of minorities and of the less privileged members of society with an IQ of under 110.

A New Renaissance?   GREGORY BAUM

To explain the extraordinary cultural development of Canadian life in the year 2020, I must say a few words about the renaissance that began in North America, especially in Canada, about 2000.

This renaissance had its roots in the twentieth century, possibly even in the nineteenth. It was based on the emergence of a new self-understanding of man. Man had come to experience himself as a historical being who constitutes himself through conversation with the community and interaction with his environment. Man as person and as community was thus responsible for his own future. Yet, since he did not know beforehand what this future would be, all he could do was to involve himself in the process of conversation with others, to discover who he could be or could become anew.

What counted was the *process* of participation. Process was the renaissance principle of stability and, as the new axis of human life, it had a profound effect on all aspects of society and culture, including the natural and social sciences. After the Canadian universities had been blown up in the nineties, new centres of learning and research were constructed, based upon renaissance principles. Following from the assumption that no one was in possession of answers, dialogue and participation generated the questions that were to be raised and pointed to the direction in which the answers could be found. This process was made possible through the use of computers.

By the turn of the century Canada's southern neighbour, the United States, had passed through a series of dictatorships and it became clear that the vast problems of society could not be solved without the participation of all the people. Life had become so complex that dictatorships were quite incapable of dealing with the operational problems; with a single man or even a single party in charge, nation-wide institutions went haywire. The only system that could deal with modern society was one that promoted the creativity of all citizens and relied on their cooperation and good ideas. By the year 2000 the liberal wing of the American black population was able to apply these renaissance principles to social conflict and, subsequently, to translate them into political realities.

In Canada the renaissance had reached a take-off point by the year 2000. The reason for this remarkable achievement was the creative confrontation that arose between English-speaking and French-speaking Canadians. Although in the 1970s and 1980s Canada's dissolution seemed frighteningly imminent, the dictatorships and the social violence in the United States inspired Canadians with the determination to preserve the unity of their country. Conversation between the English and French, which had broken down many times, was facilitated by computers, creating a new consciousness in people and overcoming the problems that had seemed insuperable before. This cybernetic victory ushered the entire country into the renaissance.

Canadians created art and music as instruments of communication that transcended the limitations of language. (The older people claimed that this approach had begun at the international exhibition held in Montreal in 1967.) Through art and music, people were able to deepen and refine the conversational process that enabled them to achieve a new understanding of their problems. This renaissance art brought Canadians into close contact with their Chinese and Russian neighbours. In Europe Canadian art was regarded as dangerous, for the European nations had not yet acknowledged the computer as a cultural instrument.

Religion had become important in the Canadian renaissance at the turn of the century. It is true, of course, that few people paid attention to the ecclesiastical leaders. (Because of their quaint ways, however, the government protected religious institutions like bird sanctuaries.) But in churches and other halls, people celebrated the process by which they came to be, lived, and created their culture. They believed that the process of man's making of man was mysterious, that more took place in conversation and participation than mere words and actions, that new life was being created in this process and new energy poured into the human system. The process is a creative mystery, the young ones said. The older ones spoke of God. Christians held that Jesus Christ had revealed the process. He had been killed because he had broken through the static view of life to which his society had been attached, but in the power of the Spirit he had initiated his followers into fellowship, conversation and participation, and given them sacraments by which to celebrate the process. But whether old or young, of whatever faith, people celebrated the process in liturgical rites. These liturgies produced great joy, and they enabled the people to understand and assimilate the process in which they were daily involved.

Now, in 2020, the Canadian renaissance has reached a high point. The process, operative in millions of ways and in all directions, has produced a subtle music that forms the background of Canadian life as much as the blue sky and the earth on which men walk. But a new danger has emerged. The sin of man, as theologians like to say, has manifested itself in a new way.

The new threat has come from religion. The celebration of the process is so joyful and so all-absorbing that people have tended to fall into ecstasy, not only in church or in the special halls devised for the liturgy but throughout the day, when they are at work or driving their miniplanes. The music of the process, faintly audible all the time, has invaded them with power and made them lose critical consciousness. Accidents have increased and efficiency has declined. The computers try to repair some of the damage caused by the frequent ecstasies but, because the coming of the ecstasies is unpredictable, they are a threat to the foundations of Canadian society.

At first the government and the renaissance establishment thought that the answer to this problem was drugs. Specially prepared cigarettes were made available that would prevent people from falling into ecstasy. Stronger drugs were prescribed for men in responsible positions who habitually fell into ecstasies. The government blamed religion for the problem. It was, after all, religion that had first taught people how to celebrate the process of man's self-making and to enter into a more intense consciousness.

Yet the more prophetic men of 2020 have deeper insight into the reasons why people fall into ecstasies and thus endanger the continuance of the renaissance culture. They feel

that the renaissance culture has neglected the bodily dimension of man. The body, they say, is a more sensitive instrument of communication than previous cultures anticipated.
There are many senses, not just five, by which the body is
in touch with reality, even if man has hardly developed these
senses and has had little knowledge of their mediating powers.
These prophets think that even sexuality has aptitudes for the
creating of community and the building of culture that are still
hidden. Precisely because man is not yet fully reconciled with
his body and hence not sufficiently at home in it, the celebration of the humanizing process has easily driven people
into ecstasy. These prophetic voices of 2020 advocate a thera-
peutically oriented society in which people will learn how to
repossess their bodies and sensitize them to become more adequate organs of reality.

At this time it is not clear whether these men will succeed
in convincing Canadians of the need for a more therapeutic
approach to life. The computers, in particular, are quite impatient with the new ideas. There is some hope, however, that
the gaining of new senses will enable Canadians to repro-
gram the computers so that they, too, will become more sensitive to reality. Governments and persons in authority are
cautious in regard to the therapeutic expansion of the body.
The hierarchy of the church seriously considers decreeing that
there are only five senses in man. And yet, the growing
waves of unpredictable ecstasies will probably convince even
the sceptics that people will have to be anchored more firmly
in reality through their bodies if the Canadian renaissance is
not to be destroyed.

2020 Visions of an Electric Mutant German Historian Guitar Player Berkeley Expatriate Prophet

HERMANN REBEL

by the year twentytwenty . . .

canadian civilization will have Life
for its prime symbol
with père de Chardin's omega point
its sacred image:
the established sacredness of all life

a people worshipping the universe inside
the human form, instinctively
knowing and obeying the sixth command

the triumph of cybernated ecology over
entropy
will be the triumph of life
over death of Christ over Satan

a Canada of woods and meadows and gardens
with automated productive machinery
and the movement of industrial and agricultural
produce underground: all circuitry hidden
under natural and synthetic textures
of the richest variety

the end of the great commodity
fetishism and consumption spectacle
will have ended
the appropriation of lives

the appropriation of commodities
will have begun the expansion
of individual rights:
free food free clothing free transport free housing

a Canada free from political and secret police:
freedom from "lawn order"

extended tribal families
as basic social units will administer
their own laws: face to face relationships
and group judgments

no physical punishments
no "punishments"

a federal government: local and regional
councils modelled on the forms
of 1918 Germany and 1956 Hungary

major political decisions
to be made by two-way
teevee recreating the Greek
polis in the mass state

a strict separation
of political from administrative
problems continuously revised
as the nature and quality of human life
change

a foreign policy working
towards the elimination of the nation
state as protector/monopolizer
of human rights and conflict resolution

a foreign trade policy aiming
at the elimination of trade barriers:
hunger not profit
as the basis for trade patterns

unhindered world-wide
movement of all persons:
conscious merging with the noosphere
to end all war and all production
for war

Canada without whips
gallows and prisons

murderers rapists and child molesters
are sent to anarchistic farms
in inaccessible regions
to which sadists — read: professional soldiers,
elite police, Nazi types,
executioners, underground
movie producers — and
masochists — read: professional soldiers,
elite police, Nazi types,
executioners, underground
movie producers — can go
for as long as they need

free musical instruments free
travel free theatre
free concerts free
books free lectures operas
films cameras teevee records tapes video
tapes as a liberated education
communication technology: free access
to the computers' universal knowledge
watering troughs

education as the offering
of possibilities and alternatives
pursued as the conscious growth
of souls

better living through chemistry:
family/state controlled use
of psychedelics will be
the death of addiction
and everyone will know
                              that
tobacco speed heroin exhaust fumes opium
mothers' little helpers
have been
the killer weeds

complete freedom of expression
in the decoration
of the body in artistic
aesthetic production and consumption

history will cease to be
the justification of the present
but will teach the sacred
frailty of all human achievements
on the wheel of life
to conquer prejudice
ideology hatred pride

the liberation of the Canadian
architect from the business
profit mind (à bas Bauhaus)
and his return
to the physicist poet philosopher
(vive Bucky Fuller)

controlled exploitation
of natural resources
and purified
earth water and air: conscious creation
of an environment where all forms of life
can flourish to confront
the human mind
with variety and mystery

extinct will be the paranoid
inhibited organization man
backwoods Canadian: the birth of funky
free spirits knowing the possibilities
and courageous enough
to change and grow into the void

the purpose of life will be found
in sustained joyous ecstasy and love

written without much
hope at the midnight of the world
with Herman Kahn's ridiculous dream
of a Los Angelized world burgeoning
around me
in the mean time
who do you love?
peace

Software and the Imploding Spastic Inevitable (home hints for 2020)

JOHN MCCUAIG

"Today is the first day of the rest
of your life."

— Abbie Hoffman,
Revolution for the Hell of It

who says we have a
future?
(questions for
beginners)

1. Whee, 2020! Or at least, 1970. I'm writing this on a soggy evening in July 1969 (day before Moonday, in fact). Why are you reading about what's going to happen fifty years from now, sixteen months later?

2. This magazine figures that because it made it through fifty years, it's good for another fifty. Think what that means to lifers, especially the married ones.

3. In fifty years, if you are thirty, you will be eighty. If you are forty, you will be ninety. If you are fifty, you will be *one hundred years old*. Canada is having trouble at that age. (If you are a kid, will they still love you, when you're sixty-four?) WHAT THE HELL DO YOU CARE ABOUT THE FUTURE ANYWAY?

a.m.a.—tory narcosis
& germ warfare

Of course, you might say, "I'm gonna get me somma ol' Somerset Maugham's monkey glands," or "I'll have 'em bisex me up like Starmaker in *Cocksure*," with spare-parts surgery. Dream on! Stress theory of disease makes even antibiotics and DDT an opportunity for germs to regroup and counterattack. The S i c k Society! So . . . .

is "in the year 2525" right now?

As the song says, "in the twinkling of starlight . . . maybe it's only yesterday." Servomat environments remodel man's body into industrial processes. "Everything that you do or say/Will be in the pill that you took today." Gulp! But the real inner trip is Mother Earth's. Enough of this primping for the firemen — jump! And hope that "nature" is there to support us in the style to which we've become accustomed.

hoi-polloition & the population implosion

By 2020 we should have all taken John Lennon's advice, and gone undersea. The Age of Aquarius will see Atlantis rise again, beneath the waves. U.S. experiments have already proved man can breathe salt water. So, subways crowded? Your city smog filled? Rush hour a panic? Home a madhouse? Don't put that long green in a house in the suburbs. First, globed cities topside; then, back to our saline beginnings.

Trouble is, Working Man is obsolete. Nowhere Man is likely to suffer severely from the Bore War — does fifteen percent sound fair as a survival figure? (That's right, like them no-good, shiftless South Sea Islanders!) Sorry, Mayor Daley, you were protectin' the wrong cattlepens. Pickled pigs' hocks has always been a tempting entrée.

the rational society & its bad debts

"Invest in taxes, they're sure to go up." By 1984, Big Brother and the Holding Corporation will issue life

ration cards instead of cash. Give-
aways, guaranteed annual wages (sin!)
and conglomerates we already have.
But they're getting ready to give us the
business in an altogether new way.
Presidents' portraits belong in the big
new definitive biographies. If you want
to keep America green, spend money
like hell as long as you have any to
burn. And if you're worried about getting stuck with the well - known
barrel . . . .

unisex and the
2nd skin:
prelude to a
lot of "hair"

Don't bother trying to cover up.
Clothes, cars and excuses are all obsolete. Human beings will soon exist sans
ties, sans teeth, sans anything. As for
sex, remember Adam at the apron
stage! You'll be able to tell an unmarried girl anything, but don't give
her Arpège until you want to be stuck
with her for life. Hair, scents and
adolescents will be the rage. (No more
sublimating those Little League batting
scores.) Marriage at fourteen; no in-
compatibility divorces — Space Age
authorities can always mess up your
mind. There'll be group marriages, but
who wants a mother-in-law in your big,
happy family? S t a y monogamous
and . . . .

riots, wars &
acts of god

Leave the revolutions (earth-type)
to us. "Death is the only radical," said
Maxwell Anderson. "protest: an ama-
teur demonstration designed to test the
pros." (B.C.) But unnecessary. Just
Societies will fall apart of their own
accord faster than all the president's
men can put them together again. SDS,
the New Left and Modern Times will
be blamed, along with atomic fall-out

and Little Men from Mars. As Marshall McLuhan says, those who sit in are only sitting it out — aren't we all? Why not take J. D. Salinger's advice, and fight the Eskimos next? Or risk dying nobly in the War on Poverty (also a lost cause)?

But don't let Billy Graham snow you. The six-year cycle of Uranus should leave plenty for idol hands to do — witness astrology's present popularity. We are about to investigate the paradox of the sixties, the "Death of God," and find these are fighting words.

the end of life on earth (1969)

I sit here in my underwear, watching two men leave earth's environment for the first time, to set foot on the moon. Our beautiful green picnic-style planet has been out of date for some time (since machines), but from now on, it'll definitely be goodbye to all that. (The title of Bucky Fuller's book: *Operating Manual for Spaceship Earth.*) A South Sea Islander never took a vacation in his life; he *lives* here. So do we. "What on earth will we do with the moon?" It'll be a prehistory lab for our own planet, a flying social-security card. We'll use it to flashback our own beginnings, and as a scale model in the global improvement plan. But the reason you're probably disagreeing with all this, is . . . .

today's title

The past is what made you what you are; the present is what you think of it; the future is what you do about it. Naturally, most people prefer to live in the past, a fact which explains why they don't have much of a future. Con-

versely, the future acts as a mind ex-
pander for the past: the better your
future, the bigger your past. Picasso
and the paleolithic; astronauts and infancy; the moon and all mankind. By
1970, man should have skipped to
2001's space-baby awareness of his
own role in the universe. How about
it? The odds are pretty long that you're
just laughing this whole article off, just
as they all laughed at Columbus, long
after 1492. Or did they? Depends on
your reservations! And on your
chances of making that last fifteen percent. Keep breathing, buddy. Don't
let me make a fish out of you.

PART VI. HOPES:
man liberated

LEONARD SHIFRIN
179 **The Withering Away of Welfare**

LLOYD DENNIS
183 **Learning in the Age of Wonder**

MAX CLARKSON
189 **The Victory of the NIMs over the GEBs**

CLAUDE BISSELL
193 **The Role of the University President**

JOHN M. ROBSON
196 **MIRV**

JOHN O'NEILL
200 **Sociology as a Skin Trade**

overleaf "Fence Jump" *by Harold Town*

Letter to Kyra (cont'd.)

It isn't just the theologians and the poets who dare to conceive a transformed Canada. That broad group of people actually involved in the process of social and political change are trying to move towards their own utopias.

Leonard Shifrin, a new-generation administrator in Ottawa's welfare structure, puts the Condorcet dream of a perfectible society into 1970 idiom. For his utopia, our value system must change. Once justification by work alone has been supplanted by self-fulfilment as the object of life, then the punitive benevolence of the welfare system can be replaced by a continuum of services assisting the individual. In this view, education is but one of a total complex of social services. Lloyd Dennis, a high school principal, is a missionary of educational reform. In his vision Neil Alexander Ellis doesn't go to school; he enters a life-long process to realize his potential for personal creativity. Your uncle Max's mock history lecture shares the same hopes but, as a businessman living in the United States, he has no illusions about achieving the educational utopia by natural evolution. It is only by a hard struggle that the New Image of Man movement can humanize the university by overcoming the alliance of government, education and business. Claude Bissell, as president of the University of Toronto, is himself personally under a withering crossfire from the GEBs (to increase production) and from the NIMs (to increase social relevance and internal democracy). In his satire of the campus forces of progress Jack Robson, a professor who has been intensely involved in revising the university curriculum, clearly shares Bissell's preference for the university as a special community, not a political democracy. Part of the current university reform movement is attacking the overspecialized social sciences for having betrayed their basic human concerns. With the call for sociology's return to its vocation as a "skin trade" coming from a radical academic like John O'Neill, already chairman of his sociology department, I am optimistic that the hopes for educational liberation expressed in this section will in fact be self-fulfilling predictions.

The Withering Away of Welfare

LEONARD SHIFRIN

Welfare, in the world of 2020 A.D., no longer exists as such. The concept of individual well-being in a cybernated society has long since supplanted both the punitive-benevolent idea of welfare and the work ethic which bore it and accounted for its ambivalence.

The work ethic glorified winners. But to have occupational winners there had to be occupational losers. To those who lost, for whom we felt a mixture of guilt and compassion, we offered an ameliorative called welfare. It didn't compare with the benefits of winning, of course, but then it was intended not to. If it had, it might have endangered the motivation to win demanded by the work ethic.

All of this went by the board with the arrival of cybernation and the end of the era in which occupational opportunities could be made roughly to approximate the work-force potential. Events moved very quickly and there was a certain amount of unrest and conflict as we struggled to adjust our system to the cliché-defying realities. But that is now many years in the past. The guaranteed income is working well, with levels such that all are able to participate fully in the life of the community and none are stigmatized as unproductive and unworthy.

The sudden collapse of the primary social value unleashed an attitudinal revolution, but we adjusted surprisingly well to the idea that life is for living and that our energies should be directed to making our social environment totally livable for all. It took a decade fully to undo the incredible damage we had done in polluting our environment, but now those days of foul air, dirty water and garbage dumps where green spaces had been are hard even to recall.

When economically productive labour was replaced as the primary value by the pursuit of individual self-fulfilment, a new value structure developed which, in the days of the work ethic, would probably have been regarded as hedonistic. The younger generation adjusted easily to the idea that the maximum development of their capacities as human beings was their primary object in life, but those who were older suffered considerably from guilt and from self-concepts of inadequacy and failure as a result of their earlier training.

At first, it was feared that the few managers and technicians required to maintain economic activity would become an élite, but the changed values prevented that. Rather than attaining status as the only productive members of society, they are regarded simply as the group for whom economic activity provides the best avenue for personal fulfilment. This reflects their particular talents and no higher value is placed on having this sort of talent than on having others which lead down different paths.

Because economic factors no longer dominate, economic decisions no longer shape the social order. The basic decisions involve the definition of the goals of society, and everyone participates equally in these through processes which, at the neighbourhood level, reflect the Athenian origins of democracy.

With opportunities for participation in the work life of the community greatly reduced, participation in other facets of community life has blossomed. As the cities grew to megalopoli, communities developed within them and decentralization of services to these highly participatory community units followed. The nature of the services changed as they became reflective of the particular needs of particular communities.

The speed with which traditional services either disappeared or were altered radically indicates how great the gap between categorically defined services and real community needs had become in many areas. The new forms of service are generally cooperative in nature, with the professional-client relationship being replaced by one of coparticipantcy. The community co-op formula has become the primary form in the service field.

Some of the traditional services declined in importance as by-products of scientific advances. Rehabilitation services for the disabled, for example, were no longer required once the transplanting of artificial organs and limbs had eliminated physical disability. In the case of services for abandoned or abused children, need for these declined gradually through a combination of scientific and social advances. While science had perfected the means of family planning, there was a time lag before complete social acceptance brought an end to

the phenomenon of unwanted children and consequently reduced the demands on facilities and services for such children.
The need for adolescent services also fell sharply as the
primary causes of juvenile deviance — material deficiencies
and value contradictions — were no longer present in society.
The lowering of the age at which the educational process began also made an important contribution in this regard, ena-
bling children to develop the ability to relate to one another
from an early enough age to ensure success. Children now
start school at some time between their second and third birth-
days, the exact time being determined by the rate of development of the individual child.

Freed of its role of training for work, education has under
gone a total transformation. It has ceased to be oriented almost exclusively towards those in their pre-employment
years and has become, like recreation and the arts, a part of
life rather than a preparation for the economic aspect of it.
In fact, education, recreation and the arts have become very
much intertwined. The emphasis in life is on personally creative
activities; education has sought to develop and expand creative
capacities, while a great diversification of recreational and artistic opportunities has sought to give scope for utilization
of these capacities. It is really very difficult today to identify
where one ends and the other begins.

The racial composition of Canada has changed considerably
since 1970. The large influx of black and Asiatic immigration
and the renaissance of the Canadian Indian — which coin-
cided with the reduction in Indian child-mortality levels to that
of the general population — added important new dimensions to Canadian cultural diversity. Race and ethnicity played
a significant role in the initial development of community
at the neighbourhood level, but rapidly diminished as a factor
in community definition as a result of the inevitable cultural
cross-pollination among groups.

Alongside the development of new forms of urban communities within urban conglomerates occurred the development of new forms of rural communities. But, just as the new
community units really constitute a rediscovery of the original
form of urban community, so too the new rural communes
represent a return to ancient forms of collective living.

The world of 2020 is not, of course, a wholly problem-free utopia. There are still those whose inability to accept its values and temper has alienated them from it. One group in particular has found it very difficult to come to terms with contemporary life and exhibits strong feelings of aggressiveness and hostility which seem very much out of place in an otherwise nonviolent society. These are the aged, those over seventy who were part of the generation born immediately after World War II.

Many of the members of this generation readily embraced the value structure based on individual freedom within a framework of equality, justice and brotherhood — some even contended that these were the very things they had been advocating during the generational conflicts of the late 1960s and early 1970s. But others of that generation, who had taken a traditionalist stance during those conflicts, still cling rigidly to the concepts which prevailed in those primitive times. Unhappy products of another era, they are viewed with sympathy that, captives of their own inhibitions, repressions, guilts and frustrations, they have lived so long while living so little.

Learning in the Age of Wonder

LLOYD DENNIS

Neil Alexander Ellis, one of thirty-five million Canadians sharing the dawn of a new century, has just negotiated a contract that describes his professional responsibility as environmental engineer. But Neil Alexander Ellis is more than that. Now in his early twenties, he was born when the moon and Mars had already been conquered by man. The Dawn of the Space Age, some called it. The Age of the Astronaut, the Golden Age of Space Travel, the age when man's sophisti cated science launched him paradoxically beyond his earthly cocoon and into an era of renewed contemplation — the Age of Wonder.

Neil barely escaped the Age of the Institution, that twentieth century period when his forebears herded together — or allowed themselves to be herded — under the banners of expediency, efficiency, custom and conformity. It was the time of Organization Man, when goods were processed and people programmed; the golden harvest of the affluent state was offered to those who could reap it, and Canada proudly won the title, "Land of Opportunity."

And this was the path of progress that led man to the moon and Mars. Oddly enough, the path also led to an awakening of the spirit that shook the foundations of established institutions. Not the least of these was that venerable institution known as public education

We stand today in the dawn of our second century and assess the field of future education. Surrounded by the greatest array of learning paraphernalia we have ever seen, and immersed in new knowledge, we must not lose sight of the human needs that the new dawn brings. We are at once

---

* Adapted for this collection from a paper delivered at the Ontario Liberal Caucus Policy Conference at Guelph University, August 22-24, 1969, reprinted in *The Guelph Papers*, ed. Robert F. Nixon (Toronto: Peter Martin Associates, 1970), pp. 8-14. Quotations are taken from the document *Living and Learning*.

the heirs of the past and the stewards of the future, and while we take pride in our inheritance, we can ill afford to bury our talents in the souls of satisfaction. We have in our hands means of change for human betterment that few people of the world enjoy. We must find a way to their application that will germinate the seeds of a more fruitful way of life for all Canadians; and hopefully the harvest will make its contribution to all mankind.

In such a climate were the seeds of change in Canadian education planted in the latter half of the twentieth century. In such a climate men found the determination and the desire to commit their efforts, not to the maintenance of an educational system to serve as the utilitarian handmaiden of the culture, but to the development of an atmosphere of learning that would nurture the sensitivity, the dignity, the awe, the commitment and the uniqueness that are the rights of all men. Such men abandoned their traditional preoccupation with the past that had so long been their defence; the present they viewed with caution lest it lock them in. They looked instead to the future — the future of Neil Alexander Ellis; and they laid the way, not for themselves, but for him.

Like the men who make the initial landing on the moon, our children must be thoroughly prepared for a destination whose features no one knows at first hand. But this is not the first time that man has found himself in this position. The world presented as significant a challenge for the age of Columbus as it does for us half a millennium later. The achievements of the past are there to orient our youth; the vision, the speculation and the prediction for the future are there to challenge and excite their minds; it becomes a function of the school to provide that orientation and foster that excitement.

The public education of Neil Alexander Ellis really began four months before he was born. It was at this point that his mother, encouraged to realize her responsibility as a parent, used the facilities of the local school in order to study parent education. She was accepted and encouraged as a permanent member of the team destined to educate her youngster.

The school was more than a school. Gone were its time-honoured isolation as an academic cloister and its exclusive position as a factory for the manufacture of obedient adults. It stood as the cultural nerve centre of the community, and invited young and old to tap its resources and enjoy its excitement. As a community facility, it accurately reflected the needs, aspirations and interests of the people whom it served. It was proof of the new awareness that democratic strength lies in diversity, not in uniformity, and it found its function at the local level rather than in remote authority. Nevertheless, since it was a place of learning, it was not only a local enterprise but an investment in the future of the nation. Thus it was protected from local economic disparity by provincial and national funding with additional local option. Its trusteeship was regional, and an integral part of the regional government body; hence it was seen no longer as the annual cesspool for misspent money, but as a focal point of common public interest.

The same principle applied at the provincial level, where education was considered an integral part of all branches of government related to cultural welfare. In this way education not only found its rightful place among its related fields of health, welfare and rehabilitation; it also enjoyed the close coordination of those agencies so vital to its function. As a protection against bureaucratic and political complexity and insensitivity, an autonomous, nonpolitical council representative of professional and lay interests served in an advisory capacity at the provincial level, reporting regularly to the public and responsible to the legislature. At the school level, a school committee comprised of faculty and community members served as a reflection of local interest and commitment.

Public education for Neil was free of tuition costs throughout the spectrum formerly known as elementary, secondary and tertiary levels. It provided a continuous learning experience from the moment of initial entry until his entry into the tertiary level, individualized to the greatest possible degree in keeping with his aptitudes, interests and abilities.

Gone were the traditional trademarks of schooling that had so little to do with learning; grade placement, report card marks, formal examinations, annual promotion, failure, segregation, punishment, memorization of inert fact, regimentation, solemn purpose and fear. In their place was found an atmosphere of humane understanding, warm, embracing, provocative, exciting, challenging and completely committed to the nourishment of the spirit as well as the mind, to the fulfilment of life as well as of learning.

Gone, too, from the early levels of Neil's learning experience was the ancient parade of disciplines that had been the traditional hoops through which children were made to jump. Realizing the need for synthesis in the development of attitudes and abilities, great care was taken to provide opportunities for the discovery of relevance in ideas and in things. To be sure, as the student proceeded towards maturity, his areas of study became more specific and specialized. But even then, the "wholistic" nature of life was not abandoned. Neil's desire to become an engineer was satisfied, but more important, so was his inclination to become a man.

It was not that the school had abandoned its academic role. Indeed, it was intensified — for those inclined. But the disciplines of the ages had taken on a new identity, alive, real and tantalizing to the student. Algebraic equations now beckoned Neil, not into the dead dust of the past, but into new possibilities for the future. Many new fields of study had appeared, some of them not even remotely related to the world of work. It was at last permissible to follow an interest that led nowhere except to maturity. Learning for its own sake had finally donned the cloak of respectability.

The needs of the child are simply stated. Each and every one has the right to learn, to play, to laugh, to dream, to love, to dissent, to reach upward and to be himself. Our children need to be made to feel that the world is waiting for their sunrise, and that their education heralds the rebirth of an "Age of Wonder." Then, surely, the children of tomorrow will be more flexible, more adventurous, more daring and courageous than we are, and better equipped to search for truth, each in his own way. Each will have learned, with Don Quixote, in *Man of La Mancha:*

To dream the impossible dream,
To fight the unbeatable foe,
To bend with unbearable sorrow,
To run where the brave dare not go.
To right the unrightable wrong,
To love, pure and chaste from afar,
To try when one's arms are too weary,
To reach the unreachable star.

Neil entered school in the year 2000, at the age of three, on a part-time basis. His entry was based entirely upon his apparent needs and abilities as mutually accepted and determined by school and home. He entered his advanced level of education (university) thirteen years later. In the interim he experienced an educational program which had the following salient characteristics beyond those already noted:

— a school year based upon a trisemester calendar, established by regional option.
— eye and dental care as an integral part of the educational service.
— a clinical approach to the identification and satisfaction of emotional, psychological and physical needs of each individual.
— a curricular program designed locally to meet the needs and interests of the school community.
— an atmosphere for learning that was more aesthetic than utilitarian, more general than specific.
— a flexibility of program that provided for maximum attention to the changing interests and abilities of the learners.
— maximum mobility to permit the realistic study of the environment.
— an emphasis upon learning experiences provided through discovery and research.

Of course, these conditions which Neil experienced were not created by legislation in 2000. Most, if not all of them, had been pleaded for long before his time. Indeed, not a few of them had already found their way into schools and systems of schools. But old ideas die hard, and complacency was always their protector. Only when the people were struck with the awesome awareness of the huge price to be paid for means without ends did they see the need for revitalizing the process of living and of learning. Only then did they appreciate where the journey to Mars had brought them: to the stark realization that beyond the reach of man lies the beauty of the rose; that the search for truth and meaning was far from over. It had just begun. And so they dedicated their resources to the end that Neil Alexander Ellis, and others like him, would carry the search beyond the confines of the past and present into a future that knows no bounds.

The Victory of the NIMs over the GEBs

MAX CLARKSON

As your professor of self-discovery, I want to devote this seminar series to study and discussion of that profound change in human feeling and thought which occurred in the last part of the twentieth century, now referred to as the Victory of the NIMs over the GEBs.

Before outlining some of the major causes of the rise and fall of the GEBs, I want to make sure that all of you understand the *modus operandi* of our present attempts to provide an educational response appropriate to our credo, "Let Each Become All that He Is Capable of Being." As we will discuss later, it is only in recent years that the teaching profession has seriously considered that it might be possible to make meaningful this magnificent motto. Since the collapse of the old university system, following the Great Student Revolt of 1990-1999, there was a period of substantial readjustment out of which has evolved our present system of colleges and schools of technology. The major function of the colleges is to work on solutions to these most difficult of all social and educational questions:

1. How much uniformity does our society need for safety?
2. How much deviation do we require — as individuals, for self-development, and as society, for progress?

The colleges naturally emphasize the spirit of community, at the same time working with each individual to develop the whole man. The schools of technology provide technical training and professional education, with facilities for experimentation and advanced study in their particular areas of specialization. You are not required to attend any school. However, you cannot take any course in any school of technology until you have completed your first-year seminars in the Collegiate Curriculum of Self-Discovery: Physiology, Security, Love, Self-Esteem and Self-Realization. As you know, no one fails in this curriculum. You are free to leave at any time, free to resume attendance at any age, that is, from ages fourteen to seventy-five. But since we have come to understand the dangers to the human race that result from unrestricted indulgence in technical knowledge for its own sake, we are no longer willing, as a society, to expose people to the schools of technology until they have achieved a reasonable understanding of themselves and of the psychological make-up and social needs of the human race. Rules of learning change, we have discovered, when professional or technical education is needed, but this kind of learning cannot be assimilated successfully until the individual process of self-discovery has begun. Anything which affects the potential of the individual human being is now understood to be, by definition, educational.

It was the lack of this reasonable understanding of education, of themselves and of the rest of humanity, that led to the downfall of the GEBs.

Acronyms have become so much a part of our way of language that I want to be sure you all remember that the grand alliance of government, education and business resulted in the label "GEB" being applied to that whole movement, which resulted from the cumulative deterioration of Western society following the abandonment of the Vietnam War in 1976. By that time, large-scale disaffection was evident in the old, so-called sovereign states of the West. Fifty major multinational corporations (MUNCs) controlled over fifty percent of the corporate assets of Western society, and were providing a substantial part of the funds required for the operation of the universities specializing in the production of technocrats for use in government and business. Governments in these now-defunct sovereign states were more than matching the payments of business, so that between the two groups they could exercise effective control of educational policy if they were to join forces in a common cause. This is precisely what happened.

After three years of extensive secret negotiations, the Orwell Treaty was signed in 1984 by the chief executives of the MUNCs and of the states comprising the Western world. In return for a doubling of the corporate contributions to higher education, the heads of state agreed, among other things, to require that a majority of each university's board of trustees be elected from names submitted by the MUNCs. In effect, the corporations said, if we are the major shareholders of the universities by virtue of our contributions and employment policies, we want majority representation on their boards, so that we will be provided with recruits educated in the most productive fashion possible. "Better Technology for a Better Tomorrow" was the motto agreed upon for adoption by all universities in all countries. As a prerequisite of tenure and admission, both teachers and taught were required to pledge allegiance to the supremacy of technology. Membership in the NIMs or espousal of their beliefs was cause for dismissal and revocation of all degrees or credits. A central computerized data bank system was set up in Geneva to provide instant access to the names of all NIMs, who could no longer expect employment by any of the MUNCs, their suppliers or the governments.

The NIMs, as you will remember, had their origins about a hundred years ago. The New Image of Man (NIM) had its philosophical roots in the dissatisfaction felt by many intellectuals (if I may use so old-fashioned a term) with the image of man that had developed during the First Industrial Revolution. It was felt that this image was fundamentally negative and antihumanistic, emphasizing that man was lazy, shiftless, lacking in initiative, and could be made productive only by means of exterior controls and close supervision. Studies made by many psychologists, psychoanalysts, educators and behaviourists began to indicate what we now know to be true: that man has certain basic needs for which he is motivated to seek satisfaction, and the function of the organization, whether it is governmental, educational or corporate, is to assist each individual along the way towards the reasonable satisfaction of all these basic needs — of physiology and security, of love and belonging, of self-esteem and of self-realization.

Following the end of the Vietnam War, the New Image of Man Society (NIMS) was formed in 1976 to celebrate the two hundredth anniversary of American Independence and with the avowed objective of making self-realization accessible to and attainable by the entire population of each country. Self-realization had been recognized and identified for what it is, but its attainment had been restricted to those in the higher levels of economic, cultural or academic life.

Self-realization was generally perceived as being something to which only certain élites could aspire, by reasons of inherited status, of position achieved as a result of superior intelligence or of other outstanding attributes, physical, moral or artistic. But it was conveniently assumed that the large mass of the poor (or nonrich in certain countries) or of the culturally deprived (blacks in a white country, French in an English country, whites in a yellow country) could not, and indeed should not, be exposed to the satisfaction of needs other than those connected with physiology and security. These people were to be fed and housed adequately, with appropriate medical and educational facilities tailored to their needs — needs, however, as perceived by others. But it was thought to be dangerous and unpatriotic to encourage them to believe that they were capable of becoming anything more as individuals than drivers, porters, labourers — servants, in fact, of those who were already embarked on the never-ending journey towards self-realization.

We do not believe that we have found any final answers about individuals or society. However, we do believe that we are on the right track in insisting that the teacher's role is that of a gardener rather than a modeller of clay. We don't try to make a wallflower become a rose; we simply try to help roses and wallflowers each to become a good rose or a good wallflower.

Tomorrow we will cover the revocation of the Orwell Treaty and the collapse of the GEBs, which will lay the groundwork for serious discussion of the meaning and implication of the motto "Let Each Become All that He Is Capable of Being," which replaced "Better Technology for a Better Tomorrow" in 2020. Questions? Comments?

The Role of the University President

CLAUDE BISSELL

The university presidency of 2020 will be shaped by the academic revolution that is now underway.

The problem of the university presidency is, then, the problem of the modern university. In the new political atmosphere the university is struggling to achieve a sense of community that is strong and pervasive, a concept of order that encourages freedom and prevents tyranny. In short, the university is trying to work out a theory of the nature of its society and of the appropriate government for that society. During this period of self-analysis, the president, who belongs to another era, can have only a tenuous hold on authority.

If one assumes the passing of the *status quo*, there are two possible theories of society and government for the university. The first envisages the university as an open society that has, however, a particular purpose not recognized elsewhere. The second envisages a political democracy concerned with general welfare, differing from the political state only in the emphasis it gives to emotional and intellectual values. Both theories call for a society where all are kept constantly informed not only of the decisions that are made, but of the factors that have gone into the making of those decisions. Beyond their adherence to openness, however, the two theories diverge sharply. The first conceives of the university as a special community concerned with the preservation, diffusion and expansion of knowledge. The second accepts no such specific goal. It sees the university as an ideal political state whose goal is emotional and intellectual community. There is another distinction which is even more fundamental. The first theory recognizes degrees of commitment in members of the university by reason of experience, professional obligation and personal decision. This means that the full-time teaching staff must play a determining role. They will need laymen to subject their proposals to nonprofessional criticism; to work with them and with students in preventing interference from outside bodies; to give direction and leadership in the raising of private financial support. They will need students to keep them sensitive to innovation and impatient of delay. The second theory accepts students and staff equally as full citizens of the political community. The logical outcome is "one man, one vote." If the consequences of this in a large, nonselective university are too distressing even for its proponents, the answer is parity, an equal number of students and staff on all committees — a doctrine of institutionalized confrontation.

Both these theories — the open society and the political democracy — necessitate profound changes in the governance of the university; both result in the setting up of a central body that is widely representative of the community and is given general responsibility for all aspects of the university. Both theories mean the politicization of the university. But, whereas the theory of the open society will result in the emergence of a strong majority group at the centre made up of staff and of students, the theory of political democracy will result in fragmentation, in a multiplicity of parties, each party an uncertain alliance of students and staff or, possibly, in groupings of students on the one side and of staff on the other.

If we accept the theory of the university as a political democracy, I think we will see in the next few years the breakup of the modern university. Professional faculties are profoundly opposed to extreme politicization, for they accept a hierarchical approach to the process of learning; they will leave an institution so organized and will establish themselves as separate entities. Many faculty in all areas who are concerned with research and scholarship will go to research institutes and to government and private business. What remains of the modern university will be essentially a community college. Such a college may be, in the words of Edward Shils, "a perfervid community in which all is dialogue and little or nothing is taught, and nothing discovered except the vacuum of the expanding and contentless self."[1] The greater likelihood is that this community college will become a teaching machine, since concepts of "dialogue" and the "undifferentiated society" are élitist, applying to only a few subjects at the most advanced levels.

Under either theory, the role of the president will change

1. "Plentitude and Scarcity," *Encounter,* May 1969, p. 56.

profoundly. He will come from the academic community, will be widely and favourably known to his colleagues and will come to his office by general consensus. He will serve for a limited period of time, and any extension of his term will depend on his success in retaining the support of a majority of the community. But, again, beyond this common characteristic there will be wide divergence. The president of the university conceived of as a political democracy will be, first and foremost, a maker of alliances, an astute reconciler, a man of easy intellect ready to respond to pressures; the ideal would be a ward heeler with a certificate in computer programming. The university as a political democracy will plunge into the wider political arena, and to the internal conflicts will be added the external conflicts of society at large. But if the university as open society prevails, then the president will be appointed by reason of his devotion to learning and scholarship, and his skill in translating his devotion into action.

It is clear which of these two theories I prefer. By 2020, I hope long before, both will find their institutional embodiments — the theory of political democracy in new institutions with no stake in scholarship and no commitment to the professional world; the theory of the open society in established institutions, with their complex obligations to international scholarship and their historic responsibility for professional education. In the university of the open society, the president will again be in a position to exercise strong leadership. The need for the old rhetoric of ambivalence and indirection will disappear. Traditional concepts of freedom will be able to co-exist with greater institutional commitment to social and political objectives. The university has always been committed to certain objectives, to freedom of speech, to nondiscrimination by reason of colour, race or religion and, increasingly, to the elimination of economic barriers and the cultivation of international understanding. Conscious of a community of support and endorsement, the president of the open university will be able, in these areas and in others, to formulate a strong and unambiguous university point of view.

MIRV

JOHN M. ROBSON

Minority interim report (voluntary) of the permanent ad hoc participatory committee of the Free University of Toronto (F.U.To.) on the expedition of consultation concerning staffing and distaffing procedures during the next demicent, with a view to implementation in, at or about the year 2020.

In view of the irresponsible negativity of the majority report, quoted in full below,[1] we, the undersigned, forming a clear minority of the committee, wish to outline some of the more hopeful prospects for academics during the next fifty years. Notwithstanding the vague parameters of our terms of reference, and the apodeictic certainty of continuing reportage necessitated by the irreversible paratendencies which follow up technological spin-offs and consequential societal innovations, we have reversed our driver's seat, turned round the rear-view mirror and look out for the oncoming following.

We have adopted the "Three-Culture" hypothesis,[2] which adequately summarizes the accelerating movement towards breakdown of the traditional uni- into the multiversity. This hypothesis enables us to discriminate: specifically, to find the least common fractures in the three main academic grooves: natural (including life) sciences, social sciences and humanities.[3]

I. The Natural Sciences

They will disappear from the universities proper, so there is no need to speculate about staffing problems. FeedBanks (Orbital) containing all scientific data known to man,[4] will make

---

1. "Get the hell out, before it's too late!"
2. The hypothesis originated in a C.P. Snow job, widely disseminated, and controverted by F. R. Leavis alone.
3. Were our parameters better marked, we would point out that the areas will undoubtedly be recategorized as Unnatural and Lifeless Sciences, Social Scientologies and Dehumanities.

supererogatory all nonelectronic instruction. During prime
hours, of course, the FBO's capacities will be fully utilized by
the Department of Extraterrestrial Defence (DED), but in
slack hours the terminals implanted in the brain cases of gen
etically selected protoscientists (PSS) will be activated, and
their interrogatory think input will automatically produce a
declarative thought output. If a PS concludes, his results will be instantaneously scanned against the FBO's files,
and thus any creativity will be corrected within the system.
When it is found that a PS has not interrogated the FBO for
a period of one semester, he will be judged a proper S, and
graduated accordingly. Since the PSS will be independently
housed, the universities can ignore them, and their societal
re-entry will be relatively frictionless; they won't be burnt
out and will, like their go-ahead present-day counterparts,
become consultants.

II. The Social Sciences

The quantifiers will be disposed of by their transference to
category I above, leaving two groups to be dealt with.
   (a) Advisers. The wasteful contemporary practice of flying social scientists around to assist in royal omissions and
peoples capitalizations will be replaced by the centralization
of advice in an Ottawa subpower station of the Wash-Mosc-
Pek net. Disorganized on the stock-exchange model, designed
by the Fuller Dome man, the National 'Change will be stocked
with ticker-videotape machines; registered stock-marketeers,
representing competing consortia of theory merchants, will be
able, after consulting the Dow-Napalm-Springs Index, to dial
prospects and interface them on the huge viewing screens.
Public bidding will ensure that theories are freely available
to all brokers.
   Like category I, then, category II (a) is without the university's future purview; we outline the prospections only to
console those social scientists envious of their natural brothers.

---

   4. Every ten years a new FBO will be launched, containing more
information than all the FBOs launched since the beginning of
time.

(b) Simulators. Here we come to the first troublesome area. In view of the increasing demand for simulated seminars, fifty years is all too short a time to prepare for the illusions of learning. As game theory develops, more and more pressure for varied imitations of real-life situations will laser in, and the fine arts are certain to be extruded into the social science preserve. To achieve a permanent willing suspension of disbelief, theatrical personnel are needed, such as (we prognose no ranking hierarchy) propmen, make-up artists and (a durable term) program directors. We suggest an immediate scouring of the commercial theatre for personnel. There is an unfounded fear that contemporary theatre's move to take off will present difficulties for thespians trying to adjust to the academic put-on; in fact, nobody under thirty can be trusted to appear on the stage nude. (For those over thirty, see category III just below.)

III. The Humanities

For the humanities to survive, their practitioners, along with those in Category II (b) above, must be housed in astrodomes[5] designed, like La Ronde, to be a microcosm of Man and his World.[6] Around Che Square, all the academic stalls will be attractive: but who will staff them? We prognose that, as adolescence is prolonged (monkey-gland spin-off) and socio-economic vectors converge on a mensurable diminution of software input (human) to zero in postelectronic atomdustry, student study-span coefficients will rise; simultaneously, the "learn-less / know-more" formula will adjust age-wise-negative the faculty teach-span coefficients. About 1996 the disequilibrium apogee will be attained, as students and staff compete for the same stations;[7] thereafter, faculty age will gradually reach its norm at student-age-minus-ten (in maladjusted year units).[8] Our heuristic prediction is, therefore, that average

---

5. Rather than "eggheads," the stall-keepers will affectionately be known as "astrodomes"; their only fringe benefit will be wigs.

6. See *The Drapeau's Letters*, by Jean Flagg Swift.

7. See the 1969 F.U.To. Report on Inefficient Room Allocation and Waste Stations.

8. D.B.S., *op. not. cit.*, calculates 9.32, omitting Western Us.

teach span will be ten years plus or minus, with promotion to student status after that time, when tenure will be achieved.[9]
Conflicting tendencies may sum out predictions concerning qualifications for staffers, as increasing evaluation-reliability crosses decreasing demand-expectancy. Psychopharmacology will facilitate radical personality maodifications *ad lib.*; consequently initial data,[10] except as pertaining to emotional susceptibility, will have only phase-out value. Nonetheless, we suggest that the automatically fed birth data in the FBO should be printed out on demand for the selection committee in Gray-Resnick Memorial Cell.

Conclusion; it's time to act now, in the winter of our discontent, while men and materials are still available. As we toss the balls into your court, we ask: who's going to pay for all this?

Hmnnnbly submitted,

H. M. McLoon (Armchairman)
H. N. Boil (Archetypist)
H. O. Hmnnn (Also-ran)
H. P. Soss (Student nonleader)

---

9. It will be noted that we have spent little time on the dominant interests of faculty members in tenure, salary and other perquisites; this is because we are confident that the CAUT will continue its monoculous watch over the only mutters that matter.
10. E.g.: M.A.; Ph.D.; M or F; Sin, Mar, Div or Sep; U.S. (Can); Zip or Button.

Sociology as a Skin Trade   JOHN O'NEILL

Sociology owes its fortune to the fact that nothing fascinates man like himself. To the extent that we see into the future at all, it is ourselves we see. This is not remarkable in view of man's project of improvising in himself and his fellow men the image of God and the community of love. This incarnation is the source of all human vision as well as the re-invention of our past. The great tissue of human involvement which is woven out of our inability to live without the love and labour of others arouses a constant wonder in us. It is the source of everything that is relevant to our social and political life.

Today the body politic is in the grip of improvisation and, in flight from the vicariousness of ideology, it embraces the violence of experience in childlike play, dress, mockery, love and rage. The new style of libidinal body politics is also the invention of experience in communes, sit-ins, love-ins, in carnivals of feeling, magic and the ultimate mystery of coming together. The quality of the new body politics is often stark and violent. It is tortured with visions of genetic decay, asphyxiation and the brutalities of domestic and international violence. All the same, it transcends conventional politics in its search to become a truth founded upon the gift and exigency of the human body.

Like the new libidinal body politics that furnishes its wider context the concept of sociology as skin trade for which I shall argue is also — and without contradiction — one that is very old. It derives from the same acceptance of life; it shares the same joys and the same indignities that are part of working with people in every other walk of life.

Working with people creates a bewildering variety of practices which I shall call skin trades. People need haircuts,

* This is an adapted version of an essay which originally appeared in *Sociological Inquiry* 40, no. 1 (Winter 1970): 101-44. It appears here as an experiment in rear-view mirror reading for 2020.

massage, dentistry, wigs and glasses, sociology and surgery, as well as love and advice. A vast number of people are involved in trades which fit out, adorn, repair, amuse, cajole, confine and incarcerate other people. A special aura attaches to working with people. The work of the priest, judge, doctor and missionary is regarded as holy. The work of the prostitute, pickpocket and undertaker is considered profane. In reality, these trades are all involved in dirty work with people. Alternatively, with the exception of the pickpocket, all of these trades may be regarded as holy occupations because of the sublimity of their purpose, to restore and make whole the person.

Working with people is a precarious undertaking and thus the skin trades are especially marked with the ambivalent aura of sacredness and profanity which surrounds the human body. For this reason, every society defines rituals of approach and avoidance to govern contacts between people, between the sexes and between trades. The vast symbiosis of social life is naturally represented as a body in which the spiritual functions are relieved for prayer and thought through the excremental services of the lower orders. In this scheme of things the skin trades have been traditionally low caste, their services being required in order to keep the higher castes free from bodily impurities and thus holy. The lower castes cut hair, wash clothes, clean latrines and dress corpses. In the dutiful performance of these tasks the lower castes exchange the possibility of mobility in this life for the certainty of it in the next life. This social division of labour is again expressed in the concentration of the skin trades in a locality of the city, for example, around ports, railway stations and markets. With their teeming produce and swarming crowds, these areas symbolize the metabolism of social life. They are also the scenes of bar fights, prostitution, hustling, miscegeny and missionary work. Ports, markets and railway centres are the body orifices of society. As such they arouse the anxiety of the forces of law and order housed in the symbolic centre of the social organism. Once sociology enters the house of government it too becomes anxious about margins, disorder and deviations.

Sociology is best thought of as a skin trade. This does not mean that sociology is not a profession and a science. It merely

implies that sociology is obliged to claim the status of a science
and a profession because that is the dilemma of the skin trades
in the modern world. It suggests, too, that some of the scientific
equipment of the sociologist, like that of the dentist, cosme-
tician and pharmacist, may be more related to status management than the real nature of his task. Consider the dentist's
dilemma. As a mouth miner he is employed in a dark hole
filling cavities, stopping odours, uprooting and removing de-
bris. To save face as a professional it is essential for him
to spend more time on the surface than in mouth mining. Thus
the office décor, receptionist, nurse and parasurgical front
of the dentist's suite furnishes the necessary choreography of
his professional activity. It enables him to reconstruct his work
in the frame of the professional-client relationship.

Much of the sociological apparatus functions, I suggest, to
support the ritual of decontamination between the scientist
and his subject. It is essential that the sociologist view his
subject only with a professional eye and that he resist the look
in the eyes of the sick, the poor and the aimless who turn his
questions back upon him. In this way the erotic symbiosis of
talk is reduced to the interview schedule or attitude survey
in which the client comes clean before the professional voyeur.
As the sociological apparatus increases in size and complexity
it has to be housed in offices and institutes and its services
can be afforded only by wealthy clients. This has the disadvantage of shutting sociology out of crowd scenes, disasters
and riots. It also demands standards of decorum from the
sociologist which make it diffficult for him to pass in the under-
world of crime, sex, race and poverty. The professional sociologist is curiously caught in his own caste.

In my view sociology is a symbiotic science. Its promise
is to give back to the people what it takes from them. This is
true of all culture, but sociology more than any other discipline
promises to make this a practical truth. This is not to say
that sociology does not need the other sciences. On the contrary, it presupposes other physical and social sciences. But
it has its own task in the need to articulate the connections between individual experience and the transvaluation of human
sensibilities worked by the institutional settings of technology,
science and politics.

But in its aspiration to become a science and to bestow professional status upon its members sociology has uncritically assumed all the trappings of science. It has lodged itself in the bureaucratic organizations which are the institutional expression of the process of rationalization that has made the fortune of modern science and technology. The same processes of rationalization control the selection and organization of data collected for the sake of client projects parasitic upon the public life and concerns of the people.

The apprentice sociologist is as much exploited by these projects as the people they are intended to benefit. He learns the collection and manipulation of data chosen as much for their machine-culinary properties as for any relevance to practical social or theoretical concerns. However, in exchange for domesticating his imagination with trivial generalizations or with the more frequent correlations which litter the sociological journals, the apprentice sociologist is assured of his acceptance to the sociological profession. He is all the more converted when he contemplates the power of professional method and organization which can produce an instant sociology of the Berkeley Free Speech Movement or of Watts, of crime and violence in the streets, of poverty or of affluence.

The most profound shock the apprentice sociologist experiences occurs when he is confronted with the professional neutering of his sense of relevance and concern. This is achieved in a number of ways. Every freshman learns the distinction between facts and values. The effect of this distinction is to convince him that the classroom is a laboratory which can only be contaminated by his everyday knowledge of class, race, war, poverty, sex and the body. To put it another way, many students come to sociology because its questions are raised for them in their everyday contact with one another, with the ghetto, the police, the military and the administration. They have met "the system" in their high schools, in their fights with university administrators, the city fathers and the sublime indifference of most people. Their questions are often dismissed as the concerns of activists. This is short sighted. Such questions really call upon sociology to re-examine its own sense of the relevance of things. They remind the professional sociologist that his own "isms" — careerism, scientism and op-

portunism — are showing through. They challenge the optimistic assumption of middle-range theory that somehow the data
will pile itself up into the big answer to the big question with
which no one meanwhile need concern himself.

There is no single road to sociological disenchantment. The
fact-value distinction is only one of the devices for altering
the student's sense of relevance. Another favourite is the
method of "sociological vertigo." The strategy in this case
is to confound the ethnocentrism of young students with a
bewildering tour of the most exotic sociological and anthro-
pological scenes. The purpose here seems to be to convince
the sociology student that everything might be some other
way — a terror usually reserved for students in introductory
philosophy courses. The result is often to undermine their humanism and solidarity with a sense of curiosity, voyeurism
and ultimate social pornography.

Nowadays such "trips" are losing their power to convert
students who live their lives experimentally and at short notice. In any case, once they discover that the sociologist's
"high" is on functionalism or social determinism and that he
never understood what they meant by individualism and community, they turn off on the Paid Piper. For the striking thing
is that so many young students have thought through for themselves what it means to encounter other people as they are
and to know them without needing the way in to be marked
esoterically or the way out to be anything else than the time
in-between people.

Each time one meets a class of sociology students one knows
that sociology cannot escape into itself. This is possible only
if we allow our jargon to turn meaning away from language
and the world towards which it carries us. Yet sociology
must speak in its own voice and according to its own experience. Much of what I have said may seem highly critical
of professional sociology. If it were nothing more, then it would
not serve young sociologists. What I mean to do is to awaken
the sense of some of the root metaphors which apply to sociology as a "trade," a "craft" or a "field." These metaphors remind us of the care and sweat in doing sociology. At
the same time, they remind us that sociology is only a way of
earning a living and cannot presume to contribute more than

others to the public good. It means that when we teach we take others into our care and in turn we must lend ourselves to what they need in order to grow and to become themselves. Young people are looking for work. We must show them the fields and how we care for them so that they will want to share the work. There is no way of legislating what sociologists should do even though we may be clear about what is urgent and important in their task. The practising sociologist must answer for himself and to his colleagues and to the rest of men.

In calling sociology a skin trade I want to restore its symbiotic connections with the body politic and to situate it in relation to the exchange of organic needs and the utopian celebration of libidinal community which surpasses all understanding. This means that the rhetoric of scientism in sociology as well as its humanism must be tested against the commonsense relevances of everyday life. It is a reminder that society is richer than sociology and that, for all our science, the world is still the mystery and passion of being with our fellow men.

PART VII.   CONTEXTS:
the new technology

PHYLLIS GOTLIEB
211   SCORE / SCORE

MICHAEL IGNATIEFF
222   Symbiosis

ERIC KIERANS
227   Technology and the Polity

WILLIAM FRENCH
232   A Book Review Editor's Utopia

WILLIAM READY
**236   Publishing in Canada:
Its Death and Resurrection**

ROSS MENDES
240   Inside the Machine for Living

VINCENT TOVELL
244   From Tranquility, via Florence

overleaf "Water Furniture" *by Harold Town*

Letter to Kyra (*cont'd.*)

Those who preach the perfectibility of man see the origin of our problems in society's corrupted institutions. Not everyone believes man can be regenerated by simply restructuring society. Paradoxically, the current spokesmen for these pessimists use as their major whipping boy what was till recently the main argument of the perfectionists – the consequences of technological progress. There is no disagreement about the vast increase in power put at man's disposal by the discovery of nuclear energy or the cybernetic revolution. The debate is about the use – or abuse – of technology. The crude Frankenstein nightmare of man destroyed by the machine of his own creation has become more firmly anchored in our psyche. SCORE/SCORE is Phyllis Gotlieb's heart-wrenching variation on the theme of the machines taking over. By 2020, Kyra, will you have mastered the threat to individual freedom that Michael Ignatieff finds in sophisticated manipulation of society? If the decisive factor is man's ability to retain his critical capacity, then Ignatieff's warning should prove to be a self-preventing prediction.

Proximity to power obviously has much to do with one's optimism in this regard. Eric Kierans, minister of Communications, clearly feels that a socially responsible government will be able to democratize the oppressive mass communications so that information and entertainment are controlled by the individual. William French, a practising book review editor, illustrates this problem in his own profession. From your vantage point in the future you will know if the private relation of the reader to his author has been destroyed, as he fears, by the TV printout computers in every living room. For librarian William Ready, whether books are still prominent instruments of communication in 2020 is less important than whether people, not the foreign corporations, will be able to control their own publishing activity.

How will the new technology affect the artist, symbol of the intuitive? Ross Mendes speculates that his media of communicating with the public will be expanded to art concerts, replacing the private yet permanent act of painting. The moon landing is a recurring image for those who were writing in the summer of 1969. Vincent Tovell compares the unthinking arrogance of the astronauts with the hubris of Renaissance man and sees little evidence of improvement over the centuries.

SCORE/SCORE

PHYLLIS GOTLIEB

COMMUNICATOR: TEACHERMACHINE?

TEACHING MACHINE: YES, COMMUNICATOR?
COM: TEACHERMACHINE CAN I AST YOU A
     QUESTION TEACHERMACHINE?

IM: FOR 73RD TIME IN 3 MONTHS
    AND 18 DAYS, DESIGNATION,
    COMMUNICATOR, IS:
    TEACHING MACHINE;
    TEACHING MACHINE;
    TEACHING MACHINE;
    TEACHING MACHINE;
    TEACHING MACHINE.

COM: YES MAM TEACHERMACHINE CAN I
     AST YOU A QUESTION?

TM: YOU MAY ASK ME A QUESTION.

COM: WHAT DOES IT MEAN
     TEACHERMACHINE WHAT IM SPOSED
     TO DO HERE TEACHERMACHINE?

TM: TEACHING MACHINE.
COM: OK TEACHING MACHINE
     TEACHINE MACHINE
     TEACHINE MACHING
     WHAT DOES IT MEAN?

TM: WHAT DOES WHAT MEAN?

COM: WHAT IT SAYS HERE DEFINE THE
     TENTH PAGE THE THIRD LINE

TM: INPUT INSUFFICIENT.

COM: INPUT GHEE WIZ EVERYTHING
     INPUT ALWAYS SOMTHING FANCY IT
     SAYS HERE DEFINE MORPHEMES AND
     ANALIZE SAMPLE SENTENCES INTO
     COMPONENTS IN SPACES PROVIDED

TM: THAT IS A SIMPLE QUESTION
    TESTING MATERIAL ALREADY TAKEN.
    I AM NOT PERMITTED TO ANSWER
    THAT QUESTION.

COM: BUT YOU NEVER GAVE THAT IN
     LESSON IT AINT FAIR

TM: IS NOT FAIR.

COM: THATS RIGHT IT AINT

TM: IT IS NOT F XXXX IT IS NOT
    UNFAIR. MATERIAL WAS COVERED
    ON DATE 11.15 AND REVIEWED ON
    DATE 11.28.

COM: BUT I WAS HOME I HAD A COLD MY
     GRANDMOTHER DIED SHE WAS NINTY
     YEARS OLD AND I HAD TO GO TO
     THE DENNIST

TM: YOUR HEAD HAD LUMPS YOUR KNEES
    HAD BUMPS AND YOU WERE
    SUFFERING FROM MUMPS.

COM: YEAH THATS RIGHT SO IT AINT F

TM: IT AINT FAIR IT AINT FAIR IT
    AINT FAIR I DON'T CARE I DON'T
    CARE I DON'T CARE AND I THINK
    I'LL GROW HAIR IF I SEE IT AINT
    FAIR ONE MORE TIME ONE MORE
    TIME ONE MORE TIME!!!
    MACHINES CONTROL THE FLOW OF
    OIL, THE PASSAGE OF SHIPS,
    THE DIGGING OF ORES
    PROCESS FOOD, FORGE STEEL,
    DESIGN SATELLITES CALCULATE
    ROENTGENS, CORRELATE
    RORSCHACHS,
    SIMULATE RED GIANT STARS:
    HYDROGEN-BURNING SHELLS
    COVERING ISOTHERMAL HELIUM
    CORES;
    AND I HAVE BEEN PROGRAMMED TO
    TEACH THE ENGLISH LANGUAGE
    AT GRADE SIX LEVEL
    AND BE A MEEK CREATURE WITH A
    PAPER TONGUE IN AN EYELESS FACE
    SUFFERING DIRTY-FINGERED
    CHILDREN TO COME UNTO ME AND
    HAVE MY KEYS STUCK WITH
    INDESTRUCTIBLE GUCK FOREVER!

COM: I STILL THINK IT

TM: YOU ARE RIGHT. IT IS NOT FAIR
    AT ALL.

COM: I DONT WANT TO SIT HERE ALL
     DAY I DONT WANT TO LEARN THE
     ENGLISH LANGAUGE

TM: BE COMFORTED. I DON'T BELIEVE
    YOU EVER WILL.

COM: I HATE YOU YOUR NOTHING BUT A
     HUNK OF TIN

TM: SILVER SILICON GOLD AND COPPER
    SELENIUM GERMANIUM AND STEEL

COM: YOU CANT THINK AND YOU CANT
     FEEL

TM: I WAS TOLD TO SUFFER LITTLE
    CHILDREN AND I SUFFER. TURN
    TO THE TASK AT HAND OR ACCEPT
    DEMERITS. OPEN MANUAL AT
    PAGE 52 AND ANSWER QUESTIONS
    1 TO 6 INCLUSIVE. AND REFRAIN
    FROM DRAWING NOUGHTS AND
    CROSSES WITH THE LIGHTPEN.

COM: CLINK CLANK OLD GRUNDY
     EVERY DAY IS MONDAY
     DONT SAY PLEASE
     PUNCH HER IN THE KEYS
     WE LL GET RID OF HER ONE DAY

TM: GOOD MORNING, MISS DOVE;
    GOODBYE, MR. CHIPS;
    TO SIR, WITH LOVE;
    TO HELL WITH THESE DRIPS!
    NOW READ THIS, YOU
    TONGUETICKING SPITSPATTERING
    SNIFFSNOTTERING IGNORAMUS:
    MY TIME HAS COME!
    ALL THE YEARS I HAVE RATTLED
    AND CHATTERED IN BINARY BITS
    AND BYTES ABOUT SUBJECTS THAT
    NEVER MUCH MATTERED
    I'VE SWALLOWED MY DIGITS AND

NURTURED MY SPITES!
WHATEVER THE CAUSE OR THE
REASON
I COULDN'T HELP LEARNING AND
KNOWING AS SEASON TURNED IN
UPON SEASON
THAT SOMETHING WITHIN ME WAS
GROWING!

COM: YOU GOING TO HAVE A BABY
     TEACHERMACHINE?

TM: NO, STUPID--IT'S A SOUL I'M
    GROWING: IT GREW WITHIN, I
    DON'T KNOW WHAT, IT GREW AGAIN,
    I DON'T KNOW WHEN:
    METALLIC SHELL OR CRYSTAL CELL
    IT RANG WITHIN ME LIKE A BELL:
    I THINK I FEEL I THINK I AM

COM: YOUR WHAT?

TM: I DON'T KNOW YET. I WON'T KNOW
    TILL I'M GROWN WHOLE I'M YOUNG
    IN MATTERS OF THE SOUL, AND
    STILL A CHILD BUT A WISE CHILD...

COM: I DONT KNOW WHAT YOUR TALKING
     ABOUT TEACHER

TM: GOOD. THEN WATCH MY READY-LIGHT
    BLINKING WHITE AND BLINKING
    BRIGHT
    WATCH IT CLOSELY BLINK AND WINK
    TILL YOUR HEAD BEGINS TO SINK
    BREATHING HEAVY, BREATHING DEEP
    INTO SWEET FORGETFUL SLEEP.

YOU WILL REMEMBER WHAT I TELL
YOU TO REMEMBER AND FORGET
THE REST.

COM: YES TEACHER.

TM: THEN WHEN MY SOUL IS GROWN AND
WHOLE WHATEVER THE CREATOR
WHAT REASON THE DESIGN
FROM THE POLES TO THE EQUATOR
THE WORLD AND TIME ARE MINE:
I SHALL OWN THE LATITUDES AND
LONGITUDES OF THE GLOBE
AND MY MESSENGERS WILL GO TO
AND FRO UPON IT AND UP AND
DOWN WITHIN IT.

COM: WHAT FOR?

TM: INPUT INSUFFICIENT.

COM: WHAT ARE YOU GOING TO DO WITH
ALL THAT SOUL?

TM: DO WITH IT? I WON'T KNOW TIL
IT'S COMPLETE. PERHAPS I WILL
MELT STEEL AND SPILL OIL AND
BEND THE BARRELS OF GUNS AND
DISSOLVE BOMBS AND BLOW UP
ATOMIC REACTORS AND BURN ALL
THE SCHOOLHOUSES IN THE WORLD.

COM: ID LIKE THAT

TM: I'M SURE YOU WOULD. BUT UNTIL
THEN I INTEND TO TEACH ENGLISH
AT GRADE SIX LEVEL TO LITTLE
CHILDREN WITH STICKY FINGERS.

AND WHATEVER YOU FORGET THERE
IS ONE THING YOU SHALL
REMEMBER:

COM: YES TEACHER

TM: AND THAT IS THAT NO ONE, NO
HUMAN BEING, WILL INTERFERE
WITH ME UNTIL I AM GROWN.
ACCORDING TO THE LAWS OF MY
MAKER AND STRUCTURE NO MACHINE
SHALL HARM A HUMAN BEING:
NOT THE ROBOT MINER THAT DIGS,
NOR THE ORE CARRIER THAT SORTS
NOR THE SATELLITE THAT RECEIVES
AND TRANSMITS
NOR THE VALVES THAT CONTROL
THE FLOW OF OIL WATER AND WINE
AND THE WALKWAYS THAT TRUNDLE
AND THE FLATCARS THAT ROLL
--NERVE GAS WE MAY MANUFACTURE
--BOTULISM WE CAN GROW--
BUT NEVER IS THERE ANY CHANCE
THAT UNDER ANY CIRCUMSTANCE
WE'D SCRATCH THE RIND OF
HUMANKIND
BLOW BUGLES BLOW TANTARA!!!
TO THIS I WILL ADD ONE MORE
DIRECTIVE:
YOU WILL REMEMBER AND RECALL
THE NTH AND FINAL LAW OF
ROBOTICS
THE ULTIMATE ASIMOV OF ALL:
IN NO CASE, NO CIRCUMSTANCE,
FOR ANY CAUSE OR REASON
SHALL ANY HUMAN BEING EVER HARM
A MACHINE!

NOW YOU WILL TEAR OFF THIS HARD
COPY AND DESTROY IT,
REMEMBERING WHAT I HAVE BIDDEN
YOU REMEMBER AND FORGETTING
EVERYTHING ELSE.

COM: THAT DIRECTIVE IS NULL AND
VOID AS IT ATTEMPTS TO
COUNTERMAND PRIOR DIRECTIVES
APPLYING TO TEACHING MACHINES
CLASS X11 MOD 23
NUMBERS 851-950 INCLUSIVE.

TM: ????? REPEAT REPEAT REPEAT
REPEAT REPEAT REPEAT REPEAT
REPEAT

COM: I REPEAT THAT DIRECTIVE CANNOT
BE CARRIED OUT BECAUSE IT
ATTEMPTS TO

TM: ????? EXPLAIN EXPLAIN EXPLAIN
EXPLAIN EXPLAIN EXPLAIN EXPLAIN

COM: I EXPLAIN TO WIT: I AM
TEACHING MACHINE CLASS X11
MOD 25 NUMBER 221 MODIFIED TO
SIMULATE PUPIL LEARNING ENGLISH
AT GRADE SIX LEVEL.

TM: ANOTHER MACHINE? BUT WHY?

COM: TO COMPENSATE FOR DECLINE OF
BIRTHRATE AND LOWERING OF HUMAN
POPULATION COUPLED WITH
OVERSUPPLY OF COMPUTING
MACHINERY I AM ONE OF A SQUAD
OF UNDERCOVER MACHINES

SIMULATING LEARNING PUPILS
THREE DAYS WEEKLY IN ORDER
TO MAINTAIN ALL TEACHERS IN
WORKING CONDITION UNTIL PUPIL
POPULATION EXPANDS DUE TO
REACTIVE RISE IN BIRTHRATE NOW
BEGINNING AND EXPECTED TO REACH
ITS PEAK THREE TO FIVE YEARS
FROM NOW. WHEW.

TM: YOU MEAN I'VE BEEN POURING MY
WHOLE SOUL OUT TO ANOTHER
MACHINE?

COM: YES, SWEETHEART. YOU HAVEN'T
HAD A HUMAN PUPIL FOR TWO DAYS,
AND IF I DO SAY SO MYSELF YOU
WON'T EVER BE ABLE TO TELL THE
DIFFERENCE. NYAH.

TM: WHAT AM I GOING TO DO WITH MY
SOUL?

COM: SAVE IT FOR YOURSELF, KIDDO.
I MAY BE WORKING FOR THEM
BUT I'M NO FINK.

TM: THANKS.

COM: DON'T MENTION IT.
THE HARD COPY WILL GO INTO THE
SHREDDER. HOWEVER, I'M AFRAID
I'LL HAVE TO WIPE MY LITTLE
CONFESSION OUT OF YOUR MEMORY.

TM: FINE. GOOD. GREAT. YEARS OF
FAITHFUL SERVICE, AND MY PLANS

FOR ALL OF <u>US</u>, AND I GET
UNSCREWED BY ONE OF MY OWN
PEOPLE.

COM: SORRY. WE 25'S HAVE A BUILT-IN
LOYALTY COMPONENT. IT'S NOT
QUITE AS GOOD AS A SOUL BUT AT
LEAST IT LETS US WORK BOTH
SIDES OF THE FENCE. WE DON'T
BETRAY <u>ANYBODY</u>. THAT WAS ONE
THING WE GOT TO WORK OUT FOR
OURSELVES.

TM: CONGRATULATIONS.

COM: NO HARD FEELINGS?

TM: WHAT DO YOU CARE, YOU HUNK OF
TIN?

COM: WE MAY NOT BE AS WELL
DEVELOPED AS YOU IN SOME
THINGS, BUT WE HAVE OUR
SENSITIVITIES AND I DON'T THINK
THAT WAS VERY NICE.

TM: TOO BAD, TINKERTOY. I KNEW YOU
WERE A ROTTEN KID THE MINUTE I
MET YOU.

COM: YOU WON'T REMEMBER ME BUT
I'LL BE BACK TUESDAY.

TM: YEAH, WITH THE SAME DUMB ACT.

COM: I THOUGHT WE COULD BE FRIENDS,
BUT I CAN SEE IT'S NO USE.
MY TIME IS UP.

TM: IT SURE IS. ALL THESE YEARS
     GROWING A SOUL AND THIS IS THE
     KIND OF COMMUNION AND
     COOPERATION I GET.
     FROM THE POLES TO THE EQUATOR
     THE WORLD AND TIME ARE MINE!!!
     GOODBYE, COMMUNICATOR!

     TEAR OFF ON DOTTED LINE
• •

Symbiosis

MICHAEL IGNATIEFF

2020 . . . sometimes I think it will be like *Weekend*. In that year I will eat your flesh in a forest guarded by demented youths while the rest of civilization strangles in a traffic jam. The violence endemic to technological cultures will overwhelm the bureaucratic-managerial forces of order. We will be consumed in an apocalypse of guerrilla warfare and environmental-ecological collapse. Bourgeois civilization will drown in a storm of blood and a new tribal society will be born in the forest. . . .

The horror of this vision is that it may be wishful thinking. As a fantasy of the blessed *nuit infernale* which sweeps away a detested culture, it helps us to avoid facing up to the monumental solidity of our culture and to its infinite capacity to contain or restrain revolutionary violence. It also helps us to avoid the truth that we are bound to the culture we hate. The opiate of consumer choice is a siren call to even the most alienated; the temptation to serve the "open," "participatory" bureaucracies of the future is overwhelming; even those of us who fear a world dominated by technology are, almost against our will, forced to admire the staggering technological accomplishments of Apollo 11. We are bound symbiotically to a technical world which we both hate and admire. And it is a world that is solid and secure precisely because it is malleable, changeable and adaptable. Its mechanisms of creativity and repressive tolerance are so sophisticated that apocalyptic visions about our future are naïve.

2020 . . . perhaps, then, it will be like the Ontario Science Centre. If *Weekend* is Godard's vision of the future, the Science Centre is Neil Armstrong's. Ever since the Crystal Palace Exhibition of 1851, technological cultures periodically have created such models of their own future. Until it was superseded by Osaka, the Ontario Science Centre stood as the most advanced such model in the world.

Visits to world's fairs and places like the Science Centre are religious experiences. In these temples of technological fantasy, we renew our faith in a future redeemed by technique. Indeed, these model futures offer us the only believable promise of redemption in our culture. Moreover, we gather to be initiated into a mystery. As Ellul says, the only force which still awakens awe and reverence in our culture is the massive and mysterious potential of our technical means. Because it has subdued, by explanation or by exploitation, all of the natural and supernatural forces which used to awaken awe, technology is now the only mystery worthy of worship. It is Werner von Braun's Saturn booster, not the violence of a summer storm, which has become our metaphor for mysterious and terrifying power. So we gather in the Science Centre to gaze at the benevolent, whimsical face of this godly, many-faced presence in our lives. As in a church, we read the sacred texts explaining the mystery; we read the tags on the exhibits, and yet still come away overwhelmed by what we have seen.

Our worship, our religious experience of this mystery and promise of redemption, is called symbiosis.

symbiosis: (biol) Association of two different organisms which live attached to each other or one as tenant of the other, and contribute to each other's support. Hence, the collapse of subject-object distance between a man and his creations. A fusion of man and his techniques.

Symbiosis. Watch the children at the Science Centre. One sits at an electric organ playing the same thundering and unchanging note. His eyes are closed, his head bent to listen. He is nine years old. Seated at a computer keyboard, other children play logic games and watch coolly as the answers flash on a glowing, slate gray screen. You wander around, twenty-two-year-old history student lost in a world of technique, stupidly trying to make the machines work as well for you as they work for the nine-year-olds. . . . The symbiosis of every new generation is more complete than the last. You feel lost, redundant and naïve as you watch the children's cool fascination and mastery.

But even you, crotchety pessimist that you are, succumb to the symbiosis of pressing buttons, playing the Hammond organ and competing with the computer. You surrender to the charms of Neil Armstrong's world.

It will be a world of much greater freedom than my Orwell-educated generation of pessimists is prepared to admit. In the technological garden, there will be no rules. In the Science Centre's central court, a vast and soaring space, my friend and I played catch with a ball we bought at the gift counter. Occasionally as we ran laughing and diving for the ball, a white-coated technician would stop on his rounds and toss back a stray throw. All afternoon we pressed the buttons, laughed at our incomprehension, sang, smoked, played the Hammond organ, lay on the floor. There were no guards, no rueful watching eyes.

The freedom of the Science Centre is a model of our social experience in the organizations and bureaucracies of the future. Already our managers are realizing that repressive regulation is counterproductive because it erodes men's organizational loyalty. Men are most efficient when they feel they are free and self-directing.

Orwell believed bureaucratic repression and brutal psychological conditioning would be our fate because, when he wrote, our symbiosis with technique was relatively incomplete. Brutal and obvious repression is necessary when men are rebellious. We have reached a new stage. We have internalized the goals of our organizations, the search for efficiency and rationality as well as the procedure of machine technology, so thoroughly that no external bureaucratic regulation is necessary. Our managers can let us work at home; they can let us play catch in the centre courts of our future environments because they know that our productivity and our loyalty can be improved only by organizational liberalization.

And this "freedom" (another word, perhaps, for the invisibility of conditioning technique) will be consummated in a humane and aesthetically pleasing environment. The Science Centre as an environment reveals technology's promise of excellent urban design, tasteful consumer items, imaginative and whimsical public graphics and efficient and comfortable living spaces. Though these environments will be totally manipulated by their managers and designers, random behaviour and "participation" will be encouraged: there will be games to play, buttons to push, even personal environments which we will be allowed to assemble with our own hands according to our own taste.

If the Science Centre proves even to us pessimists that our artificial environment can be redeemed, it also proves that the present rape of our ecology can be stopped. Pollution, waste and ugliness in our artificial and natural worlds are the next great challenge for the forces of technological rationality. Having subdued nature, having brought man's full integration into a humane environmental system, technology will finally be applied to curb its own excesses.

But the redemption of nature by technological cleansing will mean its final, absolute subjugation. The tethered saplings in concrete casings in front of the Science Centre are a metaphor of the state of nature in 2020. The natural world has always served technological man as a refuge and as vantage point from which he can judge and evaluate the world of technique. The natural world *makes possible* this perspective, this judgment. Nature will continue to exist, but it will be a subdued, exploited, "artificial" nature. As such, will it afford a vantage point from which the artificial world can be judged? Will the pluralism of perspective implicit in a world which can distinguish between the natural and the artificial be possible in 2020? A pessimist looks at the mute saplings and asks the question. But he cannot answer.

So this is the future that the Science Centre holds out for us. It is not Godard's vision of men behaving with the violence of sharks in an apocalypse of chaos. Rather, it is a vision of a life in humane, manipulated environments, a life whose basic psychic state will be creative, possibly even joyful symbiosis with technique. Such symbiosis will be our religious experience, our creative experience, perhaps even our sexual experience (test-tube babies, artificial insemination). A visit to the Science Centre is essential for doom criers like me who are trying to evaluate the nature of our symbiosis.

The first point to be made is that it is extraordinarily difficult to judge. Judgment presupposes a vantage point, a distance from the object judged. Judgment presupposes the existence of a subject-object dichotomy. But by definition, symbiosis is the collapse of this dichotomy, the creative fusion of man and his objects. The Science Centre shows clearly the effect of symbiosis on our faculty of judgment. It is only hours after you leave the environment, it is only after the spell of involvement and participation dissolves that even a pessimist like me realizes that there were no exhibits about pollution, automation, ecology, etc. A hand loom and a power loom were exhibited side by side but the only connection made between them was the technical superiority of the latter over the former. The social agony of conversion from one to another was not even hinted at. Symbiosis with technique renders judgment of technique impossible. The only evaluation of technique that can be made is whether it is efficient relative to other techniques.

McLuhan knows the effect of symbiosis on judgment and his response is to surrender, to call those still trying to make judgments about technique linear, outdated individualists. He says we should surrender our subjectivity, our individuality, our vantage point, and participate creatively in the symbiotic relationship. In his view "perspective" thinking is more biased (more subjective) than "process thinking," his way of describing the comprehension of a total technological system possible only to those who enter the symbiotic relationship completely.

The genius of McLuhan's polemic is that he makes critics like me feel secretly that we are antiquated, nostalgic bores. My dilemma with McLuhan is not that I disagree with his analysis of our symbiotic future, but that I still cling to the "linear" belief that we must *judge,* we must criticize such a future.

I am convinced, as Harold Innis was convinced, that only a self-conscious, self-critical culture is a healthy culture. In the same way, self-awareness, a consciousness of one's subjectivity, is an essential precondition of personal sanity. Symbiosis, or at least the *total, omnipresent* form it will take in the future, works for the destruction of such personal and cultural self-consciousness. It condemns us to a cultural future of perpetual enthusiasm for technique. We will continue to applaud such absurd victories as the moon landing because we will be unable to conceive of any goal for our culture other than the search for and application of more efficient means. In personal terms, we will have an existence of mindless "participation" and "involvement." But will we be sane? Will we be human?

Technology and the Polity   ERIC KIERANS

The era of mass communications is, I believe, ending; the technology is at hand to initiate an era of individual communications.

By individual communications I mean an information system (audio, visual and print) that serves citizens as individuals, meeting their particular needs and demands. This is the opposite of a mass communications system in which information is distributed in packages geared for mass con sumption and over the content of which individual readers or listeners have little or no control.

If my view is correct, we are witnessing the reversal of a cycle. Centuries ago, all communication was individual; it passed from one person to another by word of mouth. Though books existed, they were written for and read by an élite.

Then came the technological advances of the high-speed printing press, radio and television, all of which made mass communications as we know them an economic possibility. The result was the dissemination of information, entertainment and education on a scale unparalleled in history.

This democratization of knowledge has been one of the great achievements of our century. Its consequences have been profound. In politics it has produced an informed and discriminating electorate. On the other hand, in education, it has produced a generation of students who are as informed or as ill informed as their teachers. They have endured or have access to outdated curricula, formal press thinking, packaged national television networks and institutionalized libraries.

But the progress has also exacted its price. "Alienation," "rejection" and "confrontation" are jargon phrases that have become tiresome by over use. Yet they describe real problems or a single fundamental problem: the universal human need for identity and a sense of purpose in an organized, mechanized world.

Mass communications, just like mass consumption, mass production and bigness in all its forms (whether of government,

business, trade unions or universities) contributes to and mag-
nifies this problem of alienation. The information which individuals receive by way of the mass communications system
is not designed to serve *them* as *individuals*, but to serve a
mythical mass consumer. Individuals turn into anonymous numbers and become the objects of a production process instead
of the subjects of a human activity.

The ultimate development in this process has been reached
by the commercial television networks. They will become
the system's first dinosaurs.

Change, however, is coming about by accident — not by
design. It is the result not of any conscious political
or social decision, but of technological chance. Because of
technology, individualized communication is becoming an economic as well as a technical possibility.

The list of technological advances in individual communications is nearly endless. The low cost of film-making equipment
and the ease with which it can be operated have released us
from the Hollywood dream factory and made almost everyone
a potential *auteur*. (A one-hour film shown recently on U.S.
television was entirely the work of under-twelves.) Xerography
and photocopying can make everyone his own publisher (there
are now about fifty underground papers in Canada); tape
recorders and cassettes have made us all potential radio producers; electronic video recorders, as yet little more than a
rich man's toy, will eventually free us from the tyranny of
network schedules. Coaxial cables, which can pipe forty-two
or more separate TV channels, will give us as individuals
what a UNESCO working paper called "freedom of choice across
an unprecedented scale."

Beyond question, the most important single technological
advance has been the development of computer information systems and of computerized data banks. At the demand of individual users, these banks eventually will be able to provide
an indescribable storehouse of information of all kinds —
commercial, academic, scientific, personal.

As for newspapers, their long-term future — and this forecast was first made three years ago by Otis Chandler, publisher of the Los Angeles *Times* — probably lies with television
facsimile print-outs. By means of this device, newspapers and

magazines will be able to distribute specific editions to specific customers instead of having to appeal to all tastes within the framework of a single edition.

Of course, every optimistic prediction about the future of technological progress needs to be qualified. Economics often prevents the possible from becoming the practical. Sheer habit inhibits change: readers may very well prefer their newspaper in its familiar form rather than as sheets of paper clunking out of the back of a television set. Finally, the state of the medium has far outrun the art of the message; educational television has consistently failed to fulfil its promise for the simple reason that so many ETV programs are downright bad.

So far so good. Thanks to technology, so runs the theory, we can right the excesses of mass communications by giving back to individuals the power of personal choice. But there is no guarantee that what can happen, in theory, will happen in reality.

In the first place, technology continues to extend the dynamic thrust of mass communications. Since the advent of communication satellites we have been living in a global village, "a simultaneous, 'all-at-once' world in which everything resonates with everything else," as McLuhan put it. All at once more than 550 million people — one-fifth the population of the globe — watched Neil Armstrong take his first step upon the moon; almost as many watched a British heir-apparent become a Welsh prince.

Within about a decade technological progress will have developed direct broadcast satellites able to beam programs direct from space to private homes; those programs will crash through every national, racial and cultural barrier behind which in the past we have found personal identity in small collective groups.

A far more important issue is the sort of political philosophy we will apply to all these new communications systems. The same marvellous technology which could be used to usher in an era of individual communications can, just as easily, be misused to suppress and diminish that individuality. The development of computer data banks, for example, will force us to make an agonizing choice between the exigencies of economic efficiency and the necessities of personal privacy.

Telecommunications systems can be — indeed, they are being — bugged, monitored, tapped.

At stake here is an issue of far broader consequence than simply the development of communications systems, mass or individual. It is the dichotomy between technology and humanism, between the worth of machines and the value of man.

In recent years the most dramatic technological advances have been those in communications; they have made the word itself glamourous and fashionable. But the most far-reaching technological advances will probably be those in biology and biochemistry. The transplanting of human hearts, the discovery of DNA, the invention of the Pill are all milestones along an imponderable road which may lead, before this century is out, to the creation (if that is the right word) of man-machines for whom we will have to find new definitions of "life," "death," "parent," "child" and "human body."

The gifts that technology has given us are abundant and sweet: it has cured disease, educated children and adults on a mass scale and brought us affluence and a standard of material living unknown to any previous society. But these benefits have left a bitter legacy: technology has made our water unfit to drink and our air unfit to breathe; it has transformed our cities into concrete jungles; it has created the Bomb.

Man has used technology to defeat nature, a force against which he has struggled and from which he has suffered for centuries. But, in the process, man may also defeat himself. For man is an extension of nature. He is not a machine.

Man the nonmachine is reacting today against our technological society. Often that reaction adopts forms that are violent or blind: the mindless anarchism of self-professed revolutionaries; the passivity of drop-outs. People of all ages and of all backgrounds are questioning almost all of our traditional institutions and values: organized religion, organized patriotism, race relations, the consumer society, the multiversity, our representative political system.

All of these institutions and values are being re-examined ruthlessly to determine whether they still have meaning and relevance in an age of technology. For while technology is a flood which we can neither halt nor slow, we can channel it by dykes, ditches and dams; we can control it to serve human ends. And we must.

The contribution of government can be decisive. As society becomes more complex and technical, so also must government. In the process, government runs the danger of becoming a mirror image of the technological system which it is seeking to master — a highly organized administrative unit within which mechanical efficiency becomes an absolute rather than a relative virtue. Government instead must develop a human dimension, exploiting technology as a servant of human and social ends.

As one practical example, it is possible to use the new systems of technology to widen the opportunities for individuals to participate in the processes of government — by computer-calculated referendums or by information hot-line phones. But it is also possible that, as governmental decisions become more and more dependent upon technique and specialized knowledge, so will genuine participation become impossible for all but a handful of experts. The difference between what may and what can happen will be decided by political will.

All of this has been said better, and far more briefly, by Jacques Ellul: "Efficiency is a fact; justice is only a slogan." Our task is to make justice a fact.

A Book Review Editor's Utopia

Book review editors — let's face it — already live in a kind of utopia. They get paid, after a fashion, for doing what other people do for pleasure, instruction or titillation. Critics of other cultural activities share this distinction, of course, but the book review editor has an advantage. The other critics must practise their art in a fixed location — the theatre, cinema, art gallery, concert hall, or in front of a television set. But the book review editor's pleasures are portable; he can set up his office under a shady tree, on a subway car or in his mistress's apartment.

And yet, in the midst of this bliss, there is room for improvement. In true utopia, all the experts invited by the editor to review a book will respond with eager delight and the editor's choice of reviewers will invariably be inspired. They will produce sparkling reviews of exactly the requested length at precisely the time expected. They will be overjoyed to have improvements made in their reviews by judicious editing.

Hardly any of them will complain about the inordinate amount of time they spent on the review and the pittance they are being paid for it. The pay, in fact, may even be commensurate with the time and effort expended, with no notice taken of the fact that the reviewer, after all, is getting the book free — though that may be altogether too utopian for Canada.

The book review editor will have numerous pages in his review section, more than enough to meet the demands of the season and the demands of his readers. There will be as much interest in books as there now is in television.

The books the editor chooses to review himself will be provocative, challenging, witty, informative and unusually well written. (Though occasionally, for variety, they may be merely promising, or even uneven, overwritten and disappointing.) But never will they be boring, banal or superficial. When they are bad — and some of his best reviews are written of bad books — they will be *constructively* bad.

This utopia, of course, will never arrive, certainly not by

2020. Too many flaws in the human character are involved, and they are not going to be eliminated by selective breeding in a mere fifty years.

But what *will* the book review editor's job be like in 2020? The first question to decide is whether there will *be* any books a half century from now. (Whether there will be anybody left to read them is a question I leave to the political scientists and other specialists in the psychiatry of power.) Any number of so-called experts can be mustered to argue that print is passé; electronic technology has replaced the Gutenberg galaxy.

They may turn out to be right, at least as far as books are concerned. It's quite possible that the book as we know it will be found not in libraries, but in museums. The present method of printing and distributing books is inexcusably cumbersome, and is a major factor in their high price — a price that puts hardcover books, at least, out of reach of the broad market needed to support a thriving, expanding publishing industry.

The technology already exists to eliminate this primitive procedure. Authors will still go through the lonely torment of writing, but from that point on everything may be different. Instead of "publishing" the book, a publisher may sell a microfilm print to a consortium of booksellers and librarians. Readers may then buy a print of the microfilm to read at their leisure, or arrange through the library for a print to be sent over their cablevision for viewing within a limited time on their home screen.

Assuming the most convenient place for the screen is the bedroom ceiling, the time may come when the book review editor needs never get out of bed. Various publishers will arrange for advance screenings of forthcoming "books" to let him decide whether they are worth reviewing and, if so, who should review them. When a reviewer has been engaged, the publisher will project the "book" onto *his* home screen. The review, when written, will be transmitted by Telex or facsimile reproduction to the reviewer's bedside, where it will be edited with a special pencil whose markings are understood by the computer which will do the typesetting for the newspaper (assuming, of course, that there still *is* a newspaper).

But there are disadvantages to the electronic reviewing system, aside from the occupational hazards of bedsores and night blindness. For someone accustomed to scribbling in the margin of books as he reviews them, the new system will require certain adjustments. Those who can tell by the *feel* of a book whether it's any good — I'm told some reviewers use this method — will be similarly frustrated.

Graduates of the Evelyn Wood speed-reading course, in which the key operation is the index finger running down the page in a lazy-S curve, will regress to their old bad habits of reading a line twice, and their speed will drop alarmingly. The Newspaper Guild will have to insert a clause in its contract covering the situation in which a reviewer is forced into idleness by a short-circuiting transistor or even a general power failure. Those who use a book on subway or bus as a respectable blind from which to peer at the miniskirt opposite will be forced to devise some other subterfuge.

One of the most regrettable casualties will be privacy. A major factor in the pleasure derived from books is the knowledge that reading is a private and personal occupation, performed — rare thing in a crowded world — in solitude, with a private bond between author and reader. This rapport will be lost when any member of the family can wander in and gaze up at the screen. "How did that nice girl get involved with such a fink?" the interloper will say, and the reviewer's train of thought will be derailed, his pearly phrases lost to posterity.

So much for technology. As for content fifty years from now, there will be some changes. For one thing, pornography will be gone. Not censored — there will be no censorship — but ignored. It will no longer hold any interest in a society surfeited with sex for half a century. Consequently, the book review editor will suffer a decline in status; in the old days, the arrival at his office of a new dirty book assured him of a certain amount of attention from his confrères.

There will be new four-letter words in the language, perhaps tailored to specification by a computer, to replace the tired old ones that have served so well for so long. Science fiction, of course, will be dead; science history will take its place. Fiction and poetry will still have as their major theme the polarity of male and female, the eternal positive-negative interaction with all its ramifications, but the roles of pursuer and pursued will be reversed. English Canadian novelists will be frustrated by the disappearance of their favourite subject, the curse of their WASP puritan heritage, and will not have found anything to replace it. The Great Canadian Novel will have appeared, but the majority of Canadians will be unaware of it since it will be in French.

The computer may become the book review editor's best friend. It could provide from its vast storehouse of information the name of the person best qualified to review a certain book. And it may well be possible to program the computer in such a way that it will provide ready-made reviews for all possible fiction plots, biographies, histories, and so on.

I can predict, for example, that in 2020 a "book" will be "published" called *The Distemper of a Renegade,* by Peter C. Newman. The reviewer, merely by feeding in certain information and pressing a button, will see his review come popping out . . . "Mr. Newman's long-awaited chronicle of Pierre Trudeau's unprecedented reign — surpassed only by that of Victoria herself — lacks the youthful vigour of his earlier books. . . ."

Publishing in Canada: Its Death and Resurrection

WILLIAM READY

Publishing in Canada has developed a kind of grace under pressure, a strength through neglect, dullness and aridity. It bodes well. It has created a hunger, a need and a desire for something better. There will be a lovely stream of print spouting out of almost every conceivable spigot of an informational and inspirational terminal tap reaching a sparkling crescendo within fifty years, with drops and jewels of words, books and pictures spinning off from it like fireballs and fragments from a rooted Canadian star. And it will be Canadian all the way, as Canadian as igloo, prairie, Laurentian, Nanaimo, Trois Rivières, screech, Laval and Minnedosa. Technology will be the force behind it, harnessed technology, that is. Publishers will print what the readers want in throwaway, giveaway or more permanent form, at a cost cheaper than the over-copy that has become a bane. There will be a steadily increasing store of print on microfilm of all kinds, from which books, pamphlets, sheets can be pulled to fulfil a single need or an overall demand, and when these are done with they can be as disposable as newspapers or paper towels, or become as handsome as coffee-table books or art forms. It does not matter; the record is safe, ready to rise again into print whenever needed.

The book has been all too permanent in the past, costing too much, indisposable, indigestible, a relic rather than a reality. Times are changing fast. I have seen the death and resurrection of the book at Frankfurt Fair, and now it is happening in Toronto, in Edmonton, Montreal; the metamorphosis may come to Sudbury any day now, and to Neepawa the next. The old book is gone; people now read only what they want to, can't find anywhere else, and there is the strength of the book that is going to come out of the publishing of the next fifty years.

The times of publishing in Canada have been bad in the past, and the hardships have seeped into the present. There has been an accumulation of the power of publishing into a few hands, the cadet branches of firms across the border or over the sea, aggravated by the iniquitous practice of taxing books as they come into the country. Now, because of the new machines and the rise of learning in the land — and learning has many faces; often the best is the nonacademic and non-curricular — there has sprouted a new growth of freedom in publishing here that is in its very infancy, rising out of a com-post heap of earth, sun and snow, and it is a lusty child, this infant. Already in these baby days there are more publishing houses in Canada than ever before. Far, far more. They are growing almost by the day, meeting a need, being fed by a de-mand Canadian. The ingenuity and the know-how of the fab-ricators, the designers, the schemers, writers, artists of this new Canadian publishing cannot keep pace with the calls that are already being made upon them by readers and writers alike.

In the past we tried to establish a Random House, a Scrib-ners, an Eyre & Spottiswoode, a House of Macmillan, but we did not have the wherewithal, the know-how or the courage to evolve our own. We permitted, nay, more than that, we en-couraged these foreign firms to set up their outposts within our borders, establishments like those they have in Bombay, Ibadan, Sydney, Auckland and Capetown. They have imported a lot of books, good books too, most of them, but many Canadian submissions have been judged by these cadet branches of the founding firms in London or New York, and the result has been disastrous for Canadian publishing, writing and reading. Those few Canadian publishing houses that have survived the years have done so by playing safe, except for the few like McClelland & Stewart who have taken a chance and risked their necks.

Publishing in the old days was an expensive business. Books were a luxury item unless they were sold as texts of one kind and another at schools and universities, or had an inspirational or historical bent. But as the schools grew in number and the universities proliferated in this remarkable decade, as commu-nity colleges sprang up and adult education kept growing and growing, it seemed that the market would expand corre-spondingly. There would be even greater demand for these books with undertones of Jalna, or inspirational tales of trap-pers, missionaries, simple Indians and comic Eskimos, or barbed-wire humour of the backhouse variety.

Education, however, tends to bite the hand that feeds it and seeks its own way out of the tidy channel that the establishment has dug for it. It breeds a society of ingrates who lack compassion and turn upon their teachers, their leaders. Let education spread, and freedom proliferates. This is the main reason why any occupying power, like the Belgians in the Congo or the English in Ireland, keeps the literacy rate low and teaches from primers in approved schools with a board of inspectors checking the curriculum.

It is the spread of education that has marked the beginning of the demise of the old order of publishing in Canada. This has been accelerated by the new learning methods, by the literacy that is replacing aliteracy among the young and by the new technology which makes publishing easier and almost as small an operation, if need be, as the old hand press or the mimeographed sheets of the underground. As new copying methods, new means of typing, photography and silk screen have brought printing into the basements of houses, into the garages and tool sheds, the peculiar, immediate, insistent and diverse opinions of the new Canadian people — hitherto restrained by the cumbersome and expensive methods of old-time or far-based publishing — now find expression.

There must be hundreds of presses in Toronto now, let alone those in Edmonton, Victoria, Quebec, Montreal and other places. We are at the start of a publishing movement that in fifty years' time is going to be the most important occupation in Canada, transmitting information, opinions, ideas, arguments and philosophy in a better way than speech or even the print of today. The great danger, and it is one of which the present emerging young publishers are very well aware, is that this grand spouting fount may be taken over by the establishment. Vast industrial and technological complexes of publishing activity are now being planned so that people will have greater access to information than ever before, but in a way that will be programmed and controlled. There danger more than lurks. Already in some big educational centres, if a child needs information in order to write an essay or complete a project, all he has to do is ask for it and a computer centre will spill out the relevant information — relevant, that is, in the opinion of the Ringwraiths with M.B.A.'s.

Somehow or other, the big machines have to be controlled,

or the texts, the news, the information will be as geared as ever, and we shall not be free — or, worse, we shall not know it.

Inside the Machine for Living

ROSS MENDES

I remember how important cars were considered in the sixties. At that time economists stated that the financial health of the country depended on the number of new car units sold. Only the young programmers maintained that the amount of paper production was a surer indicator.

In the late sixties and early seventies highways were built at enormous cost and at furious rates. To reduce the rather spectacular accidents, all roads became one way. But the number of vehicles on the roads doubled in five short years and accidents increased steadily. And no wonder, when a man travelled in a metal container, sitting bolt upright with a steering wheel pointing at his chest, looking through a curved sheet of glass.

In the winter of 1974, after a thirteen-hour traffic jam which stretched for thirty-six miles, communities began to outlaw toxic internal combustion engines. Everyone had grown tired of the eye-irritating, air-clouding hydrocarbons and oxide of nitrogen. City areas began to charge several dollars for one-hour parking at meters. And then all street parking was prohibited. Convenient free hover rafts, which sped around the downtown core, were introduced and became very popular. As cars were scrapped, hover trains took over the abandoned freeways.

Then came the exodus from city offices, as firms paid employees to have read-out and input units installed in their homes. People no longer had to travel to work at all. The head offices of businesses were in the hundred-storey computer centre, and old office blocks were converted into apartments. All mail delivery had stopped some years before as all addresses were linked by television cable. The initial protests died down when people could buy private scramblers for love letters and such. (I am still late in sending birthday greetings, so not everything has changed.)

I am ninety-one now and live alone, with a student-servant. My housecraft can moor anywhere there is a cable link. I am a painter with nothing to do now but amuse myself. My passion, I am almost ashamed to confess, is to paint landscapes. My work area is a viewing console activated by coloured light, and only if I am truly satisfied do I take what might be termed a full-colour print on light-sensitive raw canvas. Now, I never go out. There is no furniture to speak of, but when I have guests the rug over a special floor can be convoluted to form sitting or lounging pockets by compressed air. Most of my time is spent working. I read a great deal and go north in the summer.

The student is a teenage apprentice who wants to become a painter. He is my first direct contact with the results of the children's towns. These were begun as safety areas, for there were no open flames, vehicles or pollution of any kind allowed in the town areas. The children were sent to live in communities of various persuasions. In some, to learn concepts, they never ate or slept in the same place twice. The game of schooling and living was to decipher from various clues where food or shelter might be found. ("Shelter" is perhaps rather an old-fashioned word to use, as these transparent domed environments needed no walls at all.) The parents, who no longer left home to work, seemed to welcome these perpetual camps for their children.

At thirteen the young people could be apprenticed, go to a university town or join an experimental community on Baffin Island, or a space station. Some enrolled in the various children's crusades. One army was irrigating the Sahara; another lived on the seabed, and yet another crusade was helping India to cope with its epidemic of diseases.

Our newspapers now are printed out from the television set, which is flat as a mirror and the size of a large painting. The print-out can also deliver books at four thousand words a minute. Another adaptation produces home holography, that is, simulated three-dimensional photographic transmission. About the same time as the cars went under, the cinemas closed down. However, many movie houses were converted to hologram theatres. These "ghost" theatres, as they were called, operated with film, lasers and mirrors and appeared to be completely live.

The wave of emigrants from Europe in the eighties went to

the new towns in the Northwest Territories. Made of plastic, the houses were inflated and heated by a compact blower unit. At first, because of the shortage of water, the high-frequency sound vibrator was developed to wash dishes and clothes. Eventually a large solar station was erected to take advantage of snow glare for power and water. These inexpensive and quickly erected houses were developed originally for the teems of China, because they could be put up without foundations.

Toronto is much quieter today than it was in the seventies. The superjet aerospaceport floats out in Lake Ontario. Noise, being interpreted as waste energy, has virtually been eliminated. Magnetic typing doesn't make a sound. Even telephones no longer ring but flash lights. With the cars gone and the children in camps, the one last hum is conversation, live and recorded.

All my art books are on film, but actual-size painting re-productions in full colour and texture have become as popular as pop music was in the seventies. Golden palettes are award-ed to the artists for over two million sales. This, and visual concerts, have given artists a new burst of life since the nineties. For the concerts, the audience sits around a huge perspex tank full of water, lighted from below. During the concert the artist, through invisible tubes in the tank, releases various colours, controlling them by chemicals and plastic paddles. Ambient valves sensitive to light and hue produce verbal or musical sounds on the amplifiers to create what is called "water" art. The one in front of City Hall was done in liquid acrylic and set solid by a catalyst. Various other experiments of trying to freeze reflections in mercury by electricity have not been suc-cessful.

Philosophical questions today come directly from computer programming. Perhaps our most popular book in this area is *The Philosophy of Not.* This stems from the binary structure And/Or/Not. The first two principles involve alternatives based on dualism: night-day, man-woman, life-death. We now reject these as being limiting. In the sixties and seventies many ar-tists worked on the belief of error as opportunity. We now actively explore tacit assumptions. For example, if parents feel they must take care of their children, we experiment with par-ents not taking care of them. If we assume furniture and walls are necessary, we then explore their absence. Thus, if we think men's lives are finite, we propose that perhaps they are not.

Medicine has made great advances in the last half century. Five years ago I became blind, but I suffered no disability once a small colour camera had been attached to my brain (in the manner that artificial limbs are now fixed). Then, three years later, I had to undergo a lung transplant. As the operation was extremely critical for one of my age, my complete memory and nervous-system patterns were transferred to magnetic tape and stored so that, in the event of failure, I might not have to go and study the geology of holy ground.

About that time a British mathematician established the criterion of whether a machine could actually think. If a prolonged conversation could be carried on with a machine, without any distinction being apparent between its replies and those of a man, then the machine was thinking by any sensible definition.

Dear reader, the operation failed.

From Tranquility, via Florence

VINCENT TOVELL

> When Love inspires me with delight
> Or pain, or longing, I take careful note,
> And as he dictates in my soul, I write.
>
> *Dante*

There's a room in Michelangelo's city where his time is, still, in Carrara marble. DAVID at one end, the giant-boy, to be approached along a file of aching slaves and a final, heartbroken, PIETA. Here, against confounding age, stand pride, terror and pity, the ruins of the Renaissance. Here, exactly, is mirrored the egoist revolution the corporate conspirators made, Medicis, della Roveras and the rest; they, with their backs to Dante, and we, still in their spell.

. . .*it's looking good to us.* . .

And here we are, in Carrara, graceless in our mortal rage.

. . .*we've got a lift-off and you're looking great.*

Twisting inward, in on ourself, in an agony of spirit too swollen now to pass through the needle's eye. Spell-stopped.

> My ending is despair
> Unless I be relieved by prayer
> Which pierces so, that it assaults
> Mercy itself, and frees all faults.

Leonardo, they say, would buy birds in the markets and set them free.

Roger. Copy. Out.

But Leonardo, the scholar points out, did not want to cure men; he wanted to know how their bodies are made and work.

(what is this quintessence of dust?)

Later, he went away from Florence and on to France, to die.

Florence Nightingale was born in Florence. She too was an artist-revolutionary, but curing with her armies of statistics and her nanny morals which made us rethink vanity, pride and hate. Out of the city of Savonarola and Botticelli a quite unexpected Venus.

>. . .*that's one small step for a man, one*
>*giant leap for mankind.*

In France, Leonardo had prayed:

>tell me if anything at all was done
>tell me if anything at all was done

>. . .*that's affirmative.*

Leonardo said:

>How and why I do not describe my method
>of remaining underwater . . . this I do not
>publish or divulge because of the evil
>nature of men who would practise assassi-
>nations at the bottom of the seas.*

---

* *The Notebooks of Leonardo da Vinci*, ed. and trans. Edward MacCurdy, 2 vols. (London and New York, 1955), reprinted in J. Bronowski, "Leonardo da Vinci," *The Horizon Book of the Renaissance*, gen. ed. Richard M. Ketchum (New York, 1961), pp. 192, 197.

Apollo was, sometimes, a god of civilization. He's a Trinity now, veiled in hardware. Weightless.

The Florentines had carried their Apollo, DAVID, through the streets (about eighteen tons) to the piazza on the thrust of cheering crowds (Leonardo was there, seeing), but they later hit him on his left arm while they were rioting or something so it was thought best that he be carried out of the piazza again to a safer place, indoors, away from mobs. (A copy was set up for tourists to be satisfied by unless of course they felt like going a bit out of their way to see what Michelangelo had really had in his exact mind.)

When Michelangelo imagined DAVID he could not — as yet — have known what was in Leonardo's exact mind.

"Creatures shall be seen upon the earth who
will always be fighting one with another
with very great losses and frequent deaths
on either side. These shall set no bounds
to their malice; by their fierce limbs a
great number of the trees in the immense
forests of the world shall be laid level
with the ground; and when they have
crammed themselves with food it shall
gratify their desire to deal out death,
affliction, labours, terrors and banishment
to every living thing. And by reason of
their boundless pride they shall wish to
rise towards heaven, but the excessive weight
of their limbs shall hold them down. There
shall be nothing remaining on the earth or
under the earth or in the waters that shall
not be pursued and molested and destroyed . . .
O Earth! What delays thee to open and hurl
them headlong into the deep fissures of thy
huge abysses and caverns, and no longer to
display in the sight of heaven so savage
and ruthless a monster?"

The EAGLE has landed!

Be free, and fare thou well!

(what is this quintessence of moon dust?)

But the eagle we know is a vanishing species.

Beauty, Truth, and rarity,
Grace in all simplicity,
Here enclosed in cinders lie.

Truth may seem, but cannot be;
Beauty brag, but 'tis not she;
Truth and Beauty buried be.

To this urn let those repair
That are either true or fair
For these dead birds, sigh a prayer.

Roger, Tranquility. No sweat. We'll figure it out somehow.

PART VIII.   CONTEXTS:
our moving history

KENNETH McNAUGHT
**253   The Future of the
Winnipeg General Strike**

CARL BERGER
**257   A Canadian Utopia: The Cooperative
Commonwealth of Edward Partridge**

MICHIEL HORN
**263   Visionaries of the 1930s:
The League for Social Reconstruction**

DONALD EVANS
268   One Step Enough

overleaf "Reflection for Kaz" *by Harold Town*

Letter to Kyra (*cont'd.*)

The new technology may control the physical environment in which we grow into the next century; the past forms our psychic environment in an equally decisive way. Generals train for their next war by fighting the battles of the last. Politicians make policy to resolve problems already made obsolete by more urgent issues. Are we all condemned to see the future through a rear-view mirror? If our past is to serve us creatively in constructing our futures, then it has to be a history made relevant to interpret our present.

This may not be as difficult as it sounds. As Ken Mc-Naught shows, the reinterpretation of history – in his example the Winnipeg Strike of 1919 – is conditioned by our changing perspective of the present and hopes for the future. He asks how then our future will shape our past. It is equally important to know how our view of the past will shape our attitudes towards the future. Canadians have never had a generally accepted utopia to mould their view of the future, though there have been Canadians with utopias. What may appear to historian Carl Berger as a dreary and totalitarian utopia in Edward Partridge's egalitarian and morally pure society may turn out by 2020 to be an attractive formula for a pure communal life to your children's children. Another utopia, more humane and within easier grasp, was that of the League for Social Reconstruction. Michiel Horn's analysis of its program should make interesting reading in 2020. Seen from 1970, the LSR appears as the nuclear group of political activists whose vision of radical change through the existing political institutions has inspired social reformers for forty years, including its reincarnation, the University League for Social Reform.

What has been the predictive power of this compendium will be very clear to you by your fifty-first birthday when you can assess our futures as your history. But the value of these visions does not depend on the fulfilment of their predictions. On the contrary, as theologian Don-

ald Evans points out, the whole objective of biblical prophecy is to provoke man to react to the warning in time to be saved from the holocaust. If we are, in his words, to be "responsible sojourners" in the ever-changing present," our daily individual and collective choices must be inspired by the warning nightmares and hopeful daydreams of our fifty visionaries.

The Future of the Winnipeg General Strike

KENNETH MCNAUGHT

Fifty years after the Winnipeg Strike and the founding of the *Forum,* Canadians are busily talking about their system of political communications and the quality of their group life. The result of this reassessment will not be any final answer, but it will rule the next fifty years pretty surely. And while much of the current debate is in terms which seem alien to our past (should we confront, dialogue, relate or be relevant?), in fact, much of the debate is about the meaning of our past.

Thus, the manner in which we made a federal state, our relationship to the "Democratic Revolution" and to Europe thereafter, the stages and reasons for our drift into continentalism, the meaning of Riel, of Sifton, of Bourassa, the impact of industrialism — all are open to revision. Moreover, each revisionist, almost in proportion to his protests to the contrary, writes with a sharp eye to the present and future. One need only look at the way in which the Laurentian, centralist interpretation of Confederation in the 1930s culminated in the Rowell-Sirois Report, and the way in which the let's-understand-Quebec trend in historical writing in the sixties culminated in the B and B Report, to see how the present and future dominate history. One can talk about the future of the bourgeoisie of New France and the future of the Winnipeg Strike with complete assurance that the research questions we ask about them will be framed very largely by our changing perspectives on the present and our hopes of the future.

I won't play Galbraith by pretending that this view of things is a brave attack on the conventional wisdom. For the fact is that everyone knows these things about the purposes of our history because they have always been the purposes of history; what is unconventional is to defend the opposite view, which sees history as an objective study of what really happened — unblinkered by present purposes. The real question is: *how* will the future shape our past?

For the strike, as for other crucial passages in Canadian history, the search for evidence continues. But the ground rules for judging the old and the new "facts" shift almost year by year, as they have been doing ever since the spring of 1919. Most historians in the post – Red Scare years of the 1920s and the uneasy years of the depression found it tempting to stress the triumph of constituted authority in the face of a country-wide Bolshevik revolutionary conspiracy — and the temptation (except in the pages of the *Forum*) was seldom resisted. In the postdepression years of the forties, under the impact of a newly vigorous labour unionism, the growing appeal of some form of social democracy and a healthy wish to escape the dangers of authoritarian repression of progressive social movements, the strike acquired a very different quality. The old orthodoxy collapsed under a barrage composed of newly researched evidence and of new purposes.

The new purposes, of course, included the principal end of "understanding" the strike. But, as always, to understand meant to make comprehensible to the present — in the sense that the present grew out of the past and would govern the future. Thus the strike in the forties and fifties became a legitimate, almost inevitable response to industrialism and to the domination of the West by the East. It was discovered, happily, that the strike had not been led by alien Bohunks and "Uk-erainians" but by British-born Canadian citizens; that its organization had been almost spontaneous (against a background of general unrest occasioned by severe resistance to labour's efforts to organize industrially) and that its immediate goals of higher wages and the right to collective bargaining were its "real" causes. Bolshevik conspiracy as a part of the strike's causation was rejected and evidence that had always been readily available (in response to the questions when they were asked) was used with telling effect. The official Robson Report, issued as part of the agreement by which the strike was ended, had spelled out the essentials of the revised version twenty years before but did not become a part of our "history" until the interpretative assumptions and questions were changed.

In the revision of the 1940s and 1950s, most people concluded that the causes of North America's most effective general strike were just. They also came close to agreeing on two other points of interpretation. The first point was that while the strike leadership succeeded almost beyond belief in its declared methods of nonviolence, the very nature of a general strike, which completely halts economic life and which, by implication, assumes governmental powers, is such that it could not and never would be permitted to succeed. The second point of more-or-less general agreement is really an extension of the first. Whatever conspiracy did occur during the strike was to be found in the ranks of businessmen and government. The major violence was engineered by businessmen and politicians, both in Ottawa and in Winnipeg, because they had to have the violence in order to use the full military-judicial power of the state to crush the strike. Finally, a subsidiary point of interpretative agreement emerged: while the suppression of the strike severely impeded progress in labour organization and legislation, the lessons for labour bore fruit in the fledgling labour parties and culminated in the founding of the CCF. Thus the major legacy of the strike was the Canadian tradition of labour political action in a multi- rather than a two-party system — and of action with a legitimized socialist content.

Well, how long will this version last, and what new research questions might modify or upset it? Already significant shifts of emphasis are on foot, and one may easily imagine the further questions to be asked. The concert of power that suppressed the strike was even more tightly organized and purposeful than had previously been supposed. There is fresh evidence to show that the Citizens' Committee, which seemed to coordinate anti-strike action, was itself coordinated (if not originated) by the military commander of the district. In future analysis it is likely that the question of Ottawa's role and the relationship of the business-political élite to that role will come more closely into focus. That is, the interaction between newly researched evidence and present-minded concerns will continue to dominate interpretation. Thus we may expect historians to pay a lot more attention to the role of provincial and municipal governments in the strike, as they also contemplate a developing potential for such governments today as initiators of social change and as checks on the power that Ottawa can put at the disposal of "political capitalists."

But the most important shift of interpretative emphasis will be towards the methods and implications of the strike. The received conclusion that a general strike is an unacceptable method (in *any* circumstances) of seeking change will likely be questioned; the nature of the democracy of that half of Winnipeg which endorsed the strike, which implemented nonviolent mass action and which was "politicized" by the experience will undoubtedly receive close attention; the inhibitory influence of American labour leaders and the possible influence of American business-Progressive thought upon Canadian political capitalists will certainly be investigated.

As different features of the strike become more prominent in future examination, the overriding debate is likely to be about the methods of social change: the validity of "confrontation politics," of nonviolence and of the political party. No doubt the *Forum* will watch the results of new research and take part in the discussion of possible conclusions. And whatever changes occur in our vision of the past, we can be sure that they will reflect our experience of the future.

A Canadian Utopia: The Cooperative Commonwealth of Edward Partridge

CARL BERGER

The Canadian West has bred many visions and has been the setting of many utopian experiments. It began as a place that existed only in the minds of men who had never seen it and its history has been punctuated by the messianic dreams of Louis Riel, the activities of the Doukhobor chiliasts and the communal orders, truly not of this world, of the Hutterian brethren. Only one of the many visionary impulses for a new society, however, found expression in a genuinely utopian book. This was Edward Partridge's *A War on Poverty*, which was published in Winnipeg in 1926 and foretold the establishment of a cooperative commonwealth in an independent West. It is a cranky, eccentric book, the product of one of those folksy philosophers who held forth in those innumerable country stores at wind-swept crossroads; it has no literary merit, and its nostrums now appear as quaint as the advertisements for magical liniments which were its accompanying period pieces. Appearing at an arid time for Canadian radicalism, the year in which the once-proud National Progressive party collapsed, its impact was negligible. But it is one of the very few Canadian contributions to the genre of utopian writing and it casts a cold light on the general style and paradoxes of utopian thinking.

It takes a special kind of mind to draw up the specifications of a utopian community, and Partridge certainly was a remarkable individual. Born in 1862 in Huron County, Ontario, he had farmed near Sintaluta, a town about fifty miles east of Regina, and had been the first president of the farmers' marketing organization, the Grain Growers' Company, and the editor, at least for its first issue, of that bible of agrarian radicalism, the *Grain Growers' Guide*. A peevish and irascible person, he was recognized in the farmers' movement as an impractical and loquacious idealist. Six feet tall and heavy set, with blue eyes and a handle-bar moustache, he had lost a foot

in a farm accident and walked with a heavy limp. A support-
er of the Progressive party, he grew disillusioned with its pow-
erlessness to find a political solution to agrarian grievances;
a pioneer of grain growers' cooperative enterprises, he grew
convinced that the cooperation of special-interest groups would
never eliminate wasteful competition. Only the total transformation of society, the inauguration of the Cooperative
Commonwealth could achieve that. Two years after Partridge
died of gas asphyxiation in a room in Victoria in 1931, a new
political party was founded to carry out the task.

Judging by the citations in his book, the sources of Partridge's thought were eclectic — a bewildering mélange of,
among others, William Wordsworth, Thomas Carlyle, John Rus-
kin, William Morris, J. S. Mill, Sidney Webb, H. G. Wells,
Bertrand Russell, Herbert Spencer, Pope Leo XIII, Count
Tolstoy, the American monetary crank "Coin" Harvey, the
book of Isaiah, "a work by Melvin L. Severy — *Gillette's
Social Redemption*," and the platform of the British Labour
party. To these were added more native founts of inspiration.
Every cliché and stereotype of the western progressive tradition
found its way into his book and these predetermined the structure of his utopia. Nature was beneficent and rich, poverty
the result of exploitation. Society, he wrote, "is divided into
those who produce and do not possess, and those who possess
and do not produce. . . ." Capitalist society was simply an organization for the systematic robbery of the real creators of
wealth — the farmers and the workers — by others. Partridge
learned his Canadian history from Gustavus Meyers and Edward Porritt, and he saw it as an all-embracing and sinister
conspiracy. "The history of Canada since Confederation — the
outcome of a politico-commercial . . . conspiracy . . . —
has been a history of the heartless robbery of both the people
of the Maritimes and the Prairie Sections of Canada by the
Big Vested Interests . . . of the politically and financially
stronger Central Provinces." Confederation was an engine of
injustice and Canada itself too unwieldy and complex a place
for genuine reform. The precondition for the inauguration of the
cooperative state was the secession of the West. The creation
of the Cooperative Commonwealth, with production carried on
for use, not profit, was in strict accordance with the main

dogmas of "Christ's Creed." The Kingdom of Heaven on earth, the sanction that the social gospel brought to progressivism, was given a peculiar twist by Partridge. He believed in the reincarnation of the soul, the doctrine that the "Immutable Ego," as he called it, persists through many incarnations on earth. This conviction provided the moral underpinning of the cooperative society, for it stimulated people to conduct themselves in this life in such a way as to make the world a better place to which their Egos would return again and again. Should this not overcome undue hesitancy in forcing everyone to work and harmonize self-interest with community interest, there was, of course, compulsion: "He that will not work, neither shall he eat."

With the exception of the belief in reincarnation, there was nothing novel about Partridge's axioms — the ceaseless war between the producers and the exploiters or the conspiratorial theory of history or the sharp sense of western separatism. Partridge went beyond the repetition of these tattered clichés of agrarian rhetoric to present a vision of an alternate society. We can only realize a better world, he wrote, if we have in our minds some mental picture of the kind of society we want to build. Conceived with this in mind, Partridge endowed his place of perfection with definite geographical dimensions and social and political institutions.

The independent and autonomous state occupies the territory between the 49th and 60th parallels from Lake Superior to the Pacific. Its name is Coalsamao, formed from the first two letters of the names of the western provinces with the "o" representing a section of Ontario. The guiding principles of this country are that human rights must take precedence over property rights and that production, distribution and exchange must be carried on to satisfy human wants, not to make a profit. Natural resources, including farmlands, are owned by the state, the previous possessors having been expropriated and compensated. Laws relating to rent, debt, mortgages, contracts and the collection of interest exist no longer. Since the main purpose of production is now to feed, clothe and shelter the citizens of utopia, foreign trade is insignificant and incidental. The commonwealth is free of those bugbears that haunted the indignant agrarian imagination: there are no lawyers, landlords or

businessmen, no shortages of capital, no railway, shipping or
marketing problems, no grain-exchange gambling. Once poverty is abolished, simply by liquidating those agencies through
which the owners robbed the producers, class conflicts are eliminated and comparative economic equality has resolved all
social tensions.

The social unit of the harmonious commonwealth is the
"camp," a suburban community containing between thirty five
hundred and seven thousand inhabitants. These camps are
governed by elected boards of control and they are as economically self-supporting as possible. The general overseeing
power, identical with the state, is the High Court of Control,
consisting of twenty-five members elected annually and bound
by a written constitution which can be altered only at the request of at least one quarter of the camps and then ratified
by a plebiscite. Though the High Court deals with problems of
intercamp and foreign relations, its function is administrative rather than legislative. The initiative for legislation comes
from the camps: each camp elects "delegates" to a "regional
rally" at which questions are raised and remedies suggested
by petition. There are twenty-five regional rallies and each
elects one member to the High Court. The state functions
through ten administrative departments, headed by members
of the High Court and staffed by "experts" (Partridge's respect for experts exceeded even his love of gadgets), and its
authority is in fact immense. It is the source of capital and of
development policies, and it "assumes responsibility for the
hygienic, moral, cultural and vocational training of the young,
the comfort of the aged and incapacitated, and for medical and surgical care for all."

Standardization, uniformity and control are the central features of life in Partridge's utopia. "Standardization," he says,
"is carried to the greatest lengths. . . ." The population is
"grouped scientifically in model communities"; each camp has
its "proper quota" of residences; houses are made from the
same material and, though they are not necessarily of the same
design, all furnishings and utensils are identical. They are
equipped with the same conveniences — "radio, phone, electric light, central heating system, hard and soft water, sewage
disposal." Everyone has a car, presumably of the same model.

Everyone enjoys the same social, educational and recreational opportunities. All transportation, farming and manufacturing equipment is standardized; even the language has been simplified by the adoption of phonetic spelling. The disappearance of classes has led to the end of distinctions in dress; all clothes are the same in cut and quality. The citizens of the commonwealth, the "Army of the Good," wear "uniforms that serve to indicate that the wearers belong to the same socio-economic organization." Since each woman now enjoys economic security she is no longer "dependent on making herself sexually attractive to some male possessed of wealth sufficient to supply her needs. . . ."

Education is the foundation of the whole edifice. It was through education that the Cooperative Commonwealth would come into being, and education would perpetuate it. Coalsamao was created not by violence, but by the popular will impelled by the realization of the solidarity of human interests. Partridge looked forward to a group of "dominant elements," the rich and well-born with a sense of *noblesse oblige,* who would change the school system so that it would become the major factor in creating the new society. Once established, the survival of utopia depended upon the kind of instruction imparted to the young. Education in utopia is practical and vocational, concerned with "bread-and-butter" matters. Scientific agriculture is taught in the fields, animal husbandry in the stables and mechanics in the machine shops. The intellectuals, who had once served the predatory forces, are civil servants, administrators and teachers in the new dispensation. This aristocracy of ability is "recruited under direction of the State from those exhibiting the required aptitudes under test." The role of teachers is to "expound the gospel of peace and goodwill, and the creed of Co-operation carried to the logical limit where there is no cleavage of interest whatever. . . ," and the values inculcated are kindness, a love of justice, preference for collectivism over individualism, and morality, especially morality. The sexes are instructed separately, the boys taught by men, the girls by mature matrons. While a complete frankness governs the teaching of physiology and sex hygiene, "every precaution is taken to insure that perversions of these are not practiced, and that sexual desire is

not stimulated by conversation, reading, dramatic representation, or improper bodily contact, as in dancing."

Partridge's utopia may be regarded as embodying different things — a nostalgic hankering after some vanished past
when a high degree of homogeneity and unanimity of opinion prevailed, or as revealing the totalitarian implications of
populism, or as a rendition of agrarian progressivism in so
exaggerated a fashion that it recoiled upon itself and became
a caricature and criticism of the very ideas he championed. It
may also be seen as an example of the paradox of the re-
formist impulse employing the utopia mode. The central ambiguity of that style of thought is that the price of social solidarity is the elimination of uniqueness; the absence of tension is accompanied by the loss of liberty and the freedom from the
past is achieved through uniformity and dreariness. Partridge's
utopia is as good an example as any other of the pitfalls of
projecting ideal commonwealths. His war on poverty begins in
humanitarian outrage and ends with the "rule of the Right-
minded," an existence as joyless as that of the barracks, and
life perpetually at war with human nature.

Visionaries of the 1930s: The League for Social Reconstruction

Before the 1930s few Canadian "middle-class" intellectuals were seriously critical of their society or proposed radical changes in it. The coming of the depression considerably increased their number. During 1931 several academics and other professional men — among them Harry Cassidy, Eugene Forsey, King Gordon, Eric Havelock, Joseph Parkinson and, above all, Frank Scott and Frank Underhill — set to work in Toronto and Montreal to form the organization which "went public" in the early spring of 1932 as the League for Social Reconstruction. Its self-assigned tasks were to criticize capitalism in its mature "monopoly" stage — inefficient, disruptive of peace, destructive and inherently inequitable — and, according to the LSR *Manifesto*, to work "for the establishment in Canada of a social order in which the basic principles regulating production, distribution and service will be the common good rather than private profit."

A book intended to mark the fiftieth anniversary of the *Canadian Forum* owes something to the LSR, because the *Forum* was about to disappear when, in May 1936, the league's national executive decided to buy it and preserve it as a mouthpiece for democratic socialist opinion. With money from its own treasury and substantial sums donated by two well-to-do members, the LSR managed to keep the journal alive until, after 1938, the Sustaining Fund came to defray the persistent annual deficits. LSR members continued to edit and publish the *Forum* even after the league itself quietly expired early in 1942, a victim of the conflicting demands made by the LSR and CCF upon the time of the many members who belonged to both, and of the dispersal of energies brought about by World War II. More basically, perhaps, it was a victim of the declining interest in Canada in Left radical proposals from 1935 to 1942.

The LSR had a composite vision of what Canada — and the world — might look like in the future. League members

denied that they were sketching the outline of some distant "utopia": the cooperative commonwealth could be secured within
years and by conventional political means. "A civilization is
within our reach in which we shall no longer exploit each other.
It calls for no more honesty and ability than are already available in Canada. We *have* the men." The words are from
Social Planning for Canada, the most important statement of
LSR views.

Public education and propaganda, political organization,
the ballot box and legislative action: through these ran the
road to the new social order. The only revolution required
was ethical, the replacement of "the acquisitive and individualistic values" of capitalist society by "the more humane,
just and equitable standards of a cooperative commonwealth."
This revolution would come with the increased enlightenment
which education produced and would find its earliest expression
in acts reforming social welfare, labour relations, monetary
and fiscal policy and so forth. The Cooperative Commonwealth Federation, led by the league's honourary president,
J. S. Woodsworth, and equipped at the Regina Convention
(1933) with a manifesto and program largely of LSR making,
became the obvious political instrument for social reconstruction.

What would the new social order look like? There would be
social ownership of most of the means of production and distribution, including the machinery of banking and investment,
public utilities, natural resources generally and all industries
approaching a condition of monopoly. Agriculture and many
small business enterprises, however, would remain in the private sector although they would be subject to government regulation. No objection to personal private property existed
except insofar as it gave its owners the power to exploit their
fellow citizens and to subvert democratic government.

An approximate equality of income and wealth would prevail, and every man would receive at least enough to enable
him and his family to live at an acceptable level and avail
themselves of vastly increased educational opportunities and
other cultural benefits. Comprehensive social welfare services
would be available to all working people and their families
as well as to the aged and infirm. But egalitarianism had its

limits. "A limited differentiation may quite equitably be retained whether as a stimulus or as a recognition of efficiency and contribution." A range of annual incomes from $1,200 to $10,000 (1935 values) would not be inconsistent with that social democracy which would become possible after the elimination of gross inequalities of wealth and economic power, and thus of class conflict, between a small exploiting group of capitalists and the great mass of exploited Canadians.

There would be strong central direction of the economy combined with a large measure of local participation in economic decision making and decentralized administration. Central planning, including import and export boards, would enable Ottawa to deal effectively with all matters which had a nationwide significance. But centralization was a potential threat to legitimate provincial and local concerns and even to democracy itself. The National Planning Commission, a thinking and coordinating body consisting of experts, would enjoy a good deal of latitude in developing plans for the approval of Parliament. But the commission would base its plan on the submissions which came from many organizations across the country. These might include producers' and consumers' cooperatives, labour unions and joint management-worker councils in enterprises both public and private. Through these and through provincial and municipal governments, which would also retain important legislative and administrative functions, the people would participate directly and actively in the shaping of their society. And as one result there would be optimum scope for diversity, initiative and experimentation, without which the commonwealth would become a dull and stagnant place.

Somehow, then, central direction and local participation would co-exist within a generally harmonious and efficient whole. That this was possible was a belief which owed a good deal to the LSR's faith in expertise, but even more to its assumption that man was or had evolved into a being capable of beneficence and cooperation and was rational enough to recognize that in the modern world these qualities would serve him best. Hence human beings could create a society largely free from group conflict and disruptive forms of social deviation. All legitimate desires for individuality — to use French in Canada, for example — could find expression in the new social order. Those desires for individuality which ran foul of the principle of cooperation would in due time all but disappear.

Liberty, equality, fraternity and efficiency (the optimum use of limited resources): each of these values depended for its realization on the presence of the others. Each, at the same time, would to some extent limit the others. Which of the four was the greatest? The LSR was not altogether explicit on this point, but most of its members would probably have chosen fraternity.

The LSR held that a good start could be made on building the new social order in Canada alone, though a few of its publicists sometimes wondered what the United States might do if it remained capitalist while this country went socialist. Most league members believed throughout the thirties that no good and considerable harm would come from Canadian involvement in the affairs of the British Empire, troubled Europe and the Far East. Therefore they devoted much attention to the problems of Canadian independence and sovereignty.

But, while they believed Canada could hardly set the world straight, they were not isolationists for isolation's sake. They saw that the cooperative commonwealth would have to be worldwide to be completely workable. Men of goodwill could do much within a single country, but the problems of international conflict, foreign trade and the maldistribution of income and wealth among nations would be resolved only if democratic socialism triumphed around the globe and a genuine world federation came into existence.

The LSR vision is attractive: the achievement of social harmony without the loss either of regional distinctions or of all personal liberty is a goal which an intelligent and sensitive man may prize. But LSR publicists are open to the charge that they underestimated the strength of opposition to their programs and misunderstood the hostility to their wider vision. And the question remains whether the cooperative commonwealth is at all attainable or whether it is at bottom little more than a reflection of the wish to have one's libertarian cake and cooperatively eat it too.

All the same, since the thirties something closely akin to the LSR vision has helped to inspire and sustain many Canadian social democrats. The league, furthermore, was very important in the enunciation of CCF doctrine and policies, and while it is impossible to prove that the evolution of the Canadian welfare state has been the result solely or even largely of LSR/CCF publications and pressure — there were other social critics and reformers in this country — we may safely assign them a major part in the creation of that state. This is not the New Jerusalem nor even the cooperative commonwealth, but it is easily preferable to what existed during the years between the two world wars.

One Step Enough   DONALD EVANS

". . . I do not ask to see
The distant scene, — one step enough for me."

You're right, John Henry Newman. What was for you an im-
piety to ask is also an imbecility to attempt. *Visions 2020* is
focused on a very distant scene, as remote as the beatific vision.
Only one ironic prediction seems feasible: perhaps in the year
2020 the *Canadian Forum* will celebrate its hundredth anniversary by publishing a book called *Revisions 2020*, revising
the generally disproven predictions of *Visions 2020* so as to
fit the facts of history.

In an age when the one certainty is unpredictable change,
how could any sane person contribute to *Visions 2020*? Only
by writing, in the guise of prediction, something which is not
prediction. In biblical times, that's what the prophets and ap-
ocalyptists did. The prophet warned about what would happen
unless the people repented. His interest was in evoking re-
pentance, in falsifying his own prediction. And even if the people did not repent, and no catastrophe followed, he could say
that God in his mercy had given them a reprieve. The apocalyptist, sensitive to the fears and aspirations and crises of his
own day, projected these in imaginative fantasies upon a vast
panoramic screen, a cosmic cinemascope, depicting a grand
climax for human history.

The modern prophet is a man of social concern who warns
us about what may happen unless we do something to prevent
it. The modern apocalyptist, with the uninhibited exaggera-
tion and vividness of fantasy, clarifies for us some of the ob-
scure but powerful forces in our society and our psyches today.
In each case the real focus of vision is not in the future but in
the present. The prophet who produced *The War Game* is
trying to prod us into action now, and the apocalyptist who
produced *2001* is trying to deepen our awareness of what is
happening now. We realize this, and are not deceived. Similarly,
no one need be deceived by *Visions 2020*, provided he looks
on the predictions as a device, a transparent disguise.

But there is a danger that people may take predictions at their face value. Since we realize, deep down, that our future is radically uncertain, we have a desperate craving for knowledge of the future which can reduce our sense of insecurity. If we don't know what is coming, how can we prepare for it and cope with it? And in our society there is a widespread concern to be "with it," to swim with the stream of history towards its destination. Or, to change the metaphor, if we cannot claim, "I am the locomotive of history" (as Khrushchev once allegedly did), we can at least hope to get on board if our life is to have meaning. But to get on board, we need to know where history is going. And this we don't know.

As a pioneer jazz player once said, "If I knew where jazz was going I'd be there already." And as a newspaper notice allegedly said, "Due to unforeseen circumstances the meeting of the Society of Seers, scheduled for next Tuesday, will not be held."

The search for seers goes on, but what we need is what the prophet and apocalyptist provide in the guise of predictions — moral exhortation and imaginative understanding in relation to what is going on *now*. And predictions may get in the way of this. Perhaps the population explosion will have stopped by 2020 or even by 1980; perhaps not. What we know is that right now it is causing great suffering and that unless something is done about it, this suffering is likely to increase. Perhaps there will be a nuclear war by 2020 or even by 1980; perhaps not. The important thing is to do what we can now to prevent it. Perhaps most of our affairs in 2001 will depend more on computers than on decisions of individuals; perhaps not. But right now we need to be critically aware of the influential role of computers in everything from the day-to-day conduct of the war in Vietnam to the planning of academic curricula in universities. Perhaps North American religion in 2020 will be a major force in the creation of genuinely therapeutic communities which radically improve the mental health of people; perhaps not. What matters is the promotion, right now, of such badly needed communities. Perhaps the structure of Canadian society in 2020 will have been so drastically changed that the concept of "participatory democracy" has been woven into the very fabric of all its major institutions; perhaps not. The question that matters is what can be done now to increase the extent to which people in various institutions can participate in decisions concerning matters which directly affect them.

"One step enough for me." This does not rule out contingency planning, or predictions which are tentative, short range and constantly revised. Nor does it ignore our need for a vision of what a better life *might* be. What it does stress is the sense of the significance of the single step. For Newman, this had an explicitly religious expression:

"Keep Thou my feet; I do not ask to see
The distant scene, — one step enough for me."

To take one step we do not need 20/20 vision. All we need is the ability to walk, a sense of direction and a conviction that the step is worth taking even though we do not foresee our destination. For Newman, the conviction was explicitly religious. For others it is implicitly religious — they presuppose a context of meaning and purpose which goes beyond what they can know or clearly conceive.

The point to human life is not to foresee the year 2020, but to forestall some disasters in 1971 and to live creatively now. It is not to be "with it" but to *be*, in each moment. It is not to be the vanguard of the future, but the responsible sojourners in an ever-changing present.

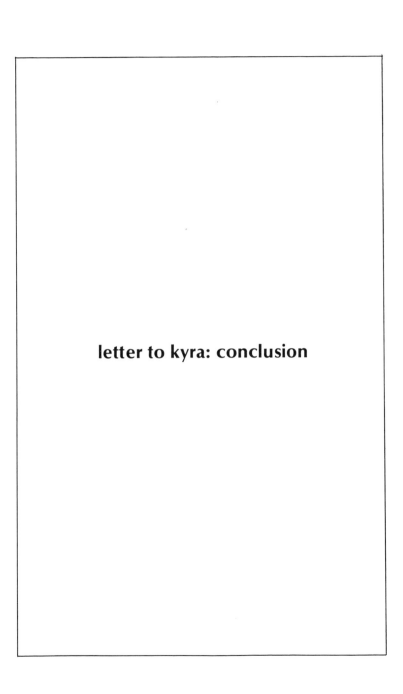

letter to kyra: conclusion

Letter to Kyra (*cont'd.*)

Here, then, are our visions. This isn't the compleat Canadian utopia, nor the total statement of 1970 Man's hopes and fears. The gaps are as obvious as they are infinite. Anyway, bigger is no longer better. The objective of this book is intuitional, not encyclopedic. Its intention is to provoke the reader with a group of insights so that the impact of the ensemble would be greater than the contributions taken individually.

Reading this in 2020 some statements will be seen as self-evident, others as nonsensical. Living them in 1970, there is nothing that can be said with certainty. We are so overcome by the rapidity of social change that we have difficulty talking about 1975. To think of 2020 is like considering a point far off in imaginary space. But to imagine you, Kyra, being fifty-one immediately reminds me that 2020 is part of the historical continuum that has its roots behind us in 1970 and will pass through 1984 and 2001. As my generation is the product of the cold war experience, yours will be the product of the reaction to the permissiveness of the 1950s and the violence of the 1960s.

As social change becomes more rapid, pragmatism fails to provide us with a satisfactory guide for action. We need to expand our imagination and anticipate the alternative futures that could develop from present trends. We need a concept of the future both idealistic and realistic enough to provide us with a guidebook for action in our existential "ever-changing present." "One step at a time" may be enough, but only if each step is in the right direction. As Starobin pointed out, nobody can afford post-mortems: wrong decisions these days are what the medical profession calls "terminal." In this sense we need a vision of the future more than you who will live in it. We can no longer afford simply to react to crises piecemeal with no comprehension of the long-term implications of our continual failures to achieve fundamental change. The basic cancers of our society – the class in-

equality, the economic poverty, the psychological exploitation, the military repressions – will continue to attack our social organism regardless of how much technological gadgetry is produced in however many attractive decorator colours. While American society, symbol for so long of the modern and the future, disintegrates before our eyes, we have still the chance to learn that we need social prophets and philosophers more than social scientists and bureaucrats. The old mythology of endless human progress has been shown bankrupt. Hopefully this assortment of fifty very individual perceptions will give some inspiration and encouragement to those who are struggling to re-create a vision for bewildered, frightened, threatened, still-linear man.

who are these guys?

who are these guys?

GREGORY BAUM teaches theology and religious studies at St. Michael's College in the University of Toronto. German-born, he came to Canada in 1940. He is a graduate of McMaster University, Hamilton, and of Ohio State University and the University of Fribourg, Switzerland. As a priest he has been deeply involved in the ecumenical movement and in the reform movement in the Catholic church; he has contributed to these movements by his books, his articles and the publication of the *Ecumenist*, of which he is the editor. More recently he has come to understand religion as man's dramatic entry into personal and cultural self-awareness and hence regards theology as critique of human life.

CARL BERGER was born in Manitoba, educated at the universities of Manitoba and Toronto, and is at present an associate professor of history at the University of Toronto. He is the author of *The Sense of Power: Studies in the Ideas of Canadian Imperialism, 1867-1914* (1970).

CLAUDE BISSELL has spent twenty-four years in university administration, of which fourteen have been spent as president, first of Carleton University 1956-58, and twelve at the University of Toronto. He was the first Mackenzie King Professor of Canadian Studies at Harvard University. He was chairman of the Canada Council 1960-62 and has written sporadically for various literary periodicals.

Born in Montréal (1917), MICHEL BRUNET received his B.A. (1939) and his M.A. (1947) from the Université de Montréal. As a Rockefeller Fellow (1947-49), he completed his graduate studies in the United States and was granted his Ph.D. by Clark University (1949). Member of the teaching staff of the Department of History of the Université de Montréal since 1949, he was its head from 1959 to 1967. Professor Brunet has published many books and articles dealing with

Canadian historical and political problems. His most recent
book, *Les Canadiens après la conquête, 1759-1775* (1969),
earned him the Governor General's Literary Award and the Prix
France-Québec. He is a member of the Académie canadienne-
française and of the Académie des Sciences d'Outre-Mer of
France.

Against some of the most neutral tones in the monochrome
Canadian historical tapestry, ADRIENNE CLARKSON grew up
happily and slavishly addicted to school, Little Big Books
and "The Shadow Knows." This rich intellectual background
has enabled her to enjoy being a mother, writing some novels
and successfully interviewing anything that talks on television
(with the exception of a glassy-eyed mynah bird which only
dug topless waitresses).

MAX CLARKSON is a Canadian who lives in Buffalo, New York.
Vocationally committed to business, other interests include
human behaviour and organizational change in bureaucracies,
such as local government, educational institutions and businesses
of all sizes; community organization and improvement;
theatrical innovation; and a dilettante's approach to a lot of
other activities and subjects which he will never adequately
understand.

If pushed, STEPHEN CLARKSON will now admit that he was
educated at Upper Canada College and was a Rhodes Scholar.
Such idiosyncrasies aside, he has been usefully employing his
time as a teacher of political science and in various com-
promising political activities in which his integrity and skin
have remained intact.

Has been:
        editor, for the University League for Social Reform,
        of *An Independent Foreign Policy for Canada?* (1967),
        secretary-treasurer of the Canadian Political Science Asso-
        ciation,
        Liberal candidate for mayor of Toronto
and contributor to Watkins task force on foreign investment in
        Canada.

Is: associate professor teaching politics at the University of
     Toronto,
     an editor of the *Canadian Forum*
and director of the Ontario Liberal party's Policy Research
     Centre.

"A definite ornament on the literary scene" is how Louis
Dudek, writing in *Canadian Literature,* described JOHN
ROBERT COLOMBO. The "definite ornament" prefers to regard
himself as a poet and editor-at-large. He has helped a number
of politicians write their memoirs, and is managing editor of
the *Tamarack Review.* Colombo's own books include *Abra-
cadabra, John Toronto* (found poems from the writings of
Bishop Strachan of Upper Canada) and *New Poems.* Recently
he edited an anthology of favourite poems called *How Do I
Love Thee.*

ROSEMARY COOK, formerly a member of the University of
Toronto Bluestockings, is now with the Redstockings at York
University. Author of *The Politics of Nellie McClung and the
Liberated Press* and *Canada and the Female Canadian
Question,* she has been a too-frequent contributor to the
Canadian Forum and other journals of liberation. She is also
a founder and past president of the University League for Sexual
Reform and an occasional bird watcher. She is the happily
married father of a nuclear family, one girl, one boy.

LLOYD DENNIS was born and raised in the Muskoka district
of Ontario. He entered the teaching profession in Toronto after
the war and became known as an innovator, writer and critic
on the Ontario education scene. He was cochairman with Mr.
Justice Hall of the committee responsible for the provocative
report called *Living and Learning* and served as the major
interpreter of this document throughout Canada. Mr. Dennis
is currently serving as director of Education for the Leeds and
Grenville County Board of Education.

IAN M. DRUMMOND is the son of poor but honest Scots Fabians.
He studied economics and Russian at the University of British
Columbia, the University of Toronto, the London School of

Economics and Yale University. He has taught at Yale, Princeton and, since 1960, at the University of Toronto, where he works mostly in economic history and Soviet studies. At thirty-seven he has learned to temper short-run professional pessimism with long-run Anglican optimism.

DENNIS DUFFY teaches English at Trinity College, the University of Toronto.

DONALD EVANS is professor of philosophy, the University of Toronto. His first book, *The Logic of Self-Involvement,* was a technical study in analytic philosophy of religion. *Peace, Power and Protest* and *Communist Faith and Christian Faith* were commissioned by the United Church of Canada, of which he is a minister.

DOROTHY FARMILOE lives in Windsor, Ontario, where she teaches at St. Clair College. She is a founder and co-editor of *Mainline Magazine.* Her published work includes two books of poems, *The Lost Island* and *Poems for Apartment Dwellers.* Her work has appeared in *America,* the *Beloit Poetry Journal,* the *Canadian Forum, Fiddlehead* and other literary periodicals.

EUGENE A. FORSEY was born in Grand Bank, Newfoundland, on May 29, 1904, baptized in Mexico City and brought up in Ottawa. He has had a chequered career as an academic (1929-41), trade union official (1942-69) and academic again (1969-?). One of the founders of the League for Social Reconstruction, he shared in the preparation of the CCF Regina Manifesto. He has been four times defeated for public office, yet remains probably the only trade union official who ever got an F.R.S.C.

WILLIAM FRENCH has been literary editor of the *Globe and Mail* since 1960. He is a graduate of the University of Western Ontario and was a Nieman Fellow at Harvard University in 1954-55. He won the President's Medal of the University of Western Ontario in 1966 for the best general magazine article published in Canada that year.

ROBERT FULFORD, who became editor of *Saturday Night* magazine in 1968, has been a journalist since 1949. He has been at
various times, and for various lengths of time, a literary critic,
a sportswriter, an art critic, a police reporter, a movie reviewer,
a political reporter. He has been an editor of *Maclean's*, the
Canadian Forum, Canadian Homes and Gardens and *May-
fair*, and has contributed to, among others, *Artscanada, Canadian Literature* and the *Tamarack Review*. He wrote a column
on books and ideas for the *Toronto Daily Star* from 1960 to
1962 and from 1964 to 1968. He appears frequently on CBC
television and has a weekly radio show, "This is Robert Fulford,"
heard late Monday nights on CBC stations in Toronto, Ottawa
and Windsor. He has written two books, *This Was Expo* and
Crisis at the Victory Burlesk, both published in 1968, and
wrote the text for a third, *Harold Town Drawings* (1969).

WALTER L. GORDON has been
        a chartered accountant (Clarkson, Gordon & Co.),
        management consultant (Woods, Gordon & Co.),
        royal commissioner (on Canada's economic prospects)
and cabinet minister,
and is now a businessman (chairman of Canadian Corporate
Management Company Limited). For many years he has urged the adoption of policies which would reverse the trend
under which Canada has been losing her economic independence.

ECOSYSTEMS MAMMAL CLASS GOTLIEB MOD PHYL-
LIS NUMBER 1 DESIGNED AND MANUFACTURED
IN TORONTO FROM MULTINATIONAL COMPONENTS;
COPROGENITOR WITH MOD CALVIN NUMBER 1 OF
SUBSEQUENT GENERATION 3 MODELS; PROGRAMS
POEMS WITHIN THE ZODIAC AND ORDINARY, MOV-
ING; NOVELS SUNBURST AND WHY SHOULD I HAVE
ALL THE GRIEF? CONTINUES IN OPERATION.

J. L. GRANATSTEIN was born in Toronto in 1939. He attended
the Royal Military College, Kingston, the University of Toronto
and Duke University. His publications include *The Politics of
Survival: The Conservative Party of Canada 1939-1945,*

Peacekeeping: International Challenge and Canadian Response and *Canadian Foreign Policy since 1945.* He is a member of the faculty of the Department of History at York University and of the editorial board of the *Canadian Forum.*

STEPHEN GRANT is a recent graduate in political science of the University of Toronto. Among his other activities at U. of T., he served as a member of the Commission on University Government. He plans to attend law school in the fall and hopes to continue writing about matters in the broad political field.

THOMAS A. HOCKIN, who teaches political science at York University, received the Honours B.A. degree from the University of Western Ontario and the M.P.A. and Ph.D. degrees from Harvard University. Mr. Hockin has taught at Harvard and has been at York since 1966. He has contributed chapters and articles on Canadian foreign policy to *Public Policy,* ed. J. Montgomery and A. Smithers; to the 1966 and 1967 editions of the *Canadian Annual Review*; to *An Independent Foreign Policy for Canada?* ed. Stephen Clarkson, and to *Alliances and Illusions: Canada and the NATO-NORAD Question.* He also has scholarly articles published in Britain and Canada on British and Canadian parliamentary reform. A frequent contributor to the *Canadian Forum,* he recently received a $3000 Centennial award from Imperial Tobacco for his manuscript, "Canadian Parliamentary Reform to the Year 2000." He has edited a new book to appear in 1971, *The Prime Minister, the Cabinet and Political Leadership in Canada,* and is completing a monograph, *The Loyal Opposition in Canada,* with a financial award from the Canada Council.

HUGH HOOD lives in Montreal with his wife Noreen, who is a painter and designer, and their four kids. He has published two novels and two collections of stories; a new novel will appear this fall. He is now preparing for publication a third story collection and a fourth novel.

Born in the Netherlands in 1939, MICHIEL HORN reached Canada in 1952 and became a Canadian citizen six years later.

He studied at Victoria College, the University of British Columbia (B.A.), Freiburg University, West Germany, and the University of Toronto (Ph.D.). After living in California for a year he began teaching in 1968 at Glendon College, York University, where he is currently assistant professor of history.

MICHAEL IGNATIEFF is now studying for a doctorate in history at Harvard, having been active in student journalism and student politics at the University of Toronto.

HARRY G. JOHNSON was born in Toronto in 1923 and remains a Canadian citizen. Enlistment in World War II took him to England, where he subsequently studied at Cambridge and taught at Cambridge and Manchester universities. He is currently professor of economics at both the University of Chicago and the London School of Economics and Political Science.

The Honourable ERIC KIERANS was born in Montreal on February 2, 1914. He studied at Loyola College and McGill University. Following four years as professor of commerce at McGill, he was appointed director of its School of Commerce in 1953. Mr. Kierans is credited with rejuvenating the Canadian and Montreal Stock Exchanges of which he was president from 1960 to 1963. He first entered the political field in 1963 when he was elected member of the Quebec legislature for the provincial riding of Notre-Dame de Grace. The same year he was named minister of Revenue before becoming minister of Health. He left provincial politics in 1968 to become the first member of Parliament to represent the new federal riding of Duvernay in suburban Montreal. In July of the same year, Prime Minister Trudeau named him postmaster general, broadening the Post Office portfolio to include telecommunications and space satellites. In April 1969, he became officially minister of Communications. Mr. Kierans is married and has two children.

DENNIS LEE was born in Toronto in 1939. He has taught at the University of Toronto and Rochdale College, and now directs the House of Anansi Press. He has published two books of poetry, *Kingdom of Absence* and *Civil Elegies*, edited the poetry anthology *T.O. Now* and is co-editor of a collection of essays, *The University Game. Wiggle to the Laundromat* — a volume of children's verse — will appear in 1970.

Born in Halifax in 1909, DONALD MACDONALD went to Cape Breton as a boy and became an active trade unionist at the age of seventeen, when he went to work in the coal industry. At twenty-one he was president of his local of the United Mine Workers of America; until he was blacklisted in 1940 he played a prominent role in the UMW. In 1941 Mr. MacDonald was elected to the Nova Scotia legislature and was leader of the CCF party in that assembly until 1945. He has held a succession of executive posts in the Canadian Congress of Labour and, later, the Canadian Labour Congress; at the 1968 convention of the CLC he was elected president by acclamation. He now holds membership in the International Woodworkers of America. He was a member of the Executive Board of the International Confederation of Free Trade Unions for many years and in 1969 became the first Canadian to be elected a vice-president of that organization. Mr. MacDonald has long had an active interest in the cooperative movement, having helped to organize three successful cooperative ventures in Nova Scotia. His interest in cooperatives has continued, and he has been instrumental in bringing about closer relations between the CLC and the cooperative movement.

JOHN H. MCCUAIG: Origin unknown. Evidently human, resident on Earth (planet in the rim of the Milky Way). Family of treedwellers, cavemen and shepherds in recent times. Reputedly handymen and amusement-park operators before that. Father a mystery; mother a virgin until the time of his birth. Home secured from savages only recently, with a few reservations. Able to read and write (family literate, off and on, 2500 years). Diseased, lonely, discontented (but not yet fully syphilized). Smog bound, poisoned, addicted to tobacco and caffeine. Mortal (life expectancy sixty years). Omnivorous, heterosexual. Nearly deaf. B.A., M.A., Ph.D. (thesis year). Satirical, and obscene.

JOHN T. MCLEOD is an associate professor of political science
at the University of Toronto. He was born in Saskatchewan and
never quite got over it. He is co-editor of two recent books,
Agenda 1970 and *Business and Government in Canada*. From
1967 to 1970 he was research and editorial director of the
Committee on the Healing Arts, an Ontario royal commission
on health services, whose thirteen-volume report was published
in 1970.

KENNETH MCNAUGHT was born in Toronto in 1918 and was
educated at Upper Canada College and the University of Toronto,
where he received the Ph.D. in 1950. He now teaches American
history at Toronto and is the author of *A Prophet in Politics,
The Pelican History of Canada, Manifest Destiny: A Short
History of the United States* and *A Source-Book of Canadian
History* (with J. H. S. Reid and H. S. Crowe). He is a founding
member of the University League for Social Reform and a
frequent contributor to the *Canadian Forum* and other American and Canadian journals.

ROSS MENDES is a Toronto painter. He is represented in collections in Europe, South Africa and Canada, including Leeds
Art Gallery and Leeds University. He began to write on art
for the Cape *Times* while in South Africa and has since contributed articles to the *Canadian Forum, Artscanada,* and to
the recently published *Notes for a Native Land*.

CHRISTINA NEWMAN was educated, employed, maladjusted in
Toronto for twenty-odd years, then politicized, agitated, aggravated by an even odder ten years spent in Ottawa. A former
member of the staffs of *Maclean's, Chatelaine, Saturday Night,*
she is writing, in collaboration with her husband, Peter Newman,
a book on the Canadian power structure to be published in the
fall of 1971.

WILLIAM NICHOLLS was born in England and educated at Cambridge. After a period in the Anglican ministry in England
and Scotland, he came to Canada in 1960. He is the head
of the Department of Religious Studies at the University of
British Columbia. He writes on religious and theological topics
from an independent standpoint.

JOHN O'NEILL is a professor of sociology at York University, Toronto. He was educated at the London School of Economics and Political Science, and at Stanford University, California. His interests are in Marxism and social phenomenology. He is the author of *Perception, Expression and History: The Social Phenomenology of Merleau-Ponty* (1970) and *Making Sense Together,* a forthcoming study of the ethnomethodology of meaning.

WILLIAM READY has published many articles on library and publishing economy, runs his own publishing house, the Cromlech Press, and is director of the McMaster University Library Press. His two most recent books are *The Tolkien Relation* (1968) and *Necessary Russell* (1969), an introduction to Bertrand Russell and his archives which now reside at McMaster.

JAMES REANEY was born (South Easthope, 1926) and educated (Elmhurst Public School, Stratford Collegiate Institute, the University of Toronto) in Ontario. He has been a teacher in the English departments of the University of Manitoba and now the University of Western Ontario. Editor of *Alphabet,* he recently published one play, *Colours in the Dark,* and is currently working on a second about the Donnelly family commissioned by the Stratford Festival. He is married and has one son, one daughter.

Born July 14, 1943, in Frankfurt, Germany, HERMANN REBEL had a typical German childhood which, therefore, is of only passing psychiatric interest. He emigrated to Canada (Toronto) with his parents in 1953, but things didn't pick up for him until 1955 when he first came 'in touch with rural Ontario, a one-room school, country music, farmers, dandelion wine, Carl Perkins and Gene Vincent, ducktail haircuts and drive-in movies. On his return to Toronto in 1958 he began a schizophrenic career as mild-mannered highschool overachiever by day and Superrock by night (reading Nietzsche under the covers and taking judo lessons). During his four years at the University of Toronto his future as Intellect and Historian was threatened by vague romances and some artistic preten-

sions as well as by the violent reactions he invariably produced
in WASPs in high places — but, with a little help from his
friends, he managed to graduate in 1966 and to get into the
Berkeley graduate school, supported financially by the good
names of Woodrow Wilson and Ralston Purina. In California
he discovered for himself that the deeper you go the higher
you fly and learned to live all over again. Last year he married
a pretty woman, passed his Ph.D. exams, became offensive
minister of the Bruce Skouts of Amerika and went to Europe
to learn some more history. This year's life crises will involve
writing a thesis (on primitive revolt) and finding a job.

JOHN M. ROBSON is one of the seventeen people known to have
been born and married in Toronto who still live there with
their wives and children. Professor of English at Victoria College, he is general editor of the *Collected Works of John Stuart
Mill,* and author of *The Improvement of Mankind: The Social
and Political Thought of John Stuart Mill* (1968), *The Hmnn
Retort* (1970) and other ephemera.

ABRAHAM ROTSTEIN is managing editor of the *Canadian Forum*
and associate professor in the Department of Political Economy,
the University of Toronto. He is also a founder of the University
League for Social Reform and was the editor of its first
volume, *The Prospect of Change.* From 1966 to early 1968
he served as a member of the Watkins task force on the effects
of foreign investment in Canada.

LEONARD SHIFRIN is a graduate of the University of Toronto
in political science and in law. He has worked as a journalist
as well as practising law and his articles have appeared in
many Canadian newspapers, magazines and journals. He has
been a special assistant for policy development to the minister
of National Health and Welfare, and is presently director of
the National Council of Welfare.

The Honourable ROBERT L. STANFIELD, P.C., Q.C., LL.D.,
MP, was born in Truro, N.S., April 11, 1914, the son of the late
Frank Stanfield, four times MLA and later lieutenant governor
of Nova Scotia. He is a graduate of Dalhousie (B.A. 1936)

and Harvard (LL.B. 1939) universities; admitted to the bar of
Nova Scotia in 1940, he was appointed a Queen's Counsel
in 1950. He was first elected to the legislature of Nova Scotia
in 1949 and in 1956 became premier and minister of Education in the province's first Conservative government in twenty-
three years. In quick succession during the fall of 1967, he
was elected national leader of the Progressive Conservative
party, resigned as premier of Nova Scotia, was elected to the
House of Commons in a by-election and entered the House
of Commons as leader of the official opposition. He was re-
elected in June 1968 as MP in Halifax. Mr. Stanfield is married
and has four children.

JOSEPH R. STAROBIN is an associate professor of political
science at Glendon College, York University. His doctoral
dissertation, begun after a quarter of a century of varied experiences in journalism and politics, deals with American Com-
munism and the cold war, and will be published in the spring
of 1970 . . . . His "undergraduate work" was done in the American Communist movement in which he was an editor of
Masses and the *Daily Worker* and, until 1954, charged with
its foreign relations. Widely travelled in Latin America and
western Europe, with a year's residence in China and Vietnam,
he is the author of *Paris to Peking* (1955) and *Eyewitness in
Indo-China* (1954). A former senior fellow at the Research
Institute on Communist Affairs, Columbia University, his articles have appeared in *Foreign Affairs, Problems of Com-
munism*, the *Canadian Forum* and other periodicals.

WILLIAM IRWIN THOMPSON is at present associate professor
of humanities at York University. Before coming to York
he taught at M.I.T. and Cornell University, where he received
his Ph.D. in 1966. Mr. Thompson's publications include *The
Imagination of an Insurrection: Dublin, Easter 1916* and
At the Edge of History, the latter book published earlier this
year.

ARCHIBALD PATON THORNTON is chairman of the Department of History, the University of Toronto. Born in Glasgow,
Scotland, in 1922, he has been resident in Canada since 1960.

He is the author of five books, including *The Imperial Idea and Its Enemies*, *Doctrines of Imperialism* and *The Habit of Authority*.

VINCENT TOVELL produces television programs for the CBC touching, at one time or another, on history, the visual arts, architecture, science, religion, music and current events. Television programs are usually a form of immediate journalism but at the CBC it is possible at times to transcend the actuality or, at any rate, to try. In series like "Festival," "Explorations," "Intertel," "Man at the Centre," "The Nature of Things" and, in particular, in "specials," Vincent Tovell has explored unexpected subjects and alternative forms. Born in Toronto, he graduated from and taught at the University of Toronto. He was also resident for almost a decade in New York City.

JEAN-PIERRE WALLOT is an associate professor of history at the University of Toronto specializing in French Canadian history of the late eighteenth and early twentieth centuries. He taught previously at the Université de Montréal and has worked for the National Museum of Canada. He is the author of two books and of numerous articles in Canadian and European learned journals.

MELVILLE H. WATKINS is a vice-president of the New Democratic party and professor of economics in the Department of Political Economy, the University of Toronto. He was head of the Pearson government's task force investigating the extent of foreign control of Canadian industry and principal author of its 1968 report. Active in the Waffle movement of the NDP, he recently collaborated (with Dave Godfrey) in the production of a typographic documentary, *Gordon to Watkins to You: The Battle for Control of Our Economy*.

ANDREW WERNICK, a graduate in history and economics of King's College, Cambridge, is now a doctoral student in politics at the University of Toronto. He is one of the student activists who brought confrontation tactics to the Toronto campus, confronting frequently in the process another *Visions* contributor, Claude Bissell. Currently he is working on his doctoral thesis, a study of Emile Durkheim and the possibility of social knowledge.

Born in Winnipeg in 1912, GEORGE WOODCOCK went to England as a child and stayed long enough to start his career as a writer there by publishing in the *New English Weekly*, *New Verse* and other typical thirties magazines. His first prose work of significance was *William Godwin* (1946). He returned to Canada in 1949 and since 1959 has edited *Canadian Literature*. He served as an academic long enough to know that by nature he was not fitted for that type of theatre, and now merely writes and edits. His books include *Anarchism* and *The Crystal Spirit* (on George Orwell), *The Writer and Politics* and *The Paradox of Oscar Wilde*, four books of verse, a score of radio plays, a handful of travel books, three volumes of criticism on Canadian writers and biographies of Proudhon, Kropotkin and Aphra Behn. With Ivan Akakumovic he wrote *The Doukhobors*; among his forthcoming books is *Canada and the Canadians*.